THE AMERICAN EXPERIENCE

The Collected Essays
of J.H. Plumb

THE
AMERICAN
EXPERIENCE

The Collected Essays
of J.H. Plumb

The University of Georgia Press
Athens

© 1989 J. H. Plumb

Published in the United States of America by
The University of Georgia Press,
Athens, Georgia 30602

First published in 1989 by
Harvester · Wheatsheaf
A Division of Simon & Schuster International Group

Printed and bound in Great Britain by
A. Wheaton & Co. Ltd, Exeter

Library of Congress Cataloging in Publication Data

(Revised for Vol. 2)

Plumb, J. H. (John Harold), 1911–
 The collected essays of J. H. Plumb.

 Includes indexes.
 Contents: v. 1. The making of an historian—
v. 2. The American experience.
 1. Plumb, J. H. (John Harold), 1911–
2. Historians—Great Britain—Biography. 3. Great
Britain—Historiography. 4. Historiography—Great
Britain. 5. Great Britain—History. I. Title.
DA3.P57A3 1989 941'.0072024 88–17290
ISBN 0-8203-1095-6 (v. 1)
ISBN 0-8203-1118-9 (v. 2)

FOR
MY FIRST AMERICAN FRIENDS
PATRICK AND ELIZABETH MOYNIHAN
GRATEFULLY

Contents

Preface

This second volume of my collected essays is about America – American History, Contemporary America, and of my own experience of America. For the last thirty years I have been deeply involved with American history, American historians, and American universities. Although most of my time has been spent in New York, I have lectured in almost all the states of America, missing only Alaska, North Dakota and Idaho. It was one of the most rewarding aspects of my middle age, for it gave me what I needed most: hope – hope about the future, hope about history as an aspect of our culture, and hope about myself. The American scholar is still far more generous than his European counterpart, freer from malice or personal paranoia, and the vast majority of American scholars believe that anyone who has devoted his life to the writing of history is engaged in a serious purpose, trying to make the best of his talents to illuminate the problems which he has set for himself. This does not mean that American scholars do not criticise. They do. Apart from a few, their criticisms are usually constructive and always made with good manners. Certainly, temperamentally I was happier in academic society in America. America became a refuge as well as a stimulant and I am deeply grateful for the generosity with which I was treated. I hope that for many years to come my heart will lift as the mid-town sky-line comes into view from Triborough bridge. 'New York,' I say to myself with joy, 'here again.'

As with the first volume of these essays I am greatly indebted to the help, and criticism, of my research assistant in this project, S. D. Smith, and to my colleague, Dr Joachim Whaley, whose sympathetic criticism has been invaluable. My secretary, Mrs Serby, has wrestled successfully with my wretched handwriting.

J. H. PLUMB

Acknowledgements

I wish to thank the following editors and publishers in whose journals or books of collected essays these articles and reviews were first published:

American Heritage, Bookworld, House and Garden, New York Review of Books, New York Times Book Review, New York Times Magazine, Saturday Review, Sunday Times, The Times Literary Supplement

PART ONE

DISCOVERY AND REVOLUTION

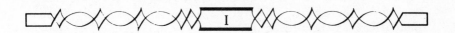

Introduction: 'O My America, My Newfoundland'

The journey to Glasgow was interminable. We stopped at stations; we stopped in the snow-sodden countryside; we stopped for good reasons – frozen points, bombing alerts, and for no reason at all. Night came early. There was no food on the train, no drinks and no heat. The light was so low, it was impossible to read. I had had to go to the office early for last instructions and got to Euston too late either for breakfast or to buy food if there was any. It took nearly eleven hours to reach the Central Hotel at Glasgow; all restaurants were closed, lights dimmed, the rooms bitterly cold and dark. A compassionate waitress had conjured up a dried egg omelette and a cup of coffee that tasted like liquid earth. Sleep proved difficult, the bed was dank and the cold intolerable and anxiety – I had to get up at 5 am – all-consuming. Fortunately, the Admiralty sent a car to meet me and I was grateful to be speeding through the dark to Greenock in reasonable comfort. Formalities which I expected to be brief (after all, I was an Intelligence Officer, albeit civilian, of the Admiralty working on code-breaking at Bletchley Park), proved lengthy. I was acting in a secondary role as a courier and packets had to be signed for, registered and goodness knows what, so that dawn was breaking as a barge took me out to the Queen Mary. I had never seen the ship before and it looked unbelievably large. Already 17,000 wounded Americans, most of them walking cases, were on board. There were five other civilian passengers apart from myself and, fortunately, I was given a superb cabin on the sun deck and was looked after by an admirable steward. We ate at strange times – 11 for lunch, 5 for dinner – but it was bliss to see a grapefruit again after six years and to be able to eat as much Virginian ham as one wanted.

There were U-boats waiting for us – lone wolves – as hunting in packs was too dangerous for them in 1945, and I knew from decoded German signals where they were – one was lurking off the approaches to New York. The Queen Mary was, however, too fast for U-boats and it would require a fluke for her to become a target. And an encounter would be made much more difficult for the U-boats because we knew, more or less, where they were. However, as soon as we left the Western Approaches, we headed south and picked up beautiful spring-like weather. The sun deck came into its own. But after sun came the gale, so furious that it bent back the bridge of the ship several inches. The great ship heaved and pitched and rolled like a vast yacht. Fortunately, I was immune to sea-sickness so I did my daily stint round the deck on my own. It was a terrible time for the wounded and an added burden to the crew. Six days had passed before we approached New York. The night before we docked I could not sleep and by the time we reached the Ambrose Light, I was pacing the deck and peering through the bitter, frosty night for a sight of land. Some miles off Long Island, I picked up the streaming headlights of cars; itself a life-enhancing sight for someone who had lived for more than five years in the Stygian gloom of the black-out, occasionally lit by bombs and fires or the indifferent moon. Dawn came up fast, soon I could pick out the cars, streaming towards Manhattan. Slowing to a gentle pace we passed through the Narrows; the great city of my dreams became reality. I had not expected anything so beautiful as the down-town skyline etched against a pellucid blue sky, or the majestic sight of the Hudson into which the Queen Mary turned.

I had no direct experience of America; only a lot of ideas derived from movies, music, especially jazz, and literature of every kind from Zane Grey to Edith Wharton. I had read very little about American history apart from the colonial period. My knowledge of contemporary American politics was derived almost entirely from Denis Brogan and *Time* magazine. Yet I felt a strong sense of gratitude to America. I had been close enough to the problems of the war to know that without America's support the defeat of Hitler would have been impossible. I was not uncritical of America as an ally but I also knew that without America I would have had no future – none at all. Without liberty I could never have been what I had longed to be since adolescence - a writer. In the 1930s America was the last refuge of liberty, or so it seemed in 1938 after Munich. Indeed, deeply worried about the possibility of further capitulation by Chamberlain to Hitler, and deeply depressed by the absurdities of the pacifism of the Labour Party, I had planned to leave England in the autumn of 1939 for the Huntington Library in California.

Fortunately, events made that unnecessary and I felt unrestrained relief, almost joy, when the Dean of King's (The Revd Eric Milner White) rushed into my bathroom at 10.45 on September 3rd and told me excitedly and elatedly that we should be at war at 11 o'clock. It seems a lifetime ago, but a lifetime in which America has played an ever-growing role, not only in military matters, but also in my own life for, once allies, we had quickly forged links with American cryptographers and we had regular liaison meetings.

In 1939 I had only spoken to one or two American students in Cambridge; by 1945 America had become a living presence, and at the official level I knew dozens. But at last my innocence about the world in which they lived and worked was about to be broken. As we were gently pushed into dock at the pier on West 50th St, I became impatient to get off. The few civilians on board were assembled with their baggage and I expected endless delay. There was none – two colleagues from the Secret Service came on board. I left the ship with them at once. We did not bother with passport control or customs. Within a minute I was in a car driving towards the Rockefeller Center. I was all wonder. The express lift to the Rainbow Room added to my amazement. I sipped my first Bourbon Old-Fashioned, I stared at Manhattan – surely one of the greatest man-made vistas of the world. It was a cloudless, cold, blue day of January, and Staten Island, the Statue of Liberty, Ellis Island, the East River and the Hudson were all visible. It was all joy. I spent three days being briefed, making arrangements for money and buying clothes – instead of frayed cuffs and collars, I had fresh, crisp, sea-island cotton shirts. There were no shortages that I could discover. I could not believe the steaks – enough for the rations of an English family for two weeks. And at night the city sparkled with light; and night after night, as long as I was in New York, I stood by the ice rink and looked at the soaring cliff of the Rockefeller Center. Years later, when I came regularly to New York, my first pilgrimage, as soon as I had settled in from the plane, was to that same spot.

After four or five days I took the train to Washington where I was to work for a month. As I lunched, a waiter quickly removed my half-drunk bottle of wine. I was bewildered but told sharply that Delaware was dry, rather as if any damn fool should know that. Later it came back with the coffee. Just in time to gulp it down before drawing up at the Union Station which seemed more like a cathedral of gleaming marble than a railway station – grander even than Penn Station – and light years away from Euston. I was whisked through Washington and finished up at the very end of Connecticut Avenue in a small suburban house, where I had a bedroom, a share of a square tub, but no hospitality. Breakfast I took on a stool at the local drugstore – spotless in its cleanliness where I learnt the mysteries of 'sunny side up' and 'once over lightly', and that sausage was not sausage. Lunch I had at the canteen and got to know for the first time 'hamburgers' and 'hot dogs', neither of which had reached England. Occasionally I ate dinner alone, and again I found a new experience – Chinese food. In England the Chinese laundered but did not cook. I was soon converted to their cuisine. Otherwise it was dinners here, there, and everywhere – at Pierre's in Dupont Circle, Halls down by the harbour, or the Mayflower Hotel and for me it was lobsters, crabs, oysters all the way, and the delectable chowders. I had been told that American food was abysmally dull, it wasn't but, alas, in those days no one drank wine with meals.

Two or three ferocious cocktails were followed by water. The cocktails loosened tongues and I was amazed with the freedom with which many wives discussed their husbands; indeed the openness of conversation, the seeming lack of any sense of hierarchy for here admirals seemed to fair no better than commanders, was both refreshing and disturbing. There was, also, a curious lack of urgency – dinner would be pushed back an hour, may be two hours, no one seemed to mind. In the office it was the same. The first day I made courtesy calls on the heads of the naval intelligence departments which I was visiting – we talked of the journey, of the weather, of the London blitzes which seemed to preoccupy most of them; of course, there was a word or two about families and mutual acquaintances and colleagues – but *no business*, not a word. And the size of offices, the equipment, the innumerable staff dazed me – five, six, seven times larger than we had back at Bletchley. When we got to business the pace was still slow. There was an obvious professionalism about the Americans – every letter, every memorandum carefully, indeed beautifully, typed, and a care for the absolute precision of detail about what was said in committee and agreed. We at Bletchley seemed by contrast amateurish. We dealt on a personal basis, avoided mountains of paper, and shared secretaries. Although the Americans slowed the pace, the result was greater efficiency, and professionalism was an aspect of American life which in the end I found wholly admirable.

Each day made my feelings about America more complex – I realised the immense area of my ignorance but what I saw strengthened my sense both of commitment to, and delight in, America – except for one aspect that I could not accept: one that profoundly shocked and disturbed me. My office was in Virginia to which I travelled every day. At the bus stop the black people stood aside while the whites went aboard and then lurched to the two or three benches allotted to them at the back. Often there was not room for them although there might be spare seats for whites. They had to wait in the snow and cold. Where I worked there were lavatories marked 'Black Men' and 'Black Women'.

I never saw, except as waiters or cooks, any black man or woman in a restaurant or on a stool in the drugstores I used. They all looked defeated as well as poor and I understood those haunting 'blues' that I loved, at a deeper level, for now understanding was combined with bitter resentment. The fair body of America was lacerated with a terrible injustice. In 1945 Britain had very few blacks. I had not visited India, so my indignation was more righteous than it should have been. After one violent argument with a Virginian woman, I understood that the rights of blacks were not a subject for discussion at an elegant dinner at Pierre's. As an historian I realised, as never before, that slavery and its aftermath had given a complexity to American history which I had not realised. How complex that was, I was to learn over the decades. The same woman, who was rather drunk (that too was a novelty for me at a semi-official dinner), switched from angry argument to self-pitying confession with alarming ease. Drink had made her Southern accent more difficult to follow but what got through to me was hair-raising enough – the detailed sexual shortcomings of her husband whose proximity across the table seemed all too close. He had a red-gleaming, boisterous, happy face; full of lobster and bourbon, deep in anecdote, he seemed to have no care in the world. As the days and the weeks passed, America and the Americans became both more fascinating and more difficult to understand. I had been captivated by its literature as a boy of seventeen – remarkably being given Faulkner's *The Sound and The Fury* as a school prize (my headmaster was too idle to bother with the contents of books). I had been overwhelmed by Thomas Wolfe's *Look Homeward Angel*, and Scott Fitzgerald had complemented my passion for jazz. So in a sense I was half in love with America before I arrived. But now, like all love affairs which become a deep commitment, my passion for America was entangled with anger, anxiety and at times even flashes of hate, such as one might feel about one's own country.

My last image, after six weeks of frantically hard work and even harder socialising in which I gave my first large formal dinner – admirals and captains galore round a vast table at the Mayflower – was the Grand Central Station – to a European unbelievably magnificent in its space, cleanliness and efficiency. I was going by train to Ottawa and through a night of fitful sleep I had a deep physical sense of the immensity of America – it was like crossing France but we crossed only one state.

Throughout the 1950s, America was in my mind. I read more and more of its history and literature, discovered Parkman, Prescott, Bancroft and Partington: Emerson and Longfellow had always been favourites of my father but I read them again: I bored myself with Poe and Melville. Towards Walt Whitman I was ambivalent. Franklin captured my imagination (surely one of the most difficult eighteenth-century men to understand) more than Jefferson, whose gifts and character were easier to comprehend. Contemporary historians and contemporary novelists I bought in large quantities but I was impressed more by writers and poets than historians and biographers – especially the latter who seemed flat-footed and tentative to a degree. The historians, however, had some men of quality – Morison, Commager, Schlesinger and a younger man still – Richard Hofstadter – all seemed to me to practise history in the grand tradition.

About 1953 I was sorely tempted to tear up my roots in England and take a post at Haverford. I had just obtained tenure at Cambridge but I had published little by 1953 and the first volume of my life of Walpole was not completed. I needed a major work without much more delay, so I was prudent and stayed in Cambridge.

Fortunately, a year or two later, my involvement with America began to burgeon. In 1957 I was approached by Oliver Jensen of *American Heritage* and asked if I would write an introductory chapter to a volume on the American Revolution which they were producing to sell by mail order. *American Heritage*, a hard-cover, no advertisement, fully illus-trated magazine in colour as well as black and white, was the brain-child of three remarkable journalists of *Time Magazine* – James Parton, Joseph Thorndike, Jr and Oliver Jensen. It had proved an immense success, bringing so much money into their coffers that they had to expand at once. They decided to print large, highly illustrated books and sell them by mail order. They were the first in the field and once again, their first book, *Great Historic Places*, had loaded the coffers with yet more cash: so they decided to do for Europe and the world what they were doing for America, publish a new magazine called *Horizon* – like *American Heritage*, no advertisements, hard covers, the best authors, and the most beautiful illustrations the printing press could create. The magazine was to be devoted to history and the arts. Arguably it was one of the finest magazines ever produced in America, both for physical beauty and literary content.

I spent the summer of 1957 at Palace House at Newmarket lent to me by Yvonne de Rothschild and wrote the chapter which *American Heritage* had commissioned for their second book, *The Revolution in America*, for what I considered a very princely sum ($1000). It gave great satisfaction and is printed below. Oliver Jensen and his new wife visited me in the spring of 1958, just after its publication, when I also learned from them about *Horizon* magazine. Subsequently, I was asked to join the Advisory Board. Naturally I accepted.

About the same time I began to plan my *History of Human Society* which Spencer Curtis Brown, my agent at that time, thought would appeal to Alfred Knopf. It certainly did for, to my astonishment, he turned up in Cambridge to discuss it and express his enthusiasm. Naturally he stressed the need for me to travel to America as soon as possible to secure American authors, but prudently deleted a clause in my contract in which Curtis Brown had suggested a yearly visit to Knopf, funded by them.

A further strand in my American destiny was woven by Richard Hofstadter's becoming Pitt Professor of American History at Cambridge for 1958–59. He was at Gonville and Caius, to which I had just lost one of the ablest of my post-war pupils, and through him I met Richard and his wife, Bede, soon after their arrival. I had long admired his work. I thought that *The Age of Reform* and *The American Political Tradition* established him in the very forefront of the new, post-war generation of American scholars. I warmed immediately to the Hofstadters – both were highly intelligent, principled, generous and witty. They both had suffered in their private lives. They had large hearts, clever heads and dedication to the intellectual tradition. I persuaded Trevelyan to come to lunch and meet them. It was a very memorable occasion for I was confident that Hofstadter was going to be the outstanding historian of his time, more intellectual than Trevelyan but with the same intuition, the same purpose: to make the writing of history an integral part of the culture of his time and generation. We became close friends and a few years later I was horrified to learn that he was dying and rushed over to New York to see him. It was one of the saddest days of my life. Frail and spent, his eyes still glowed with intelligence – and, strangely, with hope as he spoke of cutting out all lectures in the future and dedicating himself to his new large book that, of course, was never to be written. Nor shall I forget Bede in those days, her courage, her stoicism that attempted but could not conceal the tragedy of her position.

Columbia University had imposed a minor task on Hofstadter – to find a British historian to replace Ausubel, their specialist in eighteenth- and nineteenth-century British history who was taking a sabbatical year in 1959–60. Hofstadter pressed me to take it. Unfortunately I was struggling to finish volume II of my life of Walpole; the proofs would be due, probably in the autumn of 1959. Travel and communication between England and America was not so fast then as now. In the end a compromise was found: J. P. Kenyon, my pupil and colleague, took the autumn semester of 1959 and I made myself available from January 1960.

Once again I sailed on the Queen Mary: this time nearly empty – 57 only in the first class which proved a bad joke for me. I love food and wine so I had great expectations of the Silver Grill. The first night I indulged myself; the next day I was wracked with pain. In the previous October I had had severe hepatitis, since then I had lived austerely – no alcohol, no cream sauces for months and I thought myself cured. For the rest of the voyage I lived on poached fish, boiled potatoes, fruit and no drink. It was a good joke against myself and I told it to the Jensens on my first night at their apartment and so avoided the fierce martinis which everyone at *American Heritage* seemed to love. It had been very kind of the Jensens to meet me off the boat. And that night I did not realise how closely the lives of those I was meeting for the first time – James Parton, Joseph Thorndike, Richard Ketchum – would become a part of my own life as an historian. Nor did I realise that from then until now I would visit America several times a year, sometimes for long periods, or that over the next few decades I would lecture in most American States; that I would get to know innumerable universities and colleges; make some of the deepest friendships of my life in New York; or that America would make me a prosperous man. But that first night was like the moment of crystallisation in a human relationship. I was first entranced and then committed. America was my 'Newfoundland'. I wanted to see it, live in it, learn everything I could about it, and try to understand its history without which I would be lost in its complicated present.

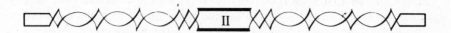

The Wider Issues

During my six months as a Visiting Professor in 1960, I put down strong roots. They might have been stronger still. Columbia wished me to stay, aroused the interest of the Ford Foundation, and began negotiations with Cambridge University to try to work out a method by which I might be shared by both universities; a common enough practice between America and Italian universities but alarmingly original to Cambridge who regarded the problems as insuperable. Urged and prodded by Columbia, they moved, but very slowly. By the time they came to a reluctant agreement, over two years had elapsed and naturally the Ford Foundation had gone cold. It would have suited me to perfection. However, increasing involvement during 1960 with *American Heritage* made this less of a disaster to my new American interests than it might have been.

I became close friends with James Parton, the President of the company and its major shareholder, and his close partners Joseph Thorndike (whose ancestor had been burnt as a witch at Salem – a fact in which this tough independently-minded New Englander took great pride) and Oliver Jensen, jokey, Anglophile, railway engine buff, and very shrewd editor. Their new magazine *Horizon* got off to a magnificent start and I drummed up a number of very good authors for them – Veronica Wedgwood, Hugh Trevor Roper, Moses Finley, Oliver Millar, Christopher Hibbert, Nancy Mitford and others in the first two years of *Horizon*'s existence – and before I returned to England I had been appointed European editor for the magazine and was deeply involved in the first book, *The Italian Renaissance*, to be published by *Horizon* and sold by mail to its readers. Twice a week I would go down to our offices in the Fred French Building on 5th Avenue and plot the book with Richard Ketchum, one of the nicest, kindest and most astute editors in the company. It was planned for publication in the spring of 1961, so we had just one year to write it, to fill it with magnificent illustration, and get it widely promoted and indeed sold before publication. I quickly convinced Richard Ketchum that no single author could do that task alone. So I undertook the narrative and background which was carefully constructed to cover all the major aspects of the Renaissance. Then we planned a star-studded cast to write a 3500-word biography of an outstanding artist or man of the Renaissance. We aimed high and up to a point I was given a free hand with finance. I had firmly objected to paying everyone the same rate; no English publisher would have taken that risk; highly competitive Americans accepted that it had more benefits than dangers.

When I got in touch with Kenneth Clark – his name was essential and I also thought he wrote better about art for the layman than anyone writing in English – he began to talk of the pressure on his time, the books in which he was involved, and I could see refusal looming ahead. So, expressing my concern about the extra burden it would put on him, I said that I thought the fee would take that into account and would be generous – $3500, i.e. $1 a word. He said he would think about it. I expected victory and achieved it. Neither Parton nor Ketchum liked the price but they realised its value; an illustrious bevy of authors was signed up - Bronowski, Mattingly, Trevor Roper, Mack Smith, Iris Origo. To fatten the volume and make it more fully illustrated we invented the portfolio – a collection of outstanding pictures on a common theme with a short text – Landscape, The Nude, Perspective, Astrology, Condottieri, etc. which meant that a third of the book could be written and designed in-house. From May to November 1960 I worked harder, thought longer and wrote with greater discipline than I had ever done before. Two manic weeks followed in early December when the text had to be adjusted to the illustrations and the captions revised, rewritten more often than not again and again to make them 'justify' with the pictures. Writing precisely to an 'em' is nightmarish. The book was published three weeks later to an extravagant success – 225,000 books sold by mail order at $15.00 a copy. It was translated into every language of Western Europe, including Finnish. The paperback edition has had an equal success and twenty-five years later maintains a steady sale. It confirmed my position with *American Heritage* for the next twenty-five years and made my name known in America. But more importantly it released me from the confines of eighteenth-century British History. This new freedom allowed me to range more widely over European and American history. I became fascinated by the interplay of cultures not only in ideas but in things. And here America, both North and South, provided enormous fascination – the way it changed Europe's life and culture dramatically; the interplay of illusion and greed; the way murder, rape, brutality of every kind could exist happily with the compassion of the Christian faith. In America I felt that there was a more complex human experience and a better documented one than was to be found in British history. By the time of the Revolution, America had become an extraordinarily complex factor in the development of European society. The problems that confronted America for centuries, that gave the Founding Fathers double-vision when they spoke of liberty and freedom, that led Americans to slaughter each other in one of the most terrible of civil wars, all these things began with Columbus.

(i) Balls of Cotton and Parrots' Feathers

The only version that we possess of the logbook of Christopher Columbus's discovery of the West Indies is derived from a copy made probably in 1552 by Las Casas, the great champion of the Indians. The original presented to Ferdinand and Isabella has long disappeared. About the existing version – *The Journal of Christopher Columbus*, here translated by Cecil Fane, with an appendix by R. A. Skelton – scholarly acerbities get razor-edged. Several suspect that Las Casas doctored the journal to strengthen his own case; others will not hear of it, conceding only that Las Casas did introduce some remarks of his own into the text of the *Journal*, but he did so 'in good faith'. I am no specialist, but it does seem to me that a man who can add place names and events is not above inserting an adjective or expanding a remark so that it glows with his own fervour. Of course, we shall never know unless another copy is unearthed in Spain.

However, it does not matter overmuch whether we are reading Columbus pure or Columbus adulterated, for the fascination of the *Journal* lies in its revelation of motive, and these were largely constant over the first great period of the Spanish conquest of America which started with Columbus's discovery and ended with the subjection of the Incas by Pizarro. And these motives, so strong, so powerful, so naïve in Columbus, have ever since pervaded the life of Europe in its involvement with the Americas, and, indeed, with primitive people everywhere.

Firstly, there was the sheer fascination, a sort of wonder at finding human beings in so totally different a state. Men and women were going about their daily lives completely naked, with the simplest weapons and tools, living what at first sight seemed like an idyll of bliss in islands that appeared to the hard-bitten salt-weakened sailors near to paradise. 'The Admiral says that it is impossible to believe that anyone has seen a people with such kind hearts and so ready to give and so timorous that they deprive themselves of everything in order to give the Christians all that they possess.' Columbus believed, perhaps rightly, that the natives believed that he and his ships came from heaven. But the simplicity and spontaneous generosity of the Indians recur again and again in Columbus's *Journal* and this aspect of his discovery is suffused with a kind of wonder. If Las Casas inserted these passages, he must have possessed great literary skill and marvellous empathy.

This contrast between primitive simplicity amidst natural abundance and the strife, violence and double-dealing of Europe was to haunt the minds of sensitive men for centuries. They shut their eyes to the disease, the savageries, the brutalities of Indian existence and dwelt, as in a dream, on what seemed the depressing contrast that civilised and sophisticated life made with the primitive and the natural. This illusion fortified the sense of loss, the concept of a Fall which had haunted Europe for millennia. And even when America had been raped and subjected, it still remained. It can be found in the novels of Fenimore Cooper as well as in the poetry of Henry Longfellow, not only in their glorification of the noble Indian, but also in the sense that living close to nature in all its wildness and majesty may bring out the finer qualities of mankind, that simple living is conducive to virtue. Even today such illusions are far from dead.

The first question, however, that Columbus asked of the simple and generous people whom he had discovered was, 'Do you know where gold can be found?' It was always on the next island, or further to the West, for these West Indians possessed only a little that they got by trade. Their few ornaments were happily traded by them for glass beads and bits of cloth. There was not enough either to satisfy Columbus or, as he rightly feared, to please his royal masters. He had come for gold and spices, to fulfil that dream of greed which haunted the more adventurous men of his time. Their imaginations had been overheated by the wondrous stories of Marco Polo. As Columbus went from island to island in his small leaky boats, first Hispaniola, and then Cuba and back again, he could not have felt anything but disappointment. There was no gold; there were no spices: only balls of cotton and parrots' feathers. And rumours! Rumours of lands to the West where there was gold in plenty. Denied gold and spices, Columbus was forced to write of the fertility of the islands and of the sweetness of the Indians' nature; particularly the latter: indeed, he said, all they lacked was knowledge of Christ.

But once given the opportunity, how could these good, these simple, sweet-natured Indians become anything but devout Christians and, therefore, a heavenly feather in the Spanish Crown. Even if there was no gold, there were souls in plenty. Columbus, and all who sailed with him, were profoundly Christian, deeply superstitious, with a need for the rituals that threaded the daily life of Europeans. They expected not only the solid rewards of this world, but also the benediction of heaven in the life to come. It never occurred to Columbus, nor to most of those who were to follow him in Europe's quest for distant worlds, that he could be conferring anything but benefit on the Indians whom he was to rob and convert. He was amazed when men and women gave him all the simple trinkets which they possessed or brought food; and his delight knew no bounds when they accepted a few trivial glass beads in return. He never thought of consequences; few makers of empire have.

Yet the signs were there. Evil lurked in this Garden of Eden. There were Caribs who ate men, which obviously put them beyond the pale of humanity. And towards the end of his journey, the Indians became distinctly less friendly and seemed to be on the point of attacking the Christians, but seven of the latter were able to rout with consummate ease more than fifty of the former. As Columbus well knew, Indians were not hard to terrify and would be easy enough to kill. He had witnessed their fears when he discharged his cannon. They possessed no metal. The future belonged, through force, to Europe. The world of the Indians was at an end.

So the future is contained in this simple journal. It is, in a curious way, a very moving book. Not only in the obvious ways, although these are powerful enough. Columbus conveys a sense of the endless waste of the sea, the growing strain on the men, the tinyness of his vessels, their dangerous conditions, the tight-rope of disaster along which they sailed, and the underlying disappointment that grew and grew as the mirage of gold disappeared as island followed island. Certainly this makes it a gripping book to read, but it moves one in a deeper, less obvious sense than this. Its simplicity possesses an almost childlike innocence. Here are the motives – greed and religious conviction that, unleashed, were to bring death and destruction to millions of men, women and children and to topple empires. They were to lead not only to the rape of America, but also Africa and to centuries of servitude and misery for blacks and mainland Indians.

The Indians of the islands had a quicker and more terrible fate. Soon these seemingly innocent and very primitive peoples whom Columbus discovered were to be obliterated, wiped right off the face of the globe by disease and by violence. Hence these simple words of Columbus are latent with the problems that were to haunt Europe for centuries. That dream of riches in this world and a harvest of souls in the next quickly turned into a nightmare of brutality and extinction.

This journal has not been reprinted, except for private circulation to the Hakluyt Society in an identical edition in 1961, since before the war. It is beautifully illustrated and possesses an admirable introduction. It deserves wide circulation, for Columbus's *Journal* is not only immensely readable, but also it raises fundamental problems. Again, we are voyaging to unknown worlds: perhaps they will be empty and barren, but if they, too, should contain life totally different from our own, one can only hope that we shall not make the same blunders, or enter into so complex a situation with the naïveté of the sixteenth-century Spaniards.

(ii) The European Vision of America

America was an experience man could only have once. Knowledge of China, knowledge of Africa, festooned as it was with the Spanish moss of myth and legend, had penetrated Europe from the days of Imperial Rome and beyond. When discovered, the animals of Australasia were stranger by far than America's, and the aborigines and the bushmen of Tasmania were more primitive, even more uniformly naked than the Caribs whose appearance was so startling to Columbus. By then the strangeness of the Americas had destroyed the sense of novelty. There could only be one New World.

When confronted by novelty, men try to domesticate what is strange and alien; they attempt to fit the exotic into their cherished intellectual schemes and to absorb it into their interpretation of the world and its past. They retain, as it were, a husk of strangeness in which to take delight, or to weave fantasies, or worse still to construct rationalisations of their own evil intentions. The discovery of America had all of these effects and more, for no event in the history of Western man provided so profound a shock to the imagination or to the mind. And yet one might argue that the most important results of this discovery were far more mundane – maize, tobacco, gold, fur – the never-ending abundance of the land that led to the rape of a continent which became a golden pasture for human locusts.

Columbus, amazed, unsure, reluctant to accept that he was *not* in the Indies, found it easier to fit the Caribs into the legend of the Golden Age. As Peter Martyr, the friend of Columbus, wrote in the early 1500s, they 'seem to live in that golden world of which old writers speak so much, wherein men lived simply and innocently without enforcement of laws, without quarrelling, judges and libels, content only to satisfy nature.' This was the beginning of that ever-lengthening legend of the innocence of America which shifts from island to the mainland, from Caribs to noble Indian chiefs. It took many centuries to die; indeed, it is hardly dead yet, for nowadays the innocence has been transferred to the wilderness, to the desert, to the primitive land still unscarred in the West.

The theory that the naked Caribs lived in innocent bliss was soon dispelled. The Spaniards learned with horror that the Caribs hung up the hams of men and women to cure in the sun like sides of bacon. They relished the taste of human flesh; for them it was a gourmet's revenge on an enemy. When the Spaniards began to root themselves inefficiently in Hispaniola, the denizens of the Golden Age rapidly became subhuman. The Spaniards stressed their cannibalism, their nakedness, their fornication, and their frequently deviant and public sexuality. This savage paganism made their salvation imperative and their servitude justifiable.

The Caribs wanted neither salvation nor servitude. Killed, hunted, tortured, beaten and worked to death, they soon began to vanish, until genocide was virtually accomplished. Today scarcely any remain, but before they almost totally disappeared they had woven themselves into the imagination of Europe, as Hugh Honour has shown us in his recent book *The New Golden Land*, which is a brilliant discussion of the way the discovery of America haunted the European artistic imagination.

These Caribs, however, did more than stimulate the imagination. The brutal treatment accorded to them unleashed the passion of Bartolomé de Las Casas, whose bitter pen damned Spanish cruelty to a believing world of French, British, Germans and Dutch – who, however, behaved no better themselves once they got a foothold in the New World. But Las Casas's fiery words and the undeniable truth of his tale of the brutalities, the killing, the torturing and the wholesale destruction of primitive peoples started an enduring theme in America's history that still resonates in our own day. It is a long, bloody, bitter and sad road that leads from Hispaniola to the slaughter at Wounded Knee or the atrocities in the forests of Brazil. Innocence and betrayal, fascination and disgust, illusion and reality, these have so often been the dual response of Europeans to the primitive peoples of America.

The discovery of America led to an appalling destruction of human life – probably over twenty million died in a half-century – a fact all too rarely depicted in the artistic vision of America. It was the strangeness, the exotic nature of the people, the ornaments, their colour that entranced the artist. They might pose them like classical heroes, but they dressed them in their own feather headdresses and feathered skirts or left them stark naked. For the first two decades these natives remained amorphous, exotic yet somewhat unreal, like strange Europeans. Many artists who painted them had never seen an Indian, although from Columbus's first voyage a few men and women had been ripped from their homes to be displayed as curiosities in the courts of Europe.

It was only quite late in the sixteenth century that Indians were depicted more accurately, placed in more exact settings, and their customs, dances, and villages shown with some appreciation of reality.

John White's water-colours of the Indians of Virginia, among whom he lived briefly in 1585–6, shows greater precision and accuracy, even though he refrained from depicting the more primitive and savage of their customs. A Frenchman, Jacques Le Moyne, had been far more candid in his sketches of Florida Indians, but true realism had to wait until the seventeenth century, when two fine Dutch painters – Frans Post and Albert Eckhout – painted Brazilian landscapes and people exactly and vividly. And yet the art of fantasy in European paintings of Indians was not eradicated for centuries; even Delacroix in the early nineteenth century could paint Indians who looked like well-bred Europeans in fancy dress. The tradition of realism started by John White developed more slowly and only reached its apogee with Catlin, Bodmer and Rosa Bonheur, just before the genocide of the Indians had begun in earnest.

It was not only the exoticism of the people that both entranced and horrified Europeans. Columbus had gone in search of riches, of the fabulous Cathay. The Spaniards wanted gold. And they found it, bountifully in Mexico and beyond their wildest hopes in Peru; and the gold in the end led to the mountains of silver in Potosí and Taxco. This success in the search for riches came slowly. There were very barren decades, so that every object that was rich and exotic to look at was valuable as propaganda in the courts of Europe, which had to finance the early voyages of exploration and colonisation. So the splendours of Central and South American civilisations were soon on their way to Europe – the great golden discs, the brilliant featherwork cloaks, the terrifying death masks in jade and greenstone, works that when Albrecht Dürer saw them in Brussels made him marvel at 'the subtle *ingenia* of men in foreign lands'.

To the emperors they were indicators of riches to come, not works of art, and the golden vases, fountains, and animals that passed into the court of Charles V were quickly melted down for the money he always lacked. The feather cloaks were thrown away or left to rot in the attics of his palaces. Only a few men of taste or obsessive curiosity found a home for them in their cabinets, and today only a handful of objects survive from the first century of European discovery.

Among the earliest collectors to appreciate the singularity and beauty of Mexican art were the emperor Ferdinand I (who died in 1564) and his two sons; the extraordinary Rudolph II, a patron of everything exotic; and not surprisingly, perhaps, the greatest family of art patrons in Italy – the Medici, who as early as 1539 had brought together, as Hugh Honour reminds us, forty-four pieces of featherwork as well as carved masks and animals in semi-precious stone. Perhaps the strangest fate of any American object in the sixteenth century was that of a Mexican obsidian disc that fell into the hands of John Dee, Queen

Elizabeth I's astrologer and magician, who used it to conjure up spirits. It was, however, the common objects, novel to Europe yet totally adaptable, that were most quickly diffused – the first being the hammock, unknown to European gardens and ships until discovered in the West Indies; equally adaptable but later in time came the canoe of the American Indians and the kayak of the Eskimos.

Just as amazing to Columbus as the inhabitants of the West Indies were the flora and fauna of the New World. Some, of course, were easy to assimilate. The rather subdued coloured parrots of Africa had been greatly prized possessions of the Europeans in the late Middle Ages, but the brilliant coloured parrots of Brazil rapidly replaced them. These were represented as early as 1502 in Europe and appeared in a painting by Carpaccio, the Venetian artist, as early as 1507. Along with hummingbirds and Mexican quail, they were used as brilliant decorative motifs in the Loggetta of Raphael at the Vatican.

Hugh Honour has demonstrated the astonishing speed with which the artists of the Renaissance seized upon American birds and animals as well as Indians to use as dramatic motifs in their painting and sculpture. The turkey – now the all-pervasive Christmas dish of English families – reached Europe almost as quickly as the parrot. It was bred in Spain shortly after 1500, and the bird had reached Britain by 1525. Ironically, a hundred years after its discovery by Columbus the turkey had reached the East Indies. But it was the odder birds and animals that excited the most curiosity – the iguana, which was thought to be a dragon, discovered at last; the armadillo, whose true nature baffled scholars for decades; the opossum, which was the first marsupial known to Europeans; and the tapir and the llama, both of which defied description.

More important than the attempt to describe and to draw the birds, animals and plants was the impact of their variety on the development of European botany and zoology. Knowledge of the new animals had reached Europe, along with specimens, from time to time. The rhinoceros had made a vivid impression on Europe, but Europeans had never been subjected to such a flood of wholly new birds, animals, fruits, vegetables, trees and flowers as they were from the New World between 1500 and 1550. And it was this variety, its strangeness, and, at times, its marvellous adaptability and usefulness that led to the beginning of a scientifically precise observation – indeed, the beginning of botany and zoology as we know them.

The flora had a far greater impact than the birds and animals, so few of which could be domesticated. Maize, which could easily be grown in Europe, was exploited at once; within ten years of its discovery it was being cultivated in Italy, where it transformed Italian agriculture. Similarly, cassava, which reached West Africa very shortly after the Portuguese discovery of Brazil, had a like dramatic effect. The potato, which took far longer to establish itself as a crop rather than as a curiosity, ultimately had a more profound effect on European history than maize. The high nutritious quality of the potato enabled the European, particularly the Irish peasant, to maintain himself and his family on tinier and tinier garden plots. Millions of men and women depended on a single crop, and the disastrous potato blight of the nineteenth century destroyed the population in a monstrous famine in 1845 and, in an ironic twist of history, sent tens of thousands of starving Irish to find a new life and a new hope in America.

The contributions of the flora of the Americas to the enrichment of Europe is nearly endless; foods such as tomatoes, tapioca, chocolate, pineapples, avocados, runner beans, Jerusalem artichokes, passion fruit, and many more: flowers now common in Europe, such as morning-glory, nasturtium, dahlia and the tobacco plant, the most dangerous and deadly of all the plants to reach not only Europe but the entire globe, certainly one of the greatest of all hazards to human health. It was thought oddly enough to be deadly and dangerous when first discovered, and no one damned it with greater vehemence than James I of England. But the habit of smoking proved contagious and the profit impossible to resist. The land of America was quickly ravaged by Europe's addiction to tobacco – and not only America but also Africa, whence came the slave labour needed for its intensive cultivation. What in 1570 was depicted as a delicately beautiful flower decoration of Albrecht V of Bavaria's prayerbook became in less than fifty years a major export for America and a sweeping addiction with traumatic economic and social effects on Africa and Europe.

The potato and tobacco, along with maize, are perhaps the best known of the vegetables that changed the eating and social habits of Europe. What, perhaps is not such common knowledge is that the great movement in landscape gardening that changed the face of the English countryside in the eighteenth century also owed a great deal to America, above all to Virginia. The Virginian oak was planted by the hundreds of thousands; so were a large number of American pines; and the *Magnolia grandiflora* became the prize possession of even small gardens. Without the influence of America the English landscape would look quite different today.

However, the mental image of America remained more powerful than the influence upon European artistic expression of its exotic people, plants and animals and surely matched even the influence of such exceptional material agents as maize, the potato or tobacco. America remained for centuries the only New World. When the northern colonies established the first federal republic, at whose birth the liberties and rights of men were proclaimed as inalienable, another New World was born, as potent as that discovered by Columbus. A new political world had come into being, utterly distinct from anything Europe had known before – and one that created as entrancing an illusion as the civilisations the conquistadors had discovered.

To the poor and downtrodden peasants and workers of Europe it held out a new hope, a glittering image of riches and freedom. It is easy to forget the bitterness and brutalities of the ghettos of Europe or the starvation and deprivation that the wretched villagers of Greece and Italy suffered. It was their despair that eventually drove them to the coffin ships in which thousands died as they made the Atlantic crossing. The reality they found in America was harsher: hunger stalked on the Lower East Side; once more deprivation for many became part of their lot in life. And yet there *was* a reality in the illusion. There was more liberty, more social hope in America than in the lands they had quitted. There still is, in spite of the black ghettos and the long-enduring memory of slavery. The destruction of primitive peoples and slavery are the harsh realities of the American experience, for whose nakedness the Constitution, with its proud declaration of liberty, proved so pathetic a rag. So often illusion provided hope, reality the fate. And yet whatever the American experience might be, it remained for most Europeans an exotic continent.

After Buffalo Bill's fabulous success small boys in Riga, in Manchester, in Lyons, in Milan, played for generation after generation at cowboys and Indians; in the twentieth century Hollywood provided the dreams for the masses, and Disney captured the imagination of the child. No longer a fairyland of exotic peoples, animals and plants, America has created a new world of fantasy.

In the lives of children, in the dream time of adolescents, even in the sexual expectations of the adult world, America still feeds Europe with its illusions. As with the illusions of the past, a harsher reality is always breaking in: the drugs, the dropouts, the divorces. Perhaps the tobacco plant with its vivid flowers, intoxicating scent and deadly leaves should be the enduring symbol of that strange combination of illusion and reality with which America has contined to haunt Europe since its discovery.

(iii) The World Beyond America At The Time Of The Revolution

1.

For the farmers in the lonely valleys and hills and plains of America and the fishermen scattered down its endless coast, Europe in the eighteenth century had little meaning. Few realised that their lives were tangled in a web of forces – diplomatic, social and economic – that stretched from London to Moscow, or that their fate might be settled on the burning plains of India or amidst the hurricane-swept isles of the Caribbean. But it was so. For nearly a century Britain had been locked in a struggle with France; on its outcome the fate of the world depended.

And there were more subtle ties than these. When Benjamin Franklin walked the streets of London and Paris, he saw and heard what was familiar to him in Boston or New York. The same lovely proportions of houses and furniture caught his eye, richer perhaps and more ostentatious in decoration, but recognisably similar. He heard voiced the same discontents and the same aspirations. Frenchmen and Britons talked to him of the tyranny of feudal privilege, of the glories of liberty, of the need for equality. He learned how they, too, felt their lives to be thwarted by kings and nobles and ancient traditional forms. He came to understand the strength of the age-old institutions by which European society was governed. Above all, he came to know that the fate of America was inextricably entwined with Europe, and that forces unleashed there would help to mould its destiny.

When George III succeeded to the English throne in 1760, the whole nation had become drunk with victory. The previous year, 'the year of miracles', London church bells had rung out day after day to celebrate fresh triumphs over France or Spain. Their colonies had dropped like ripe plums into the hands of marauding English admirals. Trade flourished, production soared. War, as William Pitt, London's hero, had forecast, brought wealth; wealth and empire as vast as his own wild dreams. This strange, lean, hawk-eyed statesman, sick in body and mind, felt called by destiny to lead England to an undreamed-of greatness. He believed that France had to be reduced to a second-rate power; Spain despoiled; his hero, Frederick of Prussia, could keep the rest of Europe in proper subjection. By 1760, this was no longer a dream but reality. In America, Canada, the West Indies, Africa and India, French power had been destroyed. British ships swept the seven seas, and the world lay at England's feet.

Neither the King nor Pitt's colleagues could bring themselves to accept so fabulous a prize. They feared, perhaps rightly, the jealousy of the defeated powers. And so, by the time peace was finally signed at Paris in 1763, Pitt had been cast out of the ministry and England's demands reduced. Nevertheless the gains proved enormous. Canada, Florida and all lands east of the Mississippi, were cleared of Frenchmen and Spaniards; in India and the West Indies the gains were nearly as large;

certainly sufficient to make the British Empire the greatest and the richest that the world had known since the fall of Rome; sufficient, too, to arouse that envy and hatred in Europe which George III and his advisers feared.

In the eyes of European monarchs, England was a wild upstart race, notable for its revolutions and its almost pathological adherence to liberty; a people who kept its kings in subjection and rioted on the least provocation; a nation of hard-drinking, beef-eating shopkeepers with the instincts of pirates. Compared with their own rigid systems of government and law, Britain might appear unstable and anarchic. Yet no one could deny that she was rich, possessing an exceptionally buoyant financial system, growing trade and technological superiority. And these things mattered more than the power of despots.

Many contemporaries thought otherwise, to them the great European powers were stronger, richer, more cultured and more secure than Britain – absolute monarchies, blessed by God and stable to eternity. And the greatest of these was France, whose language had become the *lingua franca* of science, diplomacy and the arts.

The Earl of Pembroke insisted that his son must, cost what it might, have the best fencing and dancing masters in Paris. Russian, Swedish, German, Austrian, even Spanish and Italian aristocrats shared his sentiments. The French knew how to live as no one else did. The nobility of Europe talked French, wore French clothes, sat on French furniture, bought French pictures, collected French porcelain, read French books and pretended to believe in French philosophy. No one was educated until he had lived in Paris, visited Versailles, and listened to the gossip of the famous *salons*.There they imbibed the ideas of Bayle, D'Alembert, Condorcet, Diderot, Quesnay and, above all, of Voltaire, the arch-priest of the fashionable cult of reason. These philosophers vaunted man's capacity to control his universe; insisted that law, government, religion could only be respected in so far as their principles could be justified on intellectual grounds; they derided tradition, superstition, revelation and mystery. They talked endlessly of justice, equality, reason. But the heart, too, needed its prophet and it found him in Jean-Jacques Rousseau. He detested privilege, injustice, inequality, man's brutality to man. Nature was his panacea; the primitive his ideal; all wrapped up in a golden haze of sentiment and hope. So duchesses built dairies; installed a cow in a rococo setting and, to universal applause, milked it into a *Sèvres* vase. No nobleman's park was worthy of the name without grottoes, gothic follies or lonely hermitages. Decrepit peasants could be hired cheaply to add reality to the ghostly scene. After a refreshing draft of nature, the salons shone more brightly, the witticisms crackled, and the sharp laughter blotted out the future. As Louis XV so wisely said, '*Après moi le déluge.*'

Wise, because for the earnest middle class, the lawyers, doctors, merchants, these ideas of Voltaire and Rousseau were serious matters; dynamite not fireworks. They hated the feudal privileges which warped their lives and longed for a juster, freer world. And the smart, slick talk of Versailles and Fontainebleau became revolutionary fervour in Birmingham and Boston; everywhere there was a sense of a new, brighter, more hopeful world struggling to be born; even monarchs felt it. Frederick the Great, the autocrat of Prussia, patronised both Voltaire and Rousseau. So did Catherine of Russia. Both saw the need for efficient government, both hated the Church and its privileges; but both feared the liberating influence of the new philosophy and both quarrelled with Rousseau and Voltaire. As with monarchs, so with aristocrats; they were attracted and repelled. These smart, fashionable ideas corrupted their faith in themselves, and in the institutions upon which their power was based. Only an eccentric few could swallow the consequences of the new ideas – a world in which all men were free, equal and brothers.

France led the world not only in thought but in all that adorns the life of man. The court of Louis XV, and afterwards that of his grandson, Louis XVI, achieved a standard of luxury that Europe had not witnessed since the Augustan emperors. Architects, craftsmen, painters of superlative excellence, created a world of decadent beauty. The *fêtes champêtres* of Fragonard, the luxuriant nudes of Boucher, the soft-sentiment of Greuze and the harsh realism of Chardin dominated European painting. The *ébénistes* of Paris and Versailles produced masterpiece after masterpiece of cabinet-making that renders much of the vaunted work of Chippendale and Sheraton heavy and provincial.

Nor was such excellence confined merely to Paris and the Court. France was alive to its own greatness; alive to the riches which lay in its soil and in the hands of its craftsmen. The government created the finest transport system in Europe, the best roads, the best canals. New ideas in industrial techniques were eagerly sought and if need be stolen. Population, trade, industry grew with each passing year. In science Buffon, Lavoisier and Laplace were the acknowledged masters of Europe.

With such wealth, with such intellectual and artistic supremacy, the future, most Europeans felt, must belong to France in spite of her recent setbacks in the struggle with Britain for empire. No European country could rival her. Prussia, well disciplined as she was, lacked the proper sinews of great power – coal, steel, men, money. Russia lay like a spastic elephant across the threshold of Europe. The Austrian Empire, better governed and more closely knit under the rule of Maria Theresa and her son, Joseph II, seemed greater than she was. Lacking trade, industry and proper communications, the Empire had no future; the fabulous wealth enjoyed by the Court derived from the rich but recent conquests of the Turk, and was soon dissipated. Geography denied Austria greatness. If Austria had no future, Italy and Germany had no present. A fantastic conglomeration of principalities, electorates, bishoprics, grand duchies and the like, some well, some badly governed, some homes of enlightenment, some archaic and feudal, all were too small to play any part in Europe's destinies except to provide cheap cannon fodder for the armies of their richer neighbours. Beyond the core of Europe, Spain and Portugal drifted along, sometimes energised by an active statesman, but usually content to follow in the course of their senior allies; Portugal had tied herself to Britain; Spain was strictly joined to France by a family compact between their Bourbon rulers, signed in 1761. Nor was there any rival of France to the North. The Dutch, rich and thrifty, lay moribund under a system of government that was too rigid and too decentralised, an ossified federalism which bound its energies in chains, preventing those quick decisions and desperate gambles so necessary for success in a world of armed competitive states. Scandinavia and Poland lacked force, and became mere pawns in the diplomatic game; their aristocracies grew rich and corrupt on French, English and Russian gold.

France was indisputably master of Europe. And yet in her fight for an empire beyond Europe France had failed, and continued to fail. The trouble lay in her state-system. Privilege shackled her economic strength and the system of government functioned so efficiently that a privileged nobility and Church could maintain themselves in all their feudal but anachronistic splendour. With each passing decade both the social structure and the financial organisation of the state drew further away from the realities of social and economic life, thereby creating a desperate crisis which only the exceptional authority of the monarchy and the efficiency of its centralisation could bridge. Worm-eaten with privilege, the French state in all its glory could not match in a trial of strength the brash, chaotic world of its neighbour, Britain.

2.

Britain, like France, possessed many contradictions; archaic institutions, dating from Saxon and Norman times, attempted to serve a society rapidly evolving into a modern industrial state – and naturally with little success. Political power did not always coincide with economic wealth. Feudal concepts still littered law, government and education as well as social behaviour. And yet Britain remained a mobile society, freer far than any other society in Europe. The Duke of Newcastle might plaster his coach, plate and linen with his ducal coronet and never appear in public without his stars and ribbons, but his brother had been plain Mr Henry Pelham; his relations lived modestly as country-gentlemen; his second cousins were parsons, soldiers, sailors and city merchants. Most aristocratic families sported a Lord Mayor of London in their genealogies, not a few an actress. And money, if made in sufficient quantities, bought a place in society and government, perhaps not always in one, but certainly in three generations. And the current set both ways. Younger sons of peers and squires drifted down the social scale until they became absorbed amongst the parsons, yeomen-farmers and tradesmen. Britain never became burdened with a vast, unemployable, poverty-stricken nobility. The demands of Empire for soldiers, lawyers, engineers, administrators of all kinds made ever-growing demands on the ruling classes and India was soon to absorb all the sons that they could breed. This social mobility was a vital factor in England's strength. It made for opportunity. It took the edge from privilege for those born outside the governing class; at the same time younger sons were not frustrated in their ambitions to serve their country at a profit. Usually they could make enough money to maintain the style of life into which they had been born. The same mobility, the same opportunity stretched down into the lower classes. Small manufacturers, yeoman-farmers, craftsmen lived on terms of familiarity with their workers, servants and apprentices. London and the thriving towns of the West and North – Birmingham, Manchester, Sheffield, Liverpool, Leeds and Glasgow – offered chances of wealth and success to the quickwitted men and women of their neighbourhoods.

The unadventurous – and they were the majority – stayed in their isolated villages and hamlets, treading out the same pattern of life that their ancestors had laid down long, long ago. But unperceived by them, the new wealth that seeped into Britain like an estuarine tide, had sapped their ancient traditions. From 1760 England was in the throes of a social revolution that was to change the pattern of human life not only within its own shores but in the most distant corners of the world. Its concomitants were trade, invention, liberty, sound finance and weak government. It is time to look closer at this strange land that could lose an empire and yet remain strong enough to withstand all the mighty force of the French Revolution and Napoleon.

3.

Britain in the third quarter of the eighteenth century was a strange mixture of privilege and liberty, elegance and filth, antiquated habits and new inventions; the new and the old were jostled uncomfortably together; fabulous riches mingled with dire poverty. The placid country-side and sleepy market towns witnessed rick-burnings, machine-smashing, hunger-riots. The starving poor were run down by the yeomanry, herded into jails, strung up on gibbets, transported to the colonies. No one cared. This was a part of life like the seasons, like the deep-drinking, meat-stuffing orgies of the good times and bumper harvests. The wheel turned, some were crushed, some favoured. Life was cheap enough. Boys were urged to fight. Dogs baited bulls and bears. Cocks slaughtered each other for trivial wagers. Bare-fisted boxers fought the clock round and maimed each other for a few guineas. Sailors and soldiers knew the lash and the savagery of their power-drunk officers. Each passing year saw the ferocity of the law grow greater. Death came so easily. A stolen penknife and a boy of ten was strung up at Norwich; a handkerchief, taken secretly by a girl of fourteen, brought her the noose. Every six weeks London gave itself up to a raucous fête as men and women were dragged to Tyburn to meet their end at the hangman's hands. The same violence, the same cruelty, the same wild aggressive spirit infused all ranks of society. At the great public schools boys were mercilessly flogged and bullied. Often they rebelled. Young aristocrats – the Macaronis – fantastically and extravagantly dressed, rip-roared through the town, tipping up night watchmen, beating up innocent men and women. Jails and workhouses resembled concentration camps; starvation and cruelty killed the sick, the poor and the guilty. This rough, savage life has been immortalised by Hogarth, Rowlandson and Gillray – so much truer to life than the delicate gentility of a Gainsborough or a Zoffany.

Vile slums in the overcrowded towns bred violent epidemics; typhoid, cholera, smallpox ravaged the land. And the cure of disease was as violent as the sickness itself. Young girls, given to hysterics, had their hair pulled out of their heads or they were thrown into an ice-cold well in the hope that the shock would cure them. Purges, emetics, vomits, artificial running sores; killing cures of mercury and arsenic; the surgeon's knife without anaesthetics, these things were the stock-in-trade of sickness. Children died like flies; most men got through two or three wives. Disease scourged the land and the stink of the common paupers' grave at Manchester grew too foul even for that tough age. The inhabitants of Acton pleaded for the removal from the gibbet of the rotting corpses that had become too high in the fierce summer sun. But the British were as tough and as callous as they were aggressive. Mainly they took these things in their stride, as part of life's vast gamble, a stimulant and a challenge. They grew to love risk. Betting provided an outlet. Raindrops running down a window pane, the fertility of a Dean's wife, as well as horse races, cricket matches, bear-baiting, dice and cards were fit subjects for a bet. Fortunes vanished overnight. When Lord Stavordale lost £12,000 in a single throw, he thanked God that he was not playing for high stakes. The Duchess of Devonshire bedevilled her marriage by losing nearly a million at cards. The lower classes aped their betters; cock-fighting ruined farmers; cricket bankrupted yeomen; pitch and toss and crown and anchor emptied the pockets of the labouring poor.

Yet these things provided an anodyne for the fierce, savage and uncertain life that they lived; likewise the hero-worship of highwaymen. Dick Turpin, although he finished on the gallows, became a popular, romantic hero. And so did any general or admiral who took on fearsome odds in reckless circumstances. Clive at Arcot — a young man, almost a boy — gambled his life and puny army for the wealth of India. He became a national figure whereas the wise and cautious Admiral Byng was shot on his own quarterdeck for putting discretion and the safety of his ships before glory. Others found their emotional release in religion, in the violent, passionate call to salvation from a life of sin that Wesley and Whitefield preached with such fervour. The tough miners of Bristol and Newcastle wept for the wickedness of their ways and found a new life in God. Religion, like gambling or robbery or war, became an opiate, a screen from the horrors of daily life; unlike them, it led, not to self-destruction, but to a new life of thrift and social service. Methodism reformed habits as effectively as it transformed the spirit.

Although life was hard and cruel, often violent, always shadowed by death, yet it was full, too, of light and laughter and wonder. For riches, no matter how unevenly distributed, were pouring into Britain, creating new standards of elegance and luxury for an ever-widening middle class. And in the midst of the turbulence, the anarchy and the privilege, were groups of highly intelligent, strong-minded men and women, who possessed faith in man's capacity to order his world. Believers in science, in education, in industry, in invention, in good roads, new canals, lighting, paving, sanitation, clean jails, better laws, pure administration, social discipline, good housing, higher wages for better work, they were determined to create a richer, juster, more efficient society. They knew that the future belonged to Britain and to them their faith was derived from the evidence of their own eyes.

4.

'A vast change had taken place in English social life within two generations. View the navigation, the roads, the harbours and all other public works,' wrote Arthur Young. 'Take notice of the spirit with which manufactures are carried on. Move your eye which side you will, you behold nothing but great riches and yet greater resources.'

All he said was true. Brindley's canal, constructed in the 1760s, for the Duke of Bridgwater, demonstrated so amply the reduction of costs by water transport that a mania for canal-building swept the land, thereby widening markets and cheapening raw materials – coal, iron, wool and clay. And so, too, with roads; experiment was the order of the day and fast travel the conscious aim. Mile upon mile of new roads were being engineered, and along them were speeding a new race of men, 'commercial travellers', carrying in their bags the charming miniature samples of furniture, dresses, pottery, silver – now prized antiques. They were harbingers of a more luxuriant life for the professional classes and their advent in the little market towns caused a flutter in the feminine heart. Speed widened markets; orders arrived more quickly and were more quickly dispatched; and the clumsy local crafts were replaced by metropolitan fashions. Yet nothing demonstrated England's wealth nor its origins so vigorously as her crowded seaports. London, Liverpool, Glasgow resounded to the hammer blows of thousands of workmen building the new docks to house a merchant fleet greater than the world had ever known.

British sails crowded the most distant seas. Even the Celestial Emperor in Peking, Chi'en Lung, had heard of this strange race of red marauding barbarians who were foolish enough to barter silver for tea. Little did he realise that their ideas would filter into his ancient world, bringing destruction and change to a civilisation far, far older than their own. Wherever they sailed, the British sought profit rather than empire; and great wealth poured back to fertilise expanding industrial revolution.

Navigation, roads and harbours did not tell the whole story; change was just as visible in the way of life of the prospering classes. In villages, in market towns, above all in London and in the new fashionable spas, new spacious houses were being built with a sense of elegant proportion that has given them a pre-eminence for beauty to this day. Sometimes grouped in terraces, sometimes curved in a crescent, occasionally rounded in a circle or formed into a square, these Georgian houses gave a new loveliness to the urban scene. They were decorated with exceptional taste, for their architects – the Woods at Bath, the Adams at Edinburgh and London, the Carrs of York and Smith of Warwick – were familiar with the finest work of Italy and France. The new classicism, given such impetus by the discoveries at Pompeii, controlled their exuberant delight in ostentation with a sense of proportion as exact as a mathematical theorem. Within, plasterwork, marble fireplaces, gilded panelling displayed the same faultless taste. Furniture, provincial and very plain by French standards, reached an excellence never since excelled by English craftsmen.

Silverwork of the highest order adorned the tables of the rich. The new invention, Sheffield plate, enabled the middle class to copy the aristocrats' silver at half the cost. Porcelain and ornamental pottery, both novelties to the nation at large, became manias for all who had a pound or a shilling to spare. The well-to-do bought the beautiful productions of Chelsea, Bow, Derby, Worcester or Wedgwood, the thrifty poor indulged themselves with the crude chimney ornaments of the Staffordshire potters. The huge production of useful as well as ornamental china betrayed the wealth of the nation. Clothes, too, although simpler than the exotic aristocratic fashions of earlier decades, were as rich and as ornate and as handsome as the houses and towns in which they were displayed. And the art of pleasure was cultivated with the same intensity as the art of decoration.

Balls and masquerades, plays and burlesques, concerts at which the new and lively compositions of Bach, Haydn and Mozart could be heard for the first time, took place in a setting as harmonious as the melodies themselves. Never before had the arts of social intercourse been so assiduously cultivated. And the shopkeepers and artisans were equally avid for their finery and frills. Sadlers Wells and Islington Spa provided them with tea gardens, harlequinades, rustic dancing and all the delights that their superiors enjoyed in greater elegance at Ranelagh or Vauxhall.

The aristocrats were richer, far richer than they had ever been. Rents mounted year by year; house property, coal, iron, new ventures added to their wealth and what they won so easily was often as prodigiously spent. Down went the old house and up went the new palace; Italy, France, even Germany were ransacked for treasures, pictures, sculptures, tapestries; all noblemen were connoisseurs. Whims and fancies could be indulged – private orchestras played to the musical; zoos entertained the naturalists; gardens, for which rivers were diverted and the Himalayas pillaged, delighted the botanists; private laboratories, rare libraries, hired philosophers, nourished the intellectuals. Whatever they desired, they bought. But from peer to pauper there is a gusto about life, a confidence, an ebullience and waste that argues a profound belief in their own destiny.

Certainly they felt gauche before French fashions; admittedly they respected French art and French literature profoundly. None of them believed themselves educated until they had spent some years on the Grand Tour in France and Italy. Nevertheless they knew their government and their church to be the best in the world; the most jealous of liberty, the most conducive to prosperity. Nor did their respect for antiquity blind them to their own achievement. They worshipped Shakespeare, revered Isaac Newton and John Locke – as indeed did Voltaire – took pride in Gibbon, Hume and Blackstone, and delighted in the novels of Fielding, Smollet and Richardson and in the plays of Sheridan and Goldsmith. And they were as impressed by the pontifications of Dr

Johnson as by those of any *Encyclopedist*. They were pervaded not so much by a sense of inferiority as a desire to learn.

Yet the wonders of this new age, its greatness and its hope, belonged to the few and not to the many. Old habits still clung like burrs to the minds of the majority, and behind the luxury lay the pig-sty of the poor. A world was in transition though few realised it. Great inventions and new sources of power had begun to realise the strange cunning of men; they had brought into being a ferocious, expanding world in which greater wealth would sooner or later bring greater justice, more freedom, more leisure and the final destruction of those feudal privileges under which man had laboured through the long and bitter centuries.

5.

War, commerce and invention, these were the factors that were primarily responsible for setting the social life of Britain in violent motion. Britain had been more or less continuously at war, apart from Sir Robert Walpole's twenty years of rule, for more than a century. As a young man, Chatham, in a speech of fiery eloquence, told the Commons, 'when trade is at stake, you must defend it or perish'. When he died, the City of London raised a monument to him at Guildhall upon which these words of Edmund Burke were inscribed: 'A statesman by whom commerce was united with and made to flourish by war.'

And it was true. Marlborough's wars had reaped victory's harvest in the West Indies and the Spanish trade; Clive had wrested Bengal, worth £2,000,000 p.a., from the supine hands of the decadent Moguls; at the same time he cleared the French out of the Carnatic. And Chatham's genius had won the greatest gains of all – Canada, India, West Africa had all witnessed his conquests and not only witnessed but also paid for them out of increased trade. Tobacco, sugar, rice, furs, timber, fish, silk, cottons, tea poured into British ports, a torrent of liquid wealth that fertilised all that it touched. Yet war had won trade not empire. Chatham himself spurned Clive's offer of Bengal to the nation. He preferred to leave such desperate problems of government to the East India Company. Chatham saw empire in trade, in the possession of ports and strategic points, in the denial of advantages to the enemy, France, and not in the rule and subservience of millions of his fellow-men. Hence, although a passionate imperialist, he could sympathise with the tribulations of the Americans in their struggle with Britain.

War, however, brought greater benefits, although less realised than trade, greater even than the stimulus to the production of steel and cloth and shipping. The need for larger and larger forces on land and, more particularly, at sea created an intolerable strain in William III's day on the ramshackle machinery of central government. England came near to defeat, through lack of money and lack of logistic competence. Ruin was averted by the foundation of the Bank of England, the re-coinage, the introduction of the land tax, direct administration of taxes instead of tax-farming (the bane of France), improved accountancy and a better system of budgeting and appropriation. So Britain acquired what, hitherto, the Dutch alone had achieved; a buoyant, flexible and reasonably just financial system. Such excellence bred faith; government funds were eagerly sought; money and credit abounded; interest rates fell in London to 3% and even in war rarely rose much above 5%. So war not only increased trade, but also freed money and multiplied it.

Cheap money stimulated speculation, new enterprises, invention; a risk was cheap; the effect on the industrial revolution was profound. Plentiful money created demand – for goods, for food, for those small personal luxuries that are the symbols of affluence. And as is usual in times of economic prosperity, the population began to grow, at first slowly but with ever mounting momentum until by 1780, Britain was rapidly becoming a nation dominated by youth – in itself a factor making for enterprise and expansion.

The need for labour had long been apparent, and at last, a conscious attempt to tackle problems of disease and sanitation had to be made. The wide use of inoculation against smallpox, the attention paid to midwifery, the creation of foundling hospitals for unwanted children, the increasing use of cotton (and washable) underclothing, the change from wooden platters to pottery (again washable), the encouragement of personal hygiene and the brilliant medical teaching of Smellie, Pringle and the Hunters, all contributed to keep more people alive for longer. Yet neither the improved social conditions nor the even more important economic stimulus to early marriage and parenthood, produced labour fast enough for the growing economy. This shortage of hands stimulated men's ingenuity. They broke down restrictive practices, bypassing those fearsome medieval guild regulations that were the curse of French industry.

Their attitude to the working class also changed. Instead of wanting to keep them poor to keep them working, they began to provide incentives – better wages, better housing, facilities for education and religious worship. With money to spend and goods to spend it on, the working class worked harder and spent more wisely. Again, industrialists began to pay great attention to methods of production. Division of labour became the slogan of efficiency. Instead of one craftsman making an object, each process in its manufacture became the work of one man, thereby increasing and speeding production and also enabling women and children to be employed. It is easier to teach a man to make a spring than a clock.

The factory system spread, for the factory led naturally to greater discipline and to evenly flowing production. At first workers hated it and manufacturers were forced to use women and child-labour, both more amenable to regular hours and repetitive tasks. Slowly the system spread, but in the last half of the eighteenth century it was still something of a novelty and visiting notables from Europe were always shown the great Soho works of Boulton and Watt or the new pottery works of Josiah Wedgwood at Etruria, first opened in 1769.

Yet these things were insufficient in themselves to bring about the industrial revolution. They increased production but never fast enough. All the great entrepreneurs of eighteenth-century England were also preoccupied with invention. 'Everything,' wrote Josiah Wedgwood, 'yields to experiment.' And his commonplace books are full of notes on science and technology. New materials, new machinery, new techniques, these things led to improvement and they knew it. In all industrial circles a search for invention intensified. Manufacturers joined the Royal Society — Wedgwood himself contributed a paper on the thermometer - and cultivated scientists. The close relationship between Boulton and James Watt is well known. Watt's invention of the steam engine in 1769, and more importantly, the development of an improved version with rotary motion in 1781, freed mankind for the first time from the natural sources of power, opening up the limitless vistas for industrial society. Joseph Priestley, one of the most remarkable men of his day — scientist, philosopher, reformer — numbered dozens of manufacturers amongst his close friends and admirers. In all manufacturing towns the same spirit of inquiry dominated men's minds. The result was a remarkable spate of inventions. In textiles, Arkwright's spinning frame (1769), Hargreaves's jenny (1770) and Crompton's mule (1779) revolutionised the production of yarn and turned the spinning wheel into an antique. The demand for iron, stimulated by war, led to the inventions and improvements of Smeaton, Gort and the Cranages; smelting by coal, invented earlier in the century and kept a jealous secret, spread through the industry. The great works of Carron in Scotland and Dowlais in Wales became the wonders of their age. To show his faith in iron, John Wilkinson, the great iron-master, built iron bridges, iron boats, iron chapels and was buried in an iron coffin. Human ingenuity left no industrial art unimproved.

The same vigorous spirit spread throughout England's greatest industry — the land. Improvement in agriculture was already many generations old. The great publicist, Arthur Young, sang the praises of Norfolk — its enclosures, its marling, its clover, its turnips, its rotation of crops and its long leases. Yet these things all dated back to the seventeenth century, as did the fashion for large estates which allowed so much better management through greater capital resources. From 1750 the pace of change quickened; agriculture became the rage. Robert Bakewell's farm at Dishley became an object of pilgrimage, for he bred larger and fatter and woollier sheep than men had dreamed of. New machinery, better fertilisers, stronger horses, milkier cows, fleshier bullocks were displayed with pride at county shows. The Duke of Bedford graced sheep-shearing contests with his presence; George III was nicknamed 'Farmer George' because of his passion for agriculture. The huge, beef-eating, beer-drinking caricature of all Englishmen – John Bull – was a farmer. More mouths to feed, more money for food, brought a golden age of prosperity to the land and, ironically strengthened those traditional forces in society that were most opposed to all change in politics and society – the country-gentlemen.

6.

Not so the new men; they took delight in reform and improvement. Their willingness to experiment, to risk the new against the old, did not stop at industrial organisation or agrarian management. The Arkwrights, Strutts, Wilkinsons, Wedgwoods and Cokes applied the same principles to society. They lost patience with traditional muddle. Old broken-down roads with puddles the size of ponds, in which men and horses floundered and drowned, were useless to them. Slums, pullulating with disease, were an affront to their intelligence as well as their humanity. Good houses spelt healthy workers and a better output in the factory or on the land. Paved streets, like good roads, meant lower costs. A plentiful water supply eased industrial problems, provided better sanitation and improved health. Ample street lighting permitted late shopping and so better time-keeping in the factories. Both social discipline and social opportunity seemed utterly desirable to the great entrepreneurs – Whitbread the Brewer, Wilkinson the Ironmaster, Wedgwood the Potter, Boulton the Engineer. They were to be found in the vanguard of philanthropic reform. At Liverpool, men of a like mind laid out the first public gardens; at Newcastle on Tyne they founded a literary and philosophic society. At Manchester they sponsored a privately organised police force. They swarmed in turnpike trusts and canal ventures. They acquired a host of private Acts of Parliament by which they provided their towns with rudimentary social amenities. They were active in all societies to reform the manners and habits of the working classes. The desperate insecurity of the life of the poor naturally bred a feckless attitude; wakes, fairs, church ales, riots and drunkenness took off the edge of bitterness for the labouring poor but they also destroyed regularity of work by creating absenteeism. They brought about destitution and disease. The suppression of these working-class bacchanalias became an urgent social necessity. 'I wish,' wrote Wedgwood, 'to make such machines of my men as cannot err'. His fellow manufacturers concurred and sought to relieve their workers of anxiety, fear and despair. In consequence, they gave support to Friendly Societies which provided insurance against sickness in return for a small weekly contribution; they provided schools or supported them; they built better houses and provided better shops for, above all, they wished to raise the standards of living to encourage men to work harder. They might believe that some men would always be poor but none of them wished to preserve poverty for its own sake as their forebears had done earlier in the century. These 'new men' lived, therefore, in the ethos of social reform and an unquestioning belief in progress was a part of the air they breathed.

And yet at every turn they met traditional obstacles. Often they lacked the social or political power to achieve the smallest reform. Any body of manufacturers wishing to cut a canal had to solicit, maybe for years, the country-gentlemen in whose hands effective power lay. England was still governed by a remarkable collection of ancient, unreformed institutions, the slow accretion of time and as strong as a coral reef. Often these could be circumvented but only by much effort. Hence these new men became ardent apostles of reform. Their leaders, Adam Smith, Jeremy Bentham, Joseph Priestley and Richard Price, directed their attention to reform on a national scale as well as local. In their own work, they had come to appreciate the value of a rational approach. It was easy for them to believe that reason would be equally effective if applied to human institutions. Liberty and equal rights became their watchwords; and democracy their aim. Naturally they identified themselves with the struggles of John Wilkes and of the American colonists.

Their political impotence bred despair for the future; as one of these new men wrote to his son:

'Through the folly and wickedness of the present, you of the rising generation have indeed a dark prospect before you ... Your best way will be to gather as fast as you can a good stock of the arts and sciences of this country; and if you find the night of despotism and wretchedness overwhelm this hemisphere, follow the course of the sun to that country (i.e. America) where freedom has already fixed her standard and is erecting her throne; where the sciences and arts, wealth and power will soon gather round her, and assist and strengthen her empire there.'

This black mood fell time and time again across their spirits. Opportunity they saw, and the promise of a larger future. But they lacked power. Society still revolved about its old gods – monarchy, established church, the nobility; little oligarchies of traditional reactionaries hogged political power in the countryside and corporate towns. Even Parliament whose struggle for liberty against the Crown had made their ancestors' days heroic had now become effete, unrepresentative, concerned only with its own privileges and indifferent to freedom and justice. So they felt. And naturally their sympathies swelled to all who cried out against oppression and privilege – Dissenters, Catholics, Irishmen, Americans. Powerless, they watched their country's empire break to pieces; they protested, they petitioned, they cursed George III, Lord North and the Constitution. Without avail for the traditional forces were still too strong; harbingers of a new world they might be; the old still held them in thrall.

7.

Commerce had enriched, but industry scarcely touched the traditional structure of English society. The new mushroom towns were ruled by the same officials in exactly the same way as in the days when they were villages. The Lord of the Manor remained a power in Manchester. Birmingham possessed the government of a village for it was a parish not a corporate town. Growing population, new industries, increased wealth, could create new problems of social organisation but it was left to the citizens to solve them. The methods of government remained almost untouched.

The Glorious Revolution of 1689 had been an almost unanimous revolt by the property-owning classes against interference in their local rights of government. In consequence the word *freehold* acquired almost a mystical reverence to eighteenth-century Englishmen – a *freehold* was not merely a tenure of land. It could mean a benefice, a commission in the Army or Navy, the possession of an obsolete office or ancient privilege. A blind, paralytic, mad bishop could not be deprived of his office until he died because his office was his freehold. To advocate the abolition of such sinecures as the Tastership of the King's Wines in Dublin or the Clerkship of the Pells smacked of revolution for these were some man's freehold. Also the Revolution had given a chance to the landed classes and their dependants to batten on the state. The Church, the Army and the Navy, the Court and the Administration had become a vast racket that provided outdoor relief for needy younger sons or dependent cousins. Lord Pembroke bought his son a commission so that he could wear a decent uniform on his Grand Tour. He did not see his regiment for four years but naturally he drew his pay and rose in rank. Lord Barrington was Secretary-at-War; his brother entered the Church and his career ran as follows:

1760 Royal Chaplain
1761 Prebend's stall at Oxford

1762 Two further stalls at Hereford
1768 Prebend of St Paul's: the highly prized *Consumpta per Mare*
1769 Bishop of Llandaff.

And then, with his brother out of office, his career flagged, but on his brother's return, the bishop began once more to move up the ladder of preferment.

1782 Bishop of Salisbury
1791 Bishop of Durham – one of the richest of all sees.

Any army or navy list in these years reads like *Debrett*. Ships or regiments, the natural assumption was that they were property, and property that belonged by divine hereditary right to the ruling classes. And the same was true of much of parliamentary representation. The Duke of Grafton, short of cash, sold his parliamentary borough of Gatton in Surrey and the auctioneer described the purchaser's joys in these terms:

> No tempestuous passions to ally, no tormenting claims of insolent electors to evade, no tinkers' wives to kiss, no impossible promises to make, none of the toilsome and not very clean paths of canvassing to drudge through; but his mind at ease and his conscience clear, with this elegant contingency in his pocket, the honours of state await his plucking and with its emoluments his purse will overflow.

There was no mention of electors because they were so few that they lacked importance. Lord Egremont bought the parliamentary borough of Midhurst for £40,000; the Duke of Bedford sold Camelford for £32,000. And as Chatham said, these little tiny towns that sent representatives to Westminster, but could be bought or sold like a parcel of fields, were 'the rotten parts of the constitution', yet even he would not hear of their destruction. The sanctity of the Constitution, blessed by the Glorious Revolution, could not be invaded.

At the same time, men witnessed a growing arrogance on Parliament's part, a jealous sensitivity to its privileges. Wilkes, elected for the most populous constituency in the country, Middlesex, was declared – not once but four times – not to be a Member of Parliament because he had crossed his King and had been convicted on a trumped-up charge of libel. It was Parliament's privilege to decide the question of its own membership. As with great, so with small matters.

'On one occasion,' wrote Lord Mahon,

> 'it was voted a breach of privilege to have killed a great number of rabbits from the warren of Lord Galway, a member. Another time the fish of Mr.

Joliffe was honoured by a like august protection. The same never failing shield of privilege was thrown before the trees of Mr. Hungerford, the coals of Mr. Ward and the lead of Sir Robert Grosvenor. The person of one member's porter and another's footman was held to be as sacred and as inviolable as the persons of the members themselves.'

Those that owned the land, owned the institutions of government, and ran them in their own interests. More and more crimes against property became capital offences; the game laws approached the savagery of the old forest laws of medieval kings; enclosures multiplied. More entrenched in power than they had ever been, they were also richer; rents soared, their investments grew, the state provided. Naturally many of them took a rosy view of the universe. It was the best of all possible worlds and to desire change was to fly in the face of Providence. Wilkes, the Radicals and the American colonists were not only stupid but wicked.

So it seemed for those excluded from the magic circle of government; they seized on the little acts of tyranny, the assumption of privileges and the minor corruption that was obvious to all and saw George III as a Stuart tyrant and Parliament as a complacent tool. For those within the situation was infinitely more complex, a bewildering world of duty that pressed heavily on privilege and profit.

Throughout the changing centuries Britain had been ruled by the owners of the land. They dominated her counties; they filled Parliament and all the professions. Sometimes a new family, grown rich in commerce or the law, would buy up an improvident's estate in order to acquire that gentility which was the hallmark of the establishment. But landowning, great or small, carried social responsibilities. The farmers, even the smallholders, had duties hard to escape. They ran their parishes, provided the constables, church-wardens, Overseers of the Highways and of the Poor, unpaid jobs all, and all onerous in that aggressive, litigious society. They kept order, collected taxes, shared out collective duties, provided for the sick and the destitute. Often they were harsh, rushing an expectant mother across the parish boundary so that their neighbours would have to provide for the unwanted mouth. Yet to their own kith and kin and to those whose roots in the parish went as deep as their own, they parcelled out a rough justice and engendered some human warmth. And although they frequently did themselves well out of the rates, most of them were honest after the fashion of their age. Usually they were owners of small properties – like Arnold of Kent, or Thomas Turner of Sussex, or Carrington of Hertfordshire whose diaries have been published – and they too were enjoying the rising prosperity of the land. Their attitude to life was to accept it as it was; if they were undisturbed, they were content for the gentlemen to rule.

Most of these little oligarchies of village rulers were linked by ancient friendship with the greater landowners – the nobility and country-gentlemen of long standing; often they were bound by economic ties by renting of land or supplying of services or materials to the 'great house'. The real rulers of the county were to be found amongst the squires and aristocrats and their ecclesiastical dependents. They provided the Justices of the Peace upon whose backs rested the whole burden of law and order. They also officered the militia, needed as much to suppress the rioting poor as to withstand the ever-expected invasion of the French. Many gentle families stretched back into remote antiquity and naturally enough their politics were patriarchal. Their destiny was to govern. A dozen families or so in most counties acquired a certain pre-eminence through wealth or ability or both. Often feuds divided them; like that of the Hastings and Greys in Leicestershire, dating back to before the War of the Roses; and great national issues always found the same set of families at loggerheads with one another. Since the Revolution these groups had often gone under the name of Whig or Tory but counties could be divided Whig against Whig and Tory against Tory. Family feuds and alliances had come to mean more than politics. Bitter battles for the honour of representing counties in Parliament had so beggared many families that by the accession of George III most English counties preferred to compromise on candidates than risk the expense of an election; often one Knight of the Shire was drawn from the Whiggish families, another from the Tories. In 1761 there were only four contests in the forty English counties, so the most democratic of all constituencies had little opportunity to express a political opinion. Yet such Members of Parliament were not free from political pressure. As the American revolt progressed, the rights and wrongs of it became issues even in county politics and Knights of the Shire felt the need to make their views known. For generations representation at Westminster had been settled with hardly a thought about politics. The American war changed that for ever, invigorated political discussion, and helped to bring about a rebirth of the party system.

The families of these Knights of the Shire read like a roll-call from *Debrett*. Cholmondeleys sat for Cheshire, Courtenays for Devon, Lambtons for Durham, Cokes for Norfolk and the same ancient names were to be found representing the small county towns or seaports. Over the generations a family had established its patronage over a borough; almost time out of mind Rashleighs had represented Fowey, Burrards Lymington, A'Courts Heytesbury. Such men spent much of their time on local affairs, securing Bills for workhouses, river-widening schemes, turnpike trusts and the like as well as attending to the manifold griev-ances of their constituents. Such men, like the Knights of the Shire, were self-electing, but neither bribery nor government influence got them into Parliament. They might favour this political group or that, incline to traditional Whiggery or traditional Toryism, but the security of tenure bred in them an attitude of such independence that all ministers needed to win the support of the majority of them if they were to survive. It was to their serried ranks on the back-benches that the oratory of the parliamentary leaders was directed. Although most of them called themselves Whigs it was not the Whiggery of their ancestors; tradition, the constitution as laid down in 1689, was their watchword rather than liberty. They believed in monarchy, in the established Church, in the subordination of Ireland and the Plantations. Most of them were suspicious of Wilkes, worried by Chatham, and content with George III and Lord North.

Although these men provided the background to politics they did not fill it. There were corrupt boroughs. Many belonged to borough patrons who detested Lord North and George III. They brought in their henchmen. A successful merchant with political leanings could usually pick up a seat if he wanted one; so could lawyers. And some boroughs with tiny electorates – like Bath – spurned patronage and worshipped furious independents. And there were boroughs with enormous electorates – open to any demagogue with a purse large enough to provide the gargantuan orgies of beer-drinking and beef-eating that all voters regarded as their rights. Naturally the Crown controlled many boroughs and found seats for its admirals, generals and civil servants and court officials but it would be quite wrong to think that George III or his ministers controlled very much of the membership of Parliament. Indeed it has been shown that royal influence at this time was steadily declining, that George III controlled less in 1780 than he had done in 1760; and that the winners, as might be expected, were either the *nouveaux riches* or the long-established parliamentary families. These factors gave Parliament its life and spirit, and brought it nearer to a truly representative assembly than its critics have allowed. Yet men of great estates dominated at Westminster, and their attitude of life was bound to be, except for a few eccentrics, traditional and averse to change.

Such men had little comprehension of, or interest in, the grievances of remote colonists; in their minds, the Americans were linked with the Irish, a difficult and disagreeable people, best kept under.

The heart of politics lay in the Court, for Kings in eighteenth-century England were expected to rule as well as reign; ministers were their servants as well as being responsible to Parliament. Hence the personality of the King proved to be an important factor in politics.

George III came to the throne at a very early age, but mentally he was younger still. He had developed late – he could not read until he was ten. He lacked faith in his own abilities, and dreaded the burdens which the Almighty had placed on his shoulders. Yet his sense of duty was quite remarkable and his natural obstinacy monolithic. Burdens they might be, but they were a sacred duty. Puzzled, determined, ignorant, and not apt to learn, George III turned to Lord Bute for whom he developed a schoolboyish passion. Bute, a career politician, and friend, possibly lover, of the Princess of Wales, George III's mother, was eager to exploit the King's dependence. Together they set about getting rid of George II's ministers – Chatham, Newcastle, Hardwicke, Devonshire; jealousies between rival Whigs proved easy to exploit, but the creation of a stable ministry, loyal to George III, Bute and their friends, proved impossible. George III was forced to turn from one group to another. He married, outgrew his dependence on Bute, and looked for other father-figures amongst his politicians. They all failed him – his uncle, Cumberland; Chatham who went quite mad; Grafton whose nerve cracked under the lash of Junius's letters.

Constant changes, squabbling groups of ministers, deprived the country of any settled policy. Grenville started the crisis. A careful administrator, good at arithmetic; a man who would have made a good banker but lacked even a modicum of imagination, decided, logically enough, that the Americans should pay towards the expenses of the Seven Years War which had freed them from the French menace in Canada. The furore caused by the Stamp Act astounded the ministry; naturally enough the opposition Whigs, led by Rockingham, were not slow to criticise and to make fine distinctions between direct and indirect taxation. Once in office they repealed the Stamp Act and appeased George III, who regarded the American colonists quite simply as rebels, by passing the Declaratory Act which asserted that Great Britain possessed a sovereign right to tax the colonies. The Rockinghams soon went. Chatham succeeded, but insisted on creating a ministry that would be above the strife of faction. Unfortunately he went mad and whilst the King waited for him to recover, Charles Townshend pushed America further towards rebellion by his imposition of duties on imports; and so the sorry tale went on. Blunder followed blunder as ministries came and went; conciliatory moves pressed hard on the heels of firm, authoritative action. No one realised until it was too late that America was in the throes of a social revolution, stronger far than the similar movement in England, and one less hampered by tradition.

By the time George III found Lord North, the situation in America had become almost hopeless. North and George III have become the villains of the struggle for independence. Both were men of limited intelligence, no vision and little common sense. George III knew his duty. The Americans must be made to obey for it was his sacred trust to pass on his empire unchanged and undivided to his heirs. So his policy was simple. Suppress the revolt; use force; do not negotiate. North, an adroit politician, fine debater and skilful administrator, lacked this simplicity of approach. He was a warm-hearted man, naturally timid, deeply loyal, above all, loyal to his King. He hated the war; indeed he longed to give up a situation for which he felt he lacked the abilities. He constantly hoped something would turn up – a victory, a chance of compromise, a change of heart. What he could not do was to give all his undivided energy to waging a ruthless war. As the sick and dying Chatham had long ago forecast, France and Spain seized their opportunity for revenge. And from the height of greatness, Britain plunged from defeat to despair.

North, too, had been hamstrung, not only by his own indecision and incompetence, but also by the noisy sympathy with America in England and by the growing opposition in Parliament. He was saved from defeat only by the steady support of the independent back-benchers, the self-elected country-gentlemen, whose attitude to Americans sprang from their hatred of change and reverence for tradition. Also they feared for Ireland. They had with difficulty held down that older land through the centuries; weakness to America would lead to weakness to Ireland, the loss of America to the loss of Ireland – so they feared. Nor were these fears groundless. And the terrible spectres of a break-up of Great Britain haunted the King's mind and jeopardised his sanity. So the squires supported George III and North to the sad, bitter end.

The majority of politicians whether in or out of the ministry knew little or nothing of America. The West Indies rather than the Northern Colonies were looked upon as the richest jewels of the empire. Exceptionally valuable, if kept in proper economic subjection; excellent producers of raw materials, most of them thought that the Northern Colonies might easily be a danger if allowed freedom of commerce and manufacture. Socially and politically difficult everyone knew them to be. They had been, for more than a century, the home of the discontented. The poverty-stricken malcontents from Scotland and Ireland had drifted there in droves, leavened only by religious bigots and fanatics. In one thing the colonies had proved convenient; they were admirable dumping grounds for thieves, whores, bankrupts and ne'er-do-wells. Many philanthropists cherished the strange idea that the socially incompetent would flourish in a harder environment. Only a few politicians knew the true state of America. A few, very few, had been there and even fewer had taken the trouble to learn of its economic and social problems.

This ignorance was in a sense natural. and so was the colonist's ignorance of British problems. Most resented the mother country and cared little about her struggle with France or Spain. As yet the greater achievements in art, science and technology carried little weight, and did nothing to counterbalance the sense of subjection and the resentment of an alien rule.

If ignorant of Britain, the colonists were aware of their own vast opportunities. The new lands to the west called for an independent spirit and bred a sense of freedom and democracy. But, by and large, those who drifted across the Alleghenies left government and constitutional problems behind. Their only importance was to create an attitude of mind. Like Wilkes they became a symbol of freedom and liberty in the minds of those that grappled with the problems of government in the long-established colonies. To them they gave a sense of the limitless possibilities of America's future. And so did their own economic wealth. The colonists were making money hand over fist, at least in Boston and New York. They built excellent ships and trade boomed. The antiquated navigation laws could be evaded or the fines paid and Europe, the West Indies, the great Spanish Empire needed American goods. Tobacco, fur, timber, fish, rice, sugar founded the fortunes of the great New England merchants. And yet they could not order their own world. A weak currency put their financial system at the mercy of London; many, particularly the tobacco factors, carried a mountain of debt partly due to shortage of currency and the weakness of the dollar. And although the commercial regulations could be evaded the need for evasion itself created vast annoyance. Yet there were deeper resentments. The richest offices – governorships, judgeships, registrars of customs and excise – went to Englishmen, to brothers and cousins of peers and politicians. Whatever patronage could be squeezed out of America went to feed the system of privilege in England. Many States kept up running feuds with the royal officials, creating every possible difficulty about payment of salaries or respecting the Crown's rights. Furthermore, most Americans knew themselves to be remote and provincial. Their manners were as plain as their living; birth and breeding meant less than success or wealth. And yet they were entangled in a web of ancient and traditional economic and social practices. Old privileges, old laws, planted obstacles to their future greatness. Many felt the need to break free though few guessed to what freedom might lead.

If the new spirit of the American colonies was little appreciated in England, even fewer colonists realised that many Englishmen's difficulties were in some way similar to their own, for in England, too, a new world was struggling to be born; a new industrial society, freer, less privileged, more just and more democratic was the ardent aspiration of the most forward-looking sections of society. The success of the American revolt and the wild outburst of the French Revolution did much to thwart their ambitions, so that when the new industrial society did emerge in

England, it still remained encrusted in privilege and dominated by ancient practice. Ignorance, lack of communication, and a sense of separate destinies kept the two movements apart, which, if combined, might have changed the destiny of mankind.

Chatham told Parliament that America could never be conquered and he was right. British troops were too few, too unused to guerrilla warfare; they could not be properly supported with ammunition, food and reinforcements. Communications were too slow; distances too great; the opposition of France and Spain too strong. Defeat followed defeat; no ally, not even the Dutch, came to Britain's aid. England plunged from the height of greatness. 'I wish,' wrote the Earl of Pembroke to his son in 1779, 'I was a Laplander, or anything but a Briton.'

The treatment of Wilkes and the obvious injustice of parliamentary representation had led many to cry for reform long before the American revolt but now the chorus swelled. This crisis impelled all men to think of politics and take a side. The magnificent oratory of Burke, of Charles James Fox and, above all, of Chatham, rang through the land, calling not only for an end to the war but for a change in government. All institutions were brought into disrepute; only the reformers gained. The American revolt forged a new attitude to monarchy, even in the aristocratic world; the Whigs, led by Rockingham and Fox, came to believe that kings should reign but no longer rule; that ministers should be chosen by the dominant party, not by the king. In 1782 the reluctant George III hesitated between abdication and compliance. He complied, and then outwitted his enemies; nevertheless the future belonged to Fox and Burke. And the constitutional concepts of parliamentary democracy of nineteenth-century England emerged from the struggle to defeat George III and North.

Indeed, out of this tragic combat both sides gained; the failure of the Crown and of aristocratic society was so complete that they never recovered their old powers. Indeed it so destroyed their own faith in themselves that the abnegation of their power to the middle class, to the new men of the Midlands and the North who had acclaimed America's victories, became a matter of time. America acquired freedom, Britain moved towards a less privileged society. Furthermore, for the first time she was made to realise that empire was more than trade and riches but a complex problem of duties as well as rights.

In 1783 Britain was humiliated and isolated, the shadow of its former greatness, but victories and defeats in war fade quickly; the steady dynamic power of economic expansion and technological supremacy cannot be destroyed by the loss of territory or defeat at a diplomats' conference. In spite of George III, Lord North or America, the immediate future still lay with Britain; and for another hundred years she led mankind in its triumphant march towards a richer and juster world.

British Attitudes to the American Revolution

As I went about America, lecturing and giving seminars, from 1960 onwards, it seemed to me that there were two large themes, amongst many others, where traditional American attitudes towards the American Revolution needed to be corrected. There was little comprehension both of the nature of British society in the 1760s and 1770s and even less of the role of George III. I wrote a lecture on both subjects which I gradually revised and modified as I read more, discovered more and thought more about them. During their gestation which took a number of years (more than a decade in George III's case) I used ideas and material from them for lectures.

During my semester at Columbia in 1960 I gave one or two lectures outside the University – one which was a huge success at *The Conference for British Studies* which brought me the friendship of Ruth Emery and Jean Hecht, both profound Anglophiles, particularly Hecht, a strange eccentric but a firmly principled man. Both possessed a remarkable network of contacts throughout the nation and became very eager to promote me as a lecturer; the other which I remember with some distaste was at Harvard – uncomfortable rooms, casual courtesy, desperate food and a rather grudging offer to pay my railway fare. Many years later after I had become well known in America, reviewing regularly for the *New York Times Book Review*, the reception was different, but after that first experience, so like the treatment that might have been meted out to an unknown American in Oxford or Cambridge, I decided not to bother with the Ivy League but go to places usually unfrequented by English historians. So between 1961 and 1977, I lectured very widely indeed, perhaps more widely than any other historian in Britain except Denis Brogan. I was helped by A.L. Rowse who had been asked by Stanley Trickett to visit Omaha University for ten days, and lecture to the Conference of American Historians. Leslie was too busy at the Huntington with Shakespeare, so he recommended me and I accepted with alacrity. Omaha became the core of an extremely busy programme lasting three weeks which started at Birmingham, Alabama (my first class at 8 am!) through the Middle West to Chicago, then across to Iowa, Omaha, Lincoln and then back via Columbus, Ohio. I gave eighteen lectures in three weeks, plus innumerable seminars and talks to the Faculty and students, interlaced with formal banquets preceded by fierce cocktail parties, and the only peaceful hours were on the slow, ever-stopping four-engined – sometimes even two-engined – propeller planes that lumbered over the endless plains at a convenient viewing height of about ten thousand feet. And this year after year became the pattern of my springs – and one day I must write a book on lecturing in America for my experiences were extraordinary and unforgettable – falling asleep for a few seconds at my own lecture at Reed College in Portland, Oregon. I'd flown there, with constant delays, direct from Cambridge, only to be taken sight-seeing up the Columbia River, back to a seminar and a cocktail party (very heavy martinis) and so to a formal dinner and the lecture. No wonder I dozed off. For once I had tested my stamina an inch too far; but I got away with it. Naturally there were other close calls, mostly in the air – a near-miss on the approach to O'Hare; engine failure *en route* to Boston, nearly landing off the runway at Oklahoma and just lifting clear again; iced wings, diversions, delays of all kinds, but although I travelled tens of thousands of miles, I never missed a lecture and my luggage never went astray: indeed none of the American airlines, not even the old Allegheny line, ever let me down. It was an experience such as no historian before my generation could ever have had. The visit I still cherish most was to Enid, Oklahoma.

(i) On the Road

Enid, Oklahoma, Enid, Oklahoma. I said to myself over and over again as I waited for the student driver to collect me at Norman where I had been lecturing at the University of Oklahoma. To be frank, I felt rather proud. I was sure that no other British historian had ever been invited to Phillips University. I was out West, in the prairies, the land my father and I had read about and dreamt about during my childhood in the smoke-drenched Midlands of England. I had made it – sage-bush, mesa, Zane Grey and all.

A car large enough for eight adults and a dozen children drew up at the curb and a young, freckled, sandy-haired youth of nineteen introduced himself as Vera (what tribulations that name brought to him I was never to know). He said little else for the next sixty miles, as we bumped our way to Enid along roads that would not have been entirely out of place in rural England – but no sage-bush, no mesa, scarcely a house. And on arrival Enid looked awful. Huge billboards, lots full of second-hand automobiles, the usual litter of sprawling urban America – one of the most tasteless inventions of man.

Again and again I am struck by the incongruity of suburban America, with its beautiful streets and houses, its trees and flowers, and its sense of ease, tranquility and comfort, and the glaring, yowling, hideous main roads that bawl aloud a philosophy of grab.

In the glaring heat, over ninety and rising, Enid looked terrible even for a small town. With a sinking heart I heard Vera laconically announce he had to give me a meal. The next moment we drew up to a Chinese restaurant. Inside my teeth began to chatter, a drop from 95 to 70 is not my idea of comfort: the chow mein was solid, lukewarm, and the egg rolls tasted as if they had been cooked in diesel oil, all washed down with instant coffee and iced chlorinated water. We ate and drank in silence. And so, off to the motel that looked like the scores of motel rooms that stretched like a chain of fate down the years of my lecturing life – Ramada Inns, Holiday Inns, Travel Lodges, always clean, always spacious, always smelling of the last man's tobacco – some with service, some without, some perched on converging freeways, so impossible to sleep in, others as peaceful as the prairie, most betwixt and between.

As I showered and got ready for the performance, I felt like an old war-horse in familiar harness – the dreary ride, the appalling meal, the silent Vera ceased to be depressants, my spirits rose. I was here in Enid; I felt like Livingstone reaching the heart of Africa. My stamina and my spirits were soon put to a sore test. The University was small, the buildings surprisingly beautiful and comely, but weirdly Moorish. The Faculty proved to be a sad lot. Doing good, sound work, toiling away too many hours a week teaching dumb clucks who were scarcely educable. These men loaded with work were still struggling to get their doctoral theses written, but the years had devoured their youth; hair flecked with grey; drained, tea-coloured flesh, nervous voices in which the touch of hope seemed forced; they filled me with pity and gloom.

However, mounting anxiety gave me a little time to brood over the fate of the Faculty. I found I was speaking at a banquet (such a change did not greatly disturb me; it is essential to learn to take all with ease, and often all is quite a lot), but I realised as soon as I talked to my host that this was different. He said they had sold more tickets than they expected at $5 each (just, I thought, not to be lonely in that vast outback, rather listen to me) and as we walked towards the meeting, I was astonished to see men in wide Stetson hats, high boots and very non-Faculty faces – the sort of faces I had dreamt of as a boy reading Zane

Grey. Not that I ever expected to see them getting out of enormous cars to spend the evening sipping iced tea and listening to a British historian. The hall, a temporary one, sizzled like an oven – no air-conditioner, or, if so, it was defeated. Long trestle tables, over 150 waiting to eat. Students seemed few, Faculty less, but lots of neighbourhood parties laughing, talking, chattering, their children playing around. The prospect seemed unpromising. And these laughing cowboys would have grown grim-faced had they known what I had prepared for them – *The Growth of Oligarchy in the Reign of Anne* – selected from a list of lectures by the Chairman of the Faculty.

The grapefruit slices were lukewarm, the golden Idaho baked potato, coy in its silver foil, stuck in the throat, the gello melted. I felt a thin trickle of sweat meander down my back to collect in a swamp in the seat of my pants. Moody at the best of times before a lecture, I found it almost impossible to talk to the quite stunning blonde on my right. With the temperature up to God knows what, a brain like an addled egg, and no usable script, conversation withered. These good, earnest, friendly people had spent dollars and travelled miles and miles and miles. Even the pink sirloin the size of a baby steer looked deadly, almost grotesque in that inferno, and somehow it managed, when nibbled, to taste cold. All too soon the Chairman was working steadily up from my birth, leaving no school unmentioned, no title or honour unremarked, but as soon as he reached the titles of my publications I knew time was short. I rose, almost fainting, to applause that drummed like a headache. Kind people. Go for them, I told myself, go.

So I sailed in, brushed the old title aside, and let them have *America's Last King*. For fifty minutes I ad-libbed on George III and the American Revolution, dwelt on the divided society in Britain and America, made them thoughtful and quiet with talk of guerrilla wars (it was the time of Vietnam), relieved their gloom with anecdotes of the Prince Regent and his monstrous brood of brothers and sisters, and finished on high tragedy with George at Windsor – mad, blind, deaf, talking endlessly to himself.

Their applause was sweet, even my sweat-sodden clothes felt good, and Enid acquired a kind of radiance. And, of course, miracle followed miracle, swept to the house of a friend of the Faculty, it seemed no surprise now to see excellent modern pictures or a Henry Moore maquette, to partake in a lively discussion of the American novel; to savour splendid highball after highball; no surprise at all to find a very good pool at the motel or a first-class breakfast served at 6.30 am (where, in my benighted country could you get a cup of coffee at that hour!). But it was a surprise, indeed, to find my charming hostess waiting for me in an air-conditioned Cadillac to drive me over 200 miles to

Tulsa to get a plane, because she wanted to do a little shopping and also, I am sure, to do me a good turn. And so Enid, which seemed so awful, gleams and shines in the memory – a wonderfully attentive audience, hospitality such as only Americans can give. The heat, the chow mien forgotten, how grateful I was to Zane Grey, to my father's secret dreams of riding for the Bar-Zed ranch which I suspect had drawn me to the prairies of Oklahoma, but, above all, to Phillips University. I never refused remote universities again, no matter how small the fee.

Few young British historians grow familiar with Commerce, Nagadochees, Wichita Falls, Independence, Farmington, Martin and many others which I remember with a kind of awe. Their audiences were large, earnest, eager to learn about the past of their country because they had hope in their future. George III became one of my most popular lectures but it took over a decade to reach its final form as I came to explore the Royal Archives and Royal Palaces which yielded new insights.

I was invited by the Society of Cincinnati to give their second *George Rogers Clark* lecture (the first had been given by Morison) and I thought it was particularly appropriate. What a contrast the occasion made with Enid – the wonderful rooms of the Society were breathtaking in their elegance and I was given a splendid reception, much enhanced by the presence of James Parton.

(ii) New Light on the Tyrant George III

'The History of the present king of Great Britain is a history of repeated injuries and usurpations, all having in direct object the establishment of an absolute Tyranny over these States.' After this blast at George III, the framers of the Declaration of Independence then listed twenty-eight crimes against the American people – for none of which, of course, he was responsible. At the time it was a convenient fiction; a personal scapegoat absolved the people of Britain – Franklin and others knew well enough that the British people were sharply divided about the American question, many supporting the colonists. Furthermore, America when independent and free would still need Britain – her money and her markets. Also many Americans still felt themselves to be a part of the British world, so they blamed their ruler rather than their people. Furthermore, they were only saying more truculently, more aggressively, what many Englishmen were saying and thinking – that George III was a new Stuart, bent on subverting the constitution, packing the House of Commons with his own friends, using his money to bribe electors. Such distortions were a part and parcel of opposition propaganda in Britain. Such views suited the American colonists admirably.[1]

Alas, this view that George III had a personal responsibility for the loss of America became enshrined in generations of historical works written by good Whigs – particularly in the works of Lord Macaulay and his nephew, George Otto Trevelyan.[2] It is the view one commonly still finds in British school textbooks and always in American ones.

Since 1930 that view has become increasingly modified amongst professional historians – Sir Lewis Namier, Sir Herbert Butterfield and others demonstrated that the King behaved with constitutional rectitude and that he neither packed Parliament nor bribed electors, that the policy towards America was his ministers' policy and overwhelmingly backed by the House of Commons.[3] Indeed, his latest biographer seems to believe that the American troubles were due to a few wild agitators and should never have happened.[4] However, Sir Lewis Namier did not let George III off entirely. He described him as psychologically weak, immature and of low intelligence and, of course, beset by periodic madness – a pathetic character born to problems beyond his emotional and intellectual competence. A view which to me twenty years ago seemed quite realistic and in accordance with the evidence.[5]

Now it seems, he was sane – never mad. A mother and son medical team, Macalpine and Hunter, studied the King's symptoms and decided that he suffered from porphyria: this turns urine reddish (once noticed by George III's doctors), leads to nervous disturbance – twitching, volubility, restlessness – and so, even when George III was in his straitjacket, he may have had periods of total normality yet appearing to have the physical symptoms of madness.[6]

This new portrait – a sound constitutional monarch, sane and never mad, merely drifting into senility in old age – is gaining currency. Add to this the fact that no one has ever impugned his high moral qualities, his total devotion to his wife and family, and the tyrant vanishes to be replaced by an almost model constitutional monarch.

Just as I could never accept George III as tyrant, I find it equally difficult to believe in George III as the cynosure of monarchy. We need a more balanced, a more penetrating analysis of a man who was so complex and so fascinating. To understand the monarch we need to comprehend the private man, and once the structure of his character is understood, his public character takes on new dimensions.

Nevertheless, current orthodoxy must be dealt with first, and the madness issue is easiest to deal with. The case for porphyria is complex and medical opinion is divided. It is an inherited disease, supposed to be derived from Mary Queen of Scots. It discolours the urine, makes it reddish due to excessive copper, and there is *one* reference only to George III's discoloured urine. The disease brings on hallucinations, chronic insomnia, skin rashes, uncontrollable restlessness – George III displayed all of these in 1789. Yet these symptoms are quite compatible with mental breakdown. Furthermore, if genetic, considering the procreative activities of Charles II, James II, George IV and William IV, to say nothing of their royal relations out of wedlock, and Queen Victoria's descendants in wedlock, one might reasonably expect porphyria to be rampant amidst the British aristocracy. That would not appear to be the case. However, porphyria or not is to my mind irrelevant. In 1789 George III thought that he had been mad, so did his family, so did the Parliament, so did his subjects. And they all feared, particularly the King, that he would go mad again. And he was ill again in 1805. And at these times he was, for whatever reason, mentally incompetent. And so the fear of madness was a potent factor in politics; also it was a weapon that the King used against his children and against his ministers. Porphyria, fascinating as it may be as a speculation, is largely a red herring.

And now, George III as a good Whig. Proved beyond a doubt is the fact that George III's ministers between 1760 and 1790 were overwhelmingly Whig. It is also true that he received considerable Tory support in the Commons – far more than George I and George II.[7] That does not make him or his ministers Tories, but it does mean that the policy towards America had very broad support in Parliament. Nor did George III pack Parliament or suborn members of Parliament: the parliamentary systems of the 1750s and 1760s are indistinguishable.[8] Furthermore, we now know that George III was educated by Lord Bute in the most impeccable Whig principles; we have bundles of the King's essays – two quotations must suffice, 'The pride, the glory of Britain and the direct end of its constitution is political liberty' (John Adams could hardly quarrel with that); and this, 'Charles I had too high a notion of the royal power.' There are, in the essays, paeans of praise for the Revolution of 1688.[9] When his father died, and his mother commissioned a family picture by George Knapton, there right in the middle of the picture are Magna Carta and the Act of Settlement – the cornerstones of English liberty – or so it was believed at that time.[10] And yet, it should also be said that the Whiggery in which George III was bred was an old-fashioned Whiggery, the Whiggery of *Cato's Letters* – ironically, the same intellectual diet that fed so many of the Founding Fathers. And so, Whig certainly, but old-fashioned Whig and not unpopular with Tories.[11]

However, this does not take us very far into the heart of the man, and we need to penetrate his character if we are to comprehend fully his political actions and attitudes. So let us look more closely at the private man.

Most importantly, George III possessed a very obsessive temperament. Why we cannot know. He was awkward as a child, a pathetic actor in a family that loved theatricals. His brother, Edward, close to him in age, outshone him in grace and liveliness and human response. His mother was a cool, reserved woman, and maybe there was some psychological damage to the young prince. But it is idle to speculate. At eighteen George III was capable of intense preoccupation and deep emotional concentration on people and things – a very exclusive concentration. With people he could love and hate with frightening intensity.Two examples must suffice: he hated his grandfather, George II. When he became King in 1760 he could not bring himself to live in any palace that George II had inhabited. He refused to use HamptonCourt – indeed, when there was a fire there he wished the palace had burnt down – nor could he set foot in Kensington Palace. He kept an office in St James's Palace and received ambassadors there, but he would not sleep there; that is why he bought Buckingham House as soon as he was married. He lived mainly at Kew, his parents' home, planned and half-built a huge gothic palace there which was blown up in 1828.[12] And he renovated Windsor: George II had used Windsor for hunting but lived in the house by the castle built for Queen Anne, so the castle itself was uncontaminated by the hateful grandfather. The dislike and obsessive rejection of George II was also transferred to George II's ministers – Hardwicke, Newcastle and the like.

Against his hatred must be put his obsessive devotion to Lord Bute, a pompous, graceful, learned man who became his mentor. His letters to Bute survive. They are quite astonishing. They are full of humility, anxiety for advice, despair at the thought of Bute doubting him, passionate expressions of undying loyalty and friendship; there is an almost terrifying intensity in these letters. One must hasten to add that these letters must *not* be misinterpreted – there is nothing homosexual in them. George III glued himself to Bute like a limpet. Bute was the fountain of wisdom and experience, the rock of strength. The relationship was utterly obsessive and gradually worked itself out by the time George was twenty-six or sooner. George III's first love affair, with Lady Sarah Lennox, has the same obsessive quality, the same intense concentration on an object. He plunged into utter grief if her name was casually mentioned with another man's, indeed became so distracted that he could not sleep – again the emotional fervour is almost frightening in its power.[13]

This capacity for intense obsessive personal relations is a constant theme of George III's private life. His relationship with his children was affectionate and easy so long as they were locked into his private world. At adolescence trouble started. Their independence disturbed him; he became obsessively worried about their sexuality and morals; their financial problems were a nightmare to the King. As for his daughters, he kept them under lock and key, in what they disconsolately called 'The Nunnery'. Only one married and the King regretted that; they enjoyed little freedom.[14]

Obsessive characters need to develop activities which can absorb some of the intensity of their emotional drives, to create, as it were, a protection from painful reality. Often they are drawn to collecting or to the absorption of precise and detailed scholarship. And this leads us to many of George III's private activities which have been known about but which have not seemed very germane to understanding his actions and policies as a king: indeed they have seemed very remote from these. Personally I now think that they are most important for an understanding of George III.

He was an obsessive book-collector. His grandfather, George II, had given the age-old royal library, that stretched back to Edward IV's days, as a fabulous foundation present to the British Museum, and this may have triggered George III's determination to rebuild the royal library. Before he came to the throne he started to collect books and he never ceased until he became incompetent in 1811. He is the greatest bibliophile to have sat on the English throne. By 1811 he had amassed 65,000 books and 450 important manuscripts. He was decisive and wise in his purchases. In 1762 the great collection of Thomason Tracts came on the market – 32,000 broadsheets, ballads, newspapers, sermons and pamphlets, essential material for the understanding of the English Civil War. He bought the lot and presented it to the British Museum – one of the greatest of gifts to its library, and an inestimable boon to all students of the Civil War.

Books remained a passion throughout his life – he retained a vast range of book catalogues – they fill some 54 columns in his own catalogue – and in old age he was popping once a week into the bookseller at Windsor whenever he was in residence, to rifle through his shelves to see if he could pick up a rarity as an addition to his huge library. Like all obsessive collectors he had his favourite themes. Bibles was one. He had over two hundred in most languages from Finnish to Iroquois. He also, naturally enough, concentrated on Shakespeare, and Cicero, that favourite classical author of the Whig aristocracy, but a more surprising choice was Boccaccio. However, his acquisitive instinct was very broad and certainly overcame his political prejudices, for both Voltaire and Rousseau were on his shelves. He bought two very large musical libraries: that of William Boyce, the famous and underestimated British composer, and 450 old songbooks which had been collected by Richard Meade; but his greatest treasure was a large number of Handel's autograph scores. He loved old and beautiful books, acquiring twenty-six Caxtons and many splendidly illustrated manuscripts including the jewel-like Sobieski *Book of Hours* which George IV, that great connoisseur, could not bear to part with when he gave the library to the British Museum. He held it back and it remains one of the pearls of the Royal Collection. Book collecting was an obsession and a solace and might have been a sufficient release from the pressures of emotion and reality for many obsessive men but not George III. His innate restlessness, as well as his intensive curiosity, impelled him towards other fields – he preferred to be absorbed all day long.[15]

His interest in art is a fascinating reflection of his character and the inner pressures of his temperament. He was taught architectural drawing by Sir William Chambers, and in this he took delight and performed with very considerable skill. At Windsor, there are boxes of his drawings, for the King continued to practise this art for many years – they are meticulous and exact in detail: obviously getting everything – the last acanthus leaf – exactly right absorbed the King. His capacity to concentrate on detail was intense. Also he could paint a very tolerable water colour – landscapes that he could see and depict as they were. His taste in art was a reflection of these preoccupations.[16] He never became a true connoisseur like his father, Frederick Prince of Wales, or his son, George IV. True, he purchased the very great collection of Joseph Smith, the British Consul at Venice, which contained, amongst other old masters, an excellent Vermeer, *The Girl at the Virginals*. The King had purchased these pictures in bulk to furnish Buckingham Palace, and the pictures that delighted him most were the huge series of Canalettos that took one down the Grand Canal and the rest of Venice almost palace by palace. He loved exact topography; it fascinated him. For the same reason he was attracted to Zoffany whose portraits were always very strong likenesses.[17] Otherwise the King's taste was rather quixotic – he seized on an artist for a time and then with equal alacrity dropped him. He never took to Reynolds. He concentrated on Ramsay for a time, then Gainsborough. Benjamin West lasted longer; his mythological and historical pictures contained stories that the King could read with delight for they enshrined virtues which he felt essential for social and personal stability – patriotism, courage, endurance, piety and respect.[18]

Nevertheless the King took his duties to art with all the serious intensity of his nature. He gave a great deal of time to the Royal Academy – particularly its rules and regulations, paying excessive and obsessive attention to the diploma, both its wording and its award. He pored for hours over the Academy's accounts, which he took a special interest in as he had reserved for himself the appointment of Treasurer. And with the punctiliousness which he brought to all that he did, he never missed the Academy's yearly exhibition until he went blind.[19]

More important to him than art was music. He listened to music almost every day and often made music too for both he and the Queen were more than passable performers on the harpsichord. But here again, his capacity for obsession was paramount. He listened to, indeed he patronised, the young Mozart and other distinguished contemporary musicians who came to Britain, but they meant little or nothing to him. Handel was his composer, day in, day out, week in, week out, year after year; the King could never hear enough Handel. Handel alone, to the King, was music. And he was overjoyed when he secured so many Handel manuscripts, and, of course, he owned a splendid bust of Handel by Roubilliac.[20]

Underlying all of the interest of the King that we have discussed so far are the principles of regularity, order, exactitude, cemented, one might say, by powerful, almost rigid, habits. His interests, furthermore, were never casual nor, once formed, did they easily change. It is not surprising, therefore, that he should be deeply attracted to science and technology. Indeed he had been the first British monarch to have been taught science as a boy. He was initially tutored by Francis Scott, a Fellow of the Royal Society, in mathematics, general science, and military fortification (again, George III greatly enjoyed the precise and detailed drawing which was involved in this subject). It is also very likely that Scott stimulated the young prince's interest in astronomy.

In 1754, when the King was 17, Stephen Demainbray became his science tutor and remained in his service after the King's accession and, in turn, taught his sons science. Demainbray was a remarkable, vivid, but somewhat irresponsible person. He not only made his name as a scholar at Westminster, where he was taught by Desaguliers, but he startled the school by marrying at seventeen. He became a fine astronomer as well as physicist, but more importantly he had attended, whilst at Leiden University, the lectures of 's Gravesande, as great a populariser of science as Desaguliers himself. Demainbray insisted on the demonstration of scientific principles as well as their explanation, and persuaded George III to purchase what is one of the finest collections of scientific instruments of the period 1750–70 in existence. Many of these were built by George Adams, the greatest scientific instrument-maker of his day. The bulk of George III's collection was purchased before 1768, but additions continued to be made to it during his life. When the King died in 1820, there were 384 instruments – some trivial but the majority superb – built with exquisite craftsmanship, and some were highly complex and ingenious: they certainly required a competence in science for their understanding and enjoyment. Many of these instruments were electrical and a few almost bordered on the toy rather than instrument, but there was as well an extremely complex (and very beautiful) Philosophical Table made by Adams in 1762 expressly at the King's command to demonstrate the principles of mechanics. In the same year he built a splendid exhausting and compressing pump (similar to the Air Pump in Wright of Derby's famous picture) which demonstrated in a spectacular way the properties of the atmosphere. And naturally George III possessed the finest of microscopes.[21]

Deep though George III's interest in mechanics and electricity was, it was surpassed by his preoccupation with clocks and with the stars, where regularity and order reached an even higher degree of certainty, or, shall we say, habitual repetition.

Every room in Buckingham Palace, Windsor and Kew – wherever the King lived – was full of clocks; clocks which had to be accurate, for the King had a passion for accuracy, and Benjamin Vulliamy, perhaps the greatest clockmaker of his age, was responsible for the regulation of all royal time-pieces. He was sharply supervised by the King. Naturally marine chronometers fascinated George III – their accuracy was essential for the calculation of longitude, and the King personally tested several models, keeping a very careful register in his own hand. Often the King himself was involved in the designs of his clocks and he collaborated with Sir William Chambers to produce the rightly famous *Four-Sided Astronomical Clock* in 1762.

> The four dials show, respectively, on the front: the time of the day on a twenty-four hour dial (two twelve-hour sequences) with hands showing mean and solar time; the dial also shows the time at various places of different longitude; on the back: the tides at forty-three points, mostly in the British Isles, and the phases of the moon; on the left: the days of the week and of the month, the position of the sun in the zodiac and the position of the stars; on the right: an orrery showing the motion of the six planets.

It is difficult to imagine a more elaborate time-piece. In 1765 he commissioned yet another astronomical clock for the Library at Buckingham Palace; it cost £1042.[22]

George III also had specially made a superb barograph by A. Cummings who invented for it a new escapement. And he bought a great number of clocks from Vulliamy. He collected, however, other than English clocks. He possessed a fine French one by Cressent that still graces Buckingham Palace. However, he does not seem to have been interested in old clocks. Accuracy of information enclosed in a beautiful case was the true object of his passion. Naturally his interest in watches was equally great as that in clocks, and Thomas Mudge made for the King what has been described, 'the most historically important watch in the world' – again its very accuracy was achieved through immense sophistication; this watch had an automatic device to compensate for changes in temperature – hot or cold, the King had the right time. Nor was the King a mere appreciator – he carefully wrote out in his own hand very precise and detailed instructions for what he called 'unmounting a watch' and 'mounting a watch'.[23]

Hand in hand with his passion for clocks, watches and time, and springing from the same depths of his personality, was his lifelong interest in astronomy. Sir William Chambers built an observatory for him at Kew and he watched the transit of Venus there in 1769; having first, of course, got Demainbray to draw up a meticulous account of what would happen so that the King could watch and note every stage. Later, after Herschel had discovered Uranus, the King built for him the largest telescope then in existence in a field at Slough near to Windsor. He paid £4000 for this out of his private funds. He gave Herschel a pension of £200 a year, another £50 to his sister and £200 a year for maintenance of the telescope. And there was nothing the King liked better than popping over to Slough to visit Herschel or to spend hours explaining his own observatory at Kew to foreign visitors. His passion for astronomy was intense and far more successful than his politics, for modern astronomy – the galactic theory of the universe – stems from Herschel's discoveries made with George III's telescope. Once again meticulous attention to detail and the sense of absolute accuracy and dependability were what held the King's interest.[24]

George III was, therefore, a man of considerable intellectual interests, with a strong bias towards practical technology and to subjects and techniques which enshrined regularity and order. Clocks, telescopes, scientific instruments, probably meant far more to him than music, which was, however, essential to him daily, and certainly more than did the visual arts. He possessed far greater intellectual interest than most English kings. And at this point, too, one should mention his lifelong interest in botany which may seem to be at variance with his desire for order. This is not so. Botany had been revolutionised by Linnaeus and indeed had become, through his system, one of the greatest illustrations of the orderly nature of the universe.[25] However, the quality of the King's interests which I want to stress is the obsession: a quality which is found in his private life too – for example his eating habits. He rarely ate anything but mutton with turnips and beetroot, except on Sunday when he always had roast beef. He was almost as addicted to tea as Doctor Johnson, and downed vast quantities of bread and butter – a favourite diet for supper, with fruit. And these eating habits never varied decade after decade.[26]

So George III's interests and private life give us greater insight into his character. He was a man of very strong, almost painfully strong, emotions, and he was haunted by anything which hinted at incoherence, disorder and unexpected conflict. His refuge from the pressures of his personality was powerful habits combined with intellectual activities of an obsessive nature in which order and regularity were clearly demonstrated. There was something soothing for him in the precision of time, or in the knowledge that the rarest tree or shrub or flower fell into its allotted place in the order of Creation, or in the repeated harmonies of Handel. Change, surprise, the accidental, the disorderly disturbed George III profoundly.

If we now turn the private man to the reigning monarch, we may understand both his problems and his actions both profoundly and more sympathetically. One can understand why he was not only worried but almost terrified at parting with a minister upon whose presence he had grown to rely. He had to be forced to part with Bute for whom his obsessive attachment I have described. The same quality is at the heart of his relationship with Lord North. For George III, North was bulwark of reliability in the dreadful chaos of the American problem; hence he begged, and bribed North to make him stay in office when North himself longed to resign.[27] If one reads George III's letters to North they recall the same intense obsessive attachment that is such a marked feature of his correspondence with Bute.[28] The period between the fall of North and the emergence of the Younger Pitt was a desperate time for the King, emotionally as well as politically. But once Pitt was secure in office, George III began to attach himself with the same limpet-like intensity to his Prime Minister. Not only his attachments, but his hates had a like obsessive quality – the Marquis of Rockingham or Charles James Fox, for example, or, perhaps more understandably, 'That Devil Wilkes'. He loathed John Wilkes because Wilkes was creating what the King most hated – disorder, confusion, law and authority put at risk. And the same, of course, was true of the citizens of Boston. They were flouting laws, order, authority: Americans in revolt were to the King simply seditious rebels. For him, of course they were not Americans, they were Englishmen, his subjects, who lived in America. On the other hand, it must be remembered that he adhered with exemplary recititude to the principles and conventions to which he recognised he was subject. It was his duty to accept and not reject laws passed by Parliament. Hence he signed the Stamp Act and the repeal of the Stamp Act. When the final drama ended, he accepted – when his ministers did – Independence. Realising his duties as a constitutional monarch, he welcomed with dignity and warmth John Adams to the Court of St James.[29]

He believed intensely in what was his correct role as a constitutional monarch. He knew that he had the right to warn and advise his ministers, and he often did so with great force. But once his ministers and his government had secured the consent of Parliament he accepted the decision with alacrity even if he hated it. Only what he considered to be a violation of his Coronation Oath would he refuse to accept – hence his unyielding obstinacy to the emancipation of Roman Catholics from their disabilities. One must also remember that all that the King did or said was charged with intensity. His emotional involvement, his fears and his hopes, were never – indeed could not be – disguised. And anyone in authority who radiates emotional intensity will provoke very strong reactions in others and often he will create misunderstandings about his motives. This is true of George III. His obsessive preoccupation with detail and with immediate issues was apparent to many in opposition to his own views: hence their belief that he was more politican than constitutional monarch, which, in fact, was not so. And to this highly charged emotion that he brought to politics and to government one must add a deeper fear – certainly after 1789 – the fear of future political schism and disruption which might arise from his going mad again. For a man of George III's meticulous habits and dedication, madness was the greatest of horrors. Hence his obsessive nature intensified his problems in politics.

And yet there were small compensations that stemmed directly from the singularity of the King's temperament. Naturally parliamentary procedure absorbed him – these were the rules, and he mastered them more completely than any minister who served him, and his advice on a matter of procedure was rarely, if ever, ignored. Also, in an age which cared little for efficiency and promptitude, he was quite exemplary in his despatch of business. There was never, so long as he was well, the slightest delay. Naturally his own prerogative powers greatly preoccupied him: he gave closest attention to the question of commuting the death sentence – his prerogative of mercy – and was merciful so long as the precision of the law allowed it. Likewise he would pore for hours over honours and promotions in the armed forces or the Church.[30]

Whatever he did, he did with excessive zeal, excessive concentration, with no thought for larger issues or to processes of political change. The King would have been happiest in a country that worked like a clock: every part knowing and performing its duty with accuracy and regularity. Alas, he lived in tempestuous and revolutionary times, and for such nature had not equipped him. Yet it is absurd to underrate him. He was a highly complex character: certainly no tyrant: a monarch who believed in monarchy, in the perfection of the British constitution which he had inherited. *He* knew the rules and behaved as meticulously as the stars in their courses: it was others who broke them, not George III. Alas, human society is never very adept at keeping to any rules, especially if it is free and democratic.

(iii) British Attitudes to the American Revolution

On 20 May 1779 the Earl of Pembroke was in despair. He felt a deep sense of shame that was impossible to hide. As he wrote to his son, Lord Herbert, who was making the Grand Tour in Italy: 'I wish I were a Laplander, or anything but a Briton.' Lord Pembroke was, of course, as his ancestors had been, Lord Lieutenant of Wiltshire. He was still a colonel in a most distinguished regiment, the Royals, although now too old to serve. At the accession of George III he had been made a Lord of the Bedchamber, a post that he had lost not through any political indiscretion but because of an amorous scandal. Indeed the result of that scandal, a son whom Pembroke somewhat infelicitously named Reebkomp (an anagram, of course, of Pembroke), was serving in the army in America. It was his letters as well as George III's policy that made Lord Pembroke a prey to fury and to such misery.

A month later, he explained at greater length to his son the reasons for his dissatisfaction.

> Our ministry, taken *en gros*, are certainly such as no wise nor honest man can trust, and in whom the country can conceive no hopes; men who proved themselves incapable, whose characteristic is indolence, and whose system is unwise, who are overpowered by misfortune because they are leagued with absurdity, whose obstinacy is not to be softened by advice, and whose eyes are not to be opened by experience.

As a soldier Pembroke was distressed by the defeats sustained by the British forces in America – hence his shame – but his anger with the government welled from deeper springs than this. In his quick-tempered, completely uninhibited letters to his son, he does not disguise his contempt for the members of George III's Parliament. He considered it an utterly corrupt institution, and he wondered that the people did not nail up the doors of both Houses and set fire to them. He scoffed at the idea of a parliamentary union with Ireland. They will want, he forecast, to go America's way and not join up with 'our rotten institutions'. In all cities, he told his son, there was the utmost discontent, particularly amongst manufacturers. His sympathy was with them.

Indeed the political state of England in 1779 was a sorry mess, and for nearly two decades every ministry had proved itself totally incapable of dealing with the American question. During the 1760s, harshness alternated with weakness, repression was followed by conciliation as one Whig ministry rapidly followed another. The House of Commons was composed of small Whig factions struggling for power, and George III's faith in Lord North derived from the fact that North in 1769 had brought to an end the confusion of a decade and created a stable ministry, solidly Whig at the core, but supported by many Tories and independents. Of course, North had not been able to secure the support of all the Whig groups, and the important group, led by the Marquis of Rockingham, whose formidable spokesman was Edmund Burke, stayed outside the government as did Lord Chatham (William Pitt) and his supporters. Not until rebellion flared up was North's American policy much more consistent than his predecessor's. As rebellion turned to war and the war itself grew long and difficult, many of North's erstwhile supporters began to have doubts of the wisdom of his policy. Criticism grew in volume. And criticism mattered. Public opinion was important in a crisis, even in the oligarchical structure of British politics. Since the accession of George III in 1760 the feeling that a Parliament of land-owners, dominated by the aristocracy, was becoming out of touch with the true needs of the nation had steadily strengthened. Criticism of the parliamentary system as well as of North's American policy had become widespread. There had developed an ever-increasing band of radicals whose radicalism was social, legal, religious, though not, of course, economic. They believed in a wider democratic franchise, toleration of religious belief and the rationalisation of law and administration. They were irritated by anachronism: that little girls and boys should be hanged for theft or that a duchess should draw a fat salary as a housekeeper for a non-existent palace infuriated them. These views were particularly powerful amongst the radical intellectuals and publicists, Joseph Priestley, Richard Price, Tom Paine and Junius, that savage critic of George III who still retains his anonymity. Their books and pamphlets were read as eagerly in the provinces as in London, and they had helped to make the American question a dominant issue, not only for members of Parliament, or even for parliamentary electors, but for all who could read. They appealed particularly to that mass of Englishmen who were politically dispossessed by the quaint franchises of the unreformed House of Commons, and who, therefore, felt a natural kinship with the Americans in revolt. Their attitude to America was based on their hopes for their own society, and they felt a community of interest with the rebelling colonists both in ideas and in political aspirations. Historians have underestimated the extent of British sympathy for America which flourished in the 1760s and early 1770s, just as they have overlooked the reason for its decay once rebellion turned to war.

First it is necessary to look more closely at those who sympathised, the manner of men they were. This radical sympathy for America is nowhere reflected so sharply as in Sylas Neville's *Diary*. Like Lord Pembroke's papers, the *Diary* is a comparatively recent discovery, and one that has certainly passed almost unnoticed by the political historians of George III's reign. For those who believe that radical public opinion mattered little in the eighteenth century, it is an uncomfortable document.

Neville kept his diary from 1767 to 1788, during his early manhood. He was born in 1741 and died in 1840, just a few months short of his century. His diary is remarkable for the bitterness with which he refers to George III and his ministers. Here are a few of his sentiments culled from 1767:

No person is a true friend of liberty that is not a Republican.

The evils of which monarchy is productive should deter any wise nation from submitting to that accursed government.

The Gazette says 10,000 people a year go from the North of Ireland to America and 40,000 in all. May they flourish and set up in due time a glorious free government in that country which may serve as a retreat to those Free men who may survive the final ruin of liberty in this country; an event which I am afraid is at no great distance.

Such comments would have done credit to a Boston radical, but these were not peculiar to Neville and his friends: strong, blunt sentiments such as these found their echoes elsewhere.

William Turner of Wakefield in Yorkshire urged his son to emigrate:

Through the folly and wickedness of the present, you of the rising generation have indeed a dark prospect before you. . . . Your best way will be to gather as fast as you can a good stock of the arts and sciences of this country; and if you find the night of despotism and wretchedness overwhelm this hemisphere, follow the course of the sun to that country where freedom has already fixed her standard and is erecting her throne; where the sciences and arts, wealth and power will soon gather round her; and assist and strengthen the empire there.

Neville was also in touch with many like-minded men and women; some were well-known London radicals such as Mrs Catherine Macaulay the historian, Caleb Fleming, the Unitarian minister of Pinners Hall, and Thomas Hollis whose lavish patronage of liberal ideas helped to keep republican sentiment alive in the middle decades of the eighteenth century.[1] These ardent radical intellectuals certainly fortified Neville's attitude. Fortunately, however, radical intellectuals were not the only characters in Neville's diary to share his sentiments. People who but for him would have merged into the nameless millions of history echo his republican sentiments as well as his hatred for George III's government – Kearsey, Bacon and Mrs Winnick and their friends who entertained him with tea and radical politics. Obviously in the 1760s there were little knots of republicans and radicals scattered throughout London and its suburbs.

Even more impressive, however, are the chance conversations that Neville had, or overheard, which indicate the width of public criticism and the frequency with which it was expressed. Viewing the Raphael cartoons at Hampton Court, Neville heard a man tell his wife that they would soon belong to the people of England, and at Terry's Coffee House in August 1767 he got into conversation with a stranger who said that he 'wished N. America may become free and independent, that it may be an asylum to those Englishmen who have spirit and virtue enough to leave their country, when it submits to domestic or foreign Tyranny.'

I find it hard to believe that Neville's experience was singular and untypical or that the sympathetic sentiments which he seems to have encountered so often were at all exceptional. After all when he moved from London to one of the most brutish and least enlightened parts of Norfolk – Scratsby near Great Yarmouth – he had little difficulty in finding kindred spirits to dine with him on calf's head on 30 January in honour of the execution of Charles I, or to share this treasonable toast: 'May the example of this day be followed on all like occasions.' From this it might seem that sympathy for America and tenacious adherence to liberal and radical sentiments reached down to the grass roots and was not merely a cause for opposition politicians, dissenting intellectuals and self-interested merchants, as recent American and British historians have stoutly maintained.[2] Fortunately, Neville's diary is not the only new source that illuminates the strength and intensity of pro-American feeling amongst those classes of society that wielded next to no formal political power and whose voice received little notice at the centre of affairs.

At Birmingham, then a rapidly growing manufacturing town, a group of professional men, manufacturers and dilettantes had come together for the purpose of discussion and mutual improvement. They had been fascinated by the ideas of the Enlightenment, as indeed had many similar intellectual élites from Philadelphia to Marseilles.[3] The importance of such groups – and particularly the British ones that are to be found in most large provincial towns – is that they represent people not outside the mainstream of economic and social development but right in the heart of it. This is certainly true of the West Midlands group, largely based in Birmingham. Their names are well known: James Watt, the inventor; Matthew Boulton, the manufacturer; Erasmus Darwin – grandfather of Charles – poet, philosopher, doctor; Joseph Priestley, chemist and publicist; Dr Small, the tutor of Jefferson; Thomas Day and Richard Edgeworth, both educationalists and both weirdly eccentric; and, perhaps the most interesting of the rest, Josiah Wedgwood, the potter.

Wedgwood, a man of vast intellectual appetite and broad human

sympathy, makes a strong contrast to Neville. Everything that Wedgwood did succeeded, and he rose from obscurity to international renown.
He was happily married, blessed with brilliant children, prosperous,
secure, the admired and admiring friend of many distinguished men in
all walks of eighteenth-century life. He certainly cannot be dismissed as
a social misfit, as an unkind critic might dismiss Neville, nor can he be
lumped with Price, Cartwright, Priestley, Mrs Macaulay and the rest as
a disgruntled radical intellectual. He was a supremely successful man of
affairs. He and his friends would have been thoroughly at home in the
purposeful, expanding world of Franklin's Philadelphia. They would
have shared its eupeptic self-confidence in its expanding commerce, and
discovered the same ideas about politics and government, science,
education and the arts as their own, amongst its intellectual leadership.
As with Philadelphia's élite so with the Lunar Society; its members felt
the future in their bones. They were ready for a new world, free from
tradition, closer to the rational principles upon which they modelled
their industry and commerce. After all, reason and its application, they
believed, had brought their success in life. Of course, as in Philadelphia,
not all translated their intellectual liberalism into radical politics.
Matthew Boulton supported Lord North although his friends teased
him endlessly on that score; Thomas Day, a dedicated follower of the
philosophy of Jean-Jacques Rousseau, found it difficult to support the
Americans so long as they maintained slavery. In general, however, the
members of the Lunar Society felt as Wedgwood did.

Wedgwood's views on the American problem were conveyed in his
letters to Richard Bentley, his partner, whose judgement in politics as
well as in the arts, sciences and social intercourse he revered.[4] Wedgwood
and Bentley were, of course, wholehearted supporters of the American
cause. They thought coercive measures wicked, preposterous, and
doomed to disaster. Wedgwood sent for Dr Price's *Observations on
Civil Liberty*. He wrote back enthusiastically: 'I thank you for Dr Price's
most excellent Pamphlet: those who are neither converted, nor frightened
into a better way of thinking by reading his excellent and alarming book
may be given up as hardened sinners, beyond the reach of conviction.'[5]
And he asked for more copies so that he could distribute them in the
right places. Later Bentley sent him Paine's *Common Sense* and many
other pro-American pamphlets to fortify, if fortification were needed,
his strong sympathies for America and to help in Wedgwood's work
of conversion of others. Wedgwood willingly subscribed £20 towards
alleviating the miseries of American prisoners captured by the British.
'Gratitude to their country men for their humanity to G[eneral] Burgoyne
and his army is no small motive for my mite.'[6]

Wedgwood and Bentley's views chimed not only with those of their immediate friends but were echoed in the correspondence of other industrialists. Even Elizabeth Strutt, a mere girl of sixteen, weighed down with grief by her mother's sudden death, felt compelled to write to her father: 'I read the determination of the American Congress yesterday and I am sorry to see what distress they are brought to. How sensibly they write, with what courage and what coolness. What havoc and bloodshed can a few ambitious men create amongst whole nations' (c. August 1775).[7] Doubtless, being a dutiful girl, she knew that such sentiments would please her father, Jedediah, one of the greatest figures in the industrial revolution: his great cotton mills at Belper in Derbyshire are still among the largest in Europe. In Bristol, Manchester, Birmingham and Leeds, indeed wherever the middle-class manufacturers were to be found, sympathy for the American attitude abounded.

Of course, it is not surprising that many of the leaders of the industrial revolution should have been so strongly pro-American: they too wanted a social revolution, an end to the system of oligarchy and patronage which created not only a sense of keen injustice but also real practical obstacles to their industrial activities. Whatever they wanted – a canal, improved roads, efficient lighting or paving of streets, more education, better law and order, or a new water supply – they had to struggle to get it for themselves, and not only struggle but pay. Neither local nor central government in Britain provided initially the slightest aid; and it is no wonder that the whole oligarchical, unrepresentative structure of eighteenth-century English society should become as much anathema to *them* as it was to Sam Adams. What is surprising is that these social élites, which were beginning to wield so much economic power, proved in the end to be so weak an ally for the American cause.

This was only partially due to the nature of the British political system which put all effective power into the hands of the landowning classes, for many of the industrialists had contacts with politicians, particularly those Whigs, led by the Marquis of Rockingham, who were in opposition to Lord North. The widespread sympathy for America failed to be effective for a more profound reason: the change in the nature of the conflict itself.

In the 1760s, even in the early 1770s, friendly support for America could be indulged with a clear conscience. The policy of successive ministries lacked consistency; many acts, particularly the Stamp Act, seemed to be as inimical to British commercial interests as American; both British and American merchants appeared to be the victims of these arbitrary acts, so resentment could be shared in common. But American resentment hardened, developed a programme, and became a revolt, violent, bloody, bitter, that, as Chatham had foreseen, turned itself into a European war. Doubts began to cloud sympathy and many consciences became uneasy. It required political and moral convictions of a thoroughly radical kind to support unquestioningly the right of the Americans to obtain their independence by any means whatsoever, *once rebellion had started to transform itself into war,*

Indeed this is sharply reflected in Wedgwood's correspondence. On 6 February 1775 he wrote to Bentley:

> Doctor Roe had been at Manchester about a week before – exceeding hot & violent against the Americans, Dr Percival told me he quite frothed at the mouth, and was so excessively rapid in his declamations, and exclamations, that nobody could put in a word 'till his story was told, & then away he flew to another House repeating the same Rigmorow over again. . . . And away he flew to promote the same good work at Leeds, Hallifax &c – & I find . . . from these Towns, that his labor has not been in vain. . . . Many were surpris'd to find him so amazingly alter'd in his sentiments, but nevertheless his harangues, & even those simple queries have had a very considerable effect amongst many, Dissenters & others.
>
> I do not know how it happens, but a general infatuation seems to have gone forth, & the poor Americans are deemed Rebels, now the Minister has declared them so, by a very great majority wherever I go.

Although Roe might have swung over many moderates in one of the most radical areas in Britain, the sympathy for America remained both extensive and vociferous. At a meeting at Stafford to adopt a Loyal Address in support of the policy of George III towards America, Mr Wooldridge produced a counter-petition and proposed it so vigorously that, according to Wedgwood, 'the gentlemen were cut down and could not answer it'; nevertheless most of them signed the Loyal Address. It is true that Wooldridge and his friends, not to be outdone, advertised their counter-petition in the local press and signatures were canvassed in Birmingham, Lichfield, Walsall and Hanley. Yet Wooldridge's and not Roe's proved to be the losing game.

The contrast between the effectiveness of merchant radicals in America and merchant radicals in England became quickly apparent. War strengthened the former, weakened the latter. The taking of New York by the British army brought the mob out into the streets. 'Our people at Newcastle', wrote Wedgwood, 'went wild with joy', and he was relieved that those stalwarts who refused to illuminate their houses to celebrate the victory were not attacked.[8] Elsewhere, too, the mob roared their delight at a British triumph. War had inflamed the natural xenophobia of the semi-literate, as indeed it did in America, but whereas in America mob support, the hopeless anger and despair of the dispossessed, strengthened radical and revolutionary attitudes to government and society, in England the reverse process took place. British mobs became increasingly patriotic, for the Americans could so easily be blamed for the economic tribulations which the working classes had to endure. When Wedgwood as early as 1774 came across an armed mob of four hundred working men who had been out machine-breaking, they blamed the loss of their livelihood on the decline of trade, due to the American troubles.

This, of course, was scarcely half-true, but it was good grist for the patriot's mill. And once war began it changed many minds. Indeed nothing illustrates this better than the case of Bristol, where the earlier opposition to the American policy of Lord North's government was gradually overwhelmed; in 1775 the mayor, corporation and clergy sent in a Loyal Address to George III and in 1777 so did the Merchant Adventurers, expressing support of North's policy.

Also many Bristol merchants, who like Richard Champion worked for the American cause (short of independence) and supported wholeheartedly Burke and the Rockingham Whigs, feared an open alliance with the radicals when the real test of war came. 'The Leaders,' he wrote of the radicals,

> are in themselves so little adequate to the task they have assumed, and conduct themselves with such a wildness of popularity, and so little attention to common sense, that with respect to the great point in view, the removal of the dangerous Faction at Court, which threatens destruction to the Liberties of the whole Empire, it can have no effect.[9]

Champion's attitude to radicalism, of course, was similar to that of many New England merchants who, frightened of radicalism, became loyalists as the revolution developed. In America events, however, strengthened the radicals who secured the almost total support of the working classes and sufficient of the merchants to forge a common policy of action if not of ideas.[10]

Events reversed this process in England. Many British merchants feared not only the victories of the radicals but also that American independence would lead to a ruin of trade; and their fear was enormously strengthened when Congress entered into an alliance with France. Indeed the effect of this alliance on the British attitude towards the revolution has been consistently under-stressed. And here again, the distinction between what happened in America and in Britain is of exceptional importance. In America, radicals were able to exploit patriotic sentiment and so wrest the leadership from the more doubtful and conservative Northern merchants or Southern planters. Loyalists, supporters of conciliation, could be regarded as traitors, and treated as such.[11] The radical detestation of aristocracy could be clothed in hatred for British officials and royal servants. The xenophobic moods of the American mob could be used to threaten violence against all who suggested compromise. By such means the radical theories of natural rights, of the equality of men, the belief that all men had a right not only to life, liberty and the pursuit of happiness but also to overturn and abolish governments which did not grant them, became essentially American: here radical attitudes and patriotism were united by the call of war.

In England war *divided* radicalism and patriotism and tainted the support of America with sedition. Tom Paine became not a hero but an anathema, the symbol of a violent, radical traitor. No one had been more constant in his sympathy towards America than Wedgwood; but war brought him doubts. In the summer of 1779 the extension of the war had so denuded Britain of regular troops that the government encouraged its supporters to raise subscriptions or regiments or both in their counties. On 7 August 1779 Wedgwood attended a meeting of the Lord Lieutenant, Sheriff and gentlemen of Staffordshire: 'The meeting was thin but respectable in number,' Wedgwood reported,

> and its proceedings enlightened only by a trenchant speech by Mr Eld, a man of eighty who, after complimenting the soldiers on their bravery, went on to say,
> 'In the times of our prosperity & exultation we, the gentlemen of this county, thought ourselves of consequence enough to address the throne, &, with offers of our lives & fortunes, call'd upon our sovereign to pursue the coersive measures already begun in America. In these days of our humiliation & despondency, which shd be a time for learning wisdom, I wish we cd now think ourselves of importance enough to address his majesty once more, & humbly beseech him to grant such terms to his late subjects in America *as freemen may accept.* I have heard of none such being hitherto offer'd to them. Submission without terms – Unconditional submission! are offers for slaves, & those who accept them must be such. I hope & trust we are none of us in love with slavery.' Mr Eld broke off rather abruptly, & without speaking to the specific business of the day, as I wish'd him to have done. He said ma[n]y good things, & said them well, & with great energy for an old man of 80.[12]

Wedgwood wished Eld to say more because he was troubled. He read all the arguments that he could about not subscribing, yet they did not carry conviction with him. They broke down because in the last resort they conflicted with his patriotism.

> I am not at present fully convinced by them, that it is better to fall a prey to a foreign enemy rather than defend ourselves under the present ministry. Methinks I would defend the land of my nativity, my family and friends against a foreign foe, where conquest and slavery were inseparable, under any leaders – the best I could get for the moment, and wait for better times to displace an obnoxious minister, and settle domestic affairs, rather than rigidly say, I'll be saved in my own way and by people of my own choice, or perish

and perish my country with me. If subscribing would certainly rivet the present ministry in their places, and non-subscribing would as certainly throw them over, the nation at large being in no hazard at the same time from a foreign foe, I should not hesitate a moment what to do, but none of these propositions seem clear to me.[13]

Here we see how 'hazard from a foreign foe' was circumscribing Wedgwood's radical attitude. Radicalism was becoming unpatriotic; what in America gave radicalism its opportunities, in England inhibited them.

The upsurge of patriotic sentiment that Wedgwood experienced was typical of many men of similar views. Even Major Cartwright, one of the most dedicated supporters of the American revolution, who, indeed, sacrificed his military career and chance of marriage by his refusal to serve against the Americans, nevertheless took to organising and drilling the militia in Nottinghamshire in case invasion by the French became a reality. Although such radical leaders as Cartwright continued to demand not only independence for America, but also linked it with the need for the reform of Parliament and an extension of the franchise, their support in Britain contracted rather than expanded once the country was involved in a large-scale war.

This also proved true of radicalism's best organised and strongest supporters, the freemen of the City of London. In the mid-1770s they left Lord North's government in no doubt of their sympathy for the American revolution. In 1773 they chose two Americans, Stephen Sayre of Long Island and William Lee of Virginia, as sheriffs; in 1774 they insisted on their parliamentary candidates signing pledges to support a Bill which would have given America the right to elect its own Parliament and tax itself. Naturally the Coercive Acts were denounced; even as late as 1778 they refused to give public support to the war. Yet even amongst men as tough-minded as these, there is a marked decline in their pro-American activity after 1776. The war constricted their sympathy and restrained them from an all-out attack on the institutions by which they were being governed.

In spite of the widespread radical sympathy that had existed for ten years or more, little had been done to channel it into an effective political party capable of action. It was this lack of organisational structure that permitted patriotic sentiment to corrode radical fervour and inhibit action. Yet the impotence of the radicals, particularly between 1774 and 1776, must not be exaggerated. They had captured more or less effective control of the Corporation of the City of London, and they even had one or two representatives in Parliament. And it should be remembered that in many ways the City Corporation was the most powerful single institution in Great Britain after Parliament. Although war certainly weakened the radicals' attitude and their influence, their ineffectiveness cannot be entirely explained either by the upsurge of patriotism or the incompetence of their political organisation; a contributory cause, and an important one, arose from their total inability to carry any major Whig politician with them.

Lord Brougham, a radical himself and a politician with long parliamentary experience, wrote early in the nineteenth century, 'Is any man so blind as seriously to believe that, had Mr Burke and Mr Fox been ministers of George III, they would have resigned rather than try to put down the Americans?'[14] And it should be remembered that Charles James Fox spoke in favour of the Declaratory Act as late as 1778. The Whigs brought neither consistent action nor consistent policy to the American situation. In 1774 when radical agitation was at its strongest, the Whig leaders in opposition to the government showed the utmost reluctance to concentrate their energies on the problem of America.[15] The Duke of Richmond said he was sick of politics and Edmund Burke had to convince the Marquis of Rockingham of 'the necessity of proceeding regularly, and with your whole force; and that this affair of America is to be taken up as business'.

Here was no realisation of the profound social causes at work both in America and Britain; no sense of the future, nor of the need to reform political institutions as well as change ministries. The American problem was a useful weapon for Rockingham with which to attack North's administration, but he and his friends did not welcome the wider political and social implications of the American revolt. And yet without some effective leadership in Parliament, radicalism was hamstrung. Dissatisfaction with the oligarchical and aristocratic structure of British political and social life was widespread, but the frustration was neither deep enough nor savage enough to create an organisation bent on forcing change.

Lacking political leadership in Parliament, smeared with anti-patriotism, the widespread radical sentiments of the late 1760s and early 1770s failed, except in the City of London itself, to become a powerful factor in the American revolution.

In the end neither the attitude of politicians nor radicals, not even the voice of merchants or industrialists, and least of all the pressure of the mob, proved significant. It was the disillusion of Lord Pembroke and his kind that brought about North's fall. The acceptance by Britain of America's independence was secured by those country gentlemen who had decided every major political issue in Great Britain since the Reformation. The country interest, the independent members who sat in Parliament as Knights of the Shire, who never spoke in debates and usually voted with the government, finally rebelled, for the very same reason that they had given their initial support to George III and Lord North – taxation. Self-interest, the need to lighten their own taxes, to relieve themselves of the costly burden of defending America, had combined with their traditional respect for the Crown and the sovereignty of Parliament to make them tolerant of the ramshackle confusion, the endless contradictions of what passed for American policy in the 1760s and 1770s. What broke their spirit was defeat at Yorktown and, more especially, the cost of defeat. They could not face the prospect of a protracted war of uncertain outcome.

Lord Pembroke's cry that he wished that he was a Laplander or anything but a Briton was the true patriot's cry, wrung from him by his deep sense of shame at his nation's failure. And basically this was the attitude of the country gentlemen. Indeed patriotic sentiment deeply influenced all British attitudes to the American revolution – perhaps more than any other factor. It was only to be expected that sympathy towards America should be rarest amongst those who were content with the fabric of British society – the aristocrats, gentry, government officers, admirals, generals, lawyers and ecclesiastics, and that it should be strongest amongst those new men – the industrial and aggressive commercial classes – to whom the future belonged. The extent of that sympathy was much wider, the identity of their interests with America much closer, than has been generally believed. Radical sentiment was very widespread in the late 1760s and early 1770s but its ineffectiveness became ever more apparent once the American revolution had become a European war: by that fact a terrible dilemma was created for the radicals and this, as much as anything, weakened resolve and helped to inhibit action – in such marked and vivid contrast with the developments of radicalism in America itself.

And this proved to be more than a transitory handicap to the development of radicalism in Britain, for although radicalism, especially in its demands for parliamentary reform, began to climb back to respectability under the aegis of William Pitt and William Wilberforce, the revolutionary wars with France reimposed, even more markedly, the stigma of disloyalty upon it. Demands for political and social equality became seditious: the ancient institutions – monarchy, aristocracy, landed gentry – were sanctified by patriotic gore. And this sanctification took place when the archaic institutions by which Britain was governed – an extraordinary hotchpotch of feudal custom, medieval chartered rights and Tudor legislation – were becoming even more inadequate to meet the needs of the rising tide of industrialism. So when reform came in the nineteenth century, it was piecemeal, *ad hoc* never radical in any fundamental sense: and Britain never enjoyed, as did America and France, the purging joys of a social and political revolution. In consequence a radical attitude to political institutions and social organisation was in England always tainted with disloyalty. And, perhaps, it should be stressed once again that eighteenth- and early nineteenth-century British radicalism demanded no more than political and social equality, no more, in fact, than Americans were guaranteed by their Constitution. Such ideas, however, were no longer regarded as British; they were alien, Jacobin, Yankee or French.

Of course traditional institutions were strengthened by other factors apart from the alienation that took place between radicalism and patriotism at the time of the American and French revolutions; the possession of empire, particularly in India, fortified aristocratic and patriotic attitudes as well as the monarchy. Nevertheless the American revolution was almost as much a watershed in the development of British society as of American, for it rendered feeble a widespread middle-class intellectual radicalism that was beginning to take root in many of the socially and commercially aggressive sections of British society. Its failure to develop and grow; its relegation to political insignificance; its exclusion from the heart of British society, was to taint its middle-class radicalism with oddity, eccentricity, social neurosis, and so justify the continuing anti-intellectualism of the British Establishment. And the corollary was to link patriotism with George III, with monarchy no matter how stupid, with aristocracy no matter how incompetent. As a future of social equality and equal opportunity opened for America, Britain became more firmly saddled with its feudal past.

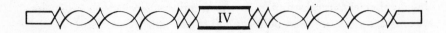

IV

Aspects of the Revolution

Because the early days of American history were so exotic – the conquests of Mexico and Peru; the haunting drama of Jamestown and the heroic Pilgrims – the decades and centuries that followed seemed cast in a minor key – even the War of Independence unfolded slowly and, until Yorktown, largely moved forward through the incompetence and follies of the British rather than through glorious American victories. And yet the American Revolution was, in many ways, as important for Europe as the discovery of America itself. For the first time a number of far-flung non-aristocratic communities had defeated a major power. Together they had deliberately created institutions of government on agreed political principles not only for themselves but for posterity. They did not know whether it would work or last. Indeed, one might argue that America experienced the only successful constitutional, political and social revolutions. And yet the very principles which the Founding Fathers formulated, the institutions which they formed, were not as it were of native growth. Their house was fashioned from other people's timbers, largely British but some French. The interplay of European, particularly British, and American culture was and still is fascinating to me, indeed as fascinating as many of the enigmatic figures of the Revolution. America discovered within its own small population men of incomparable ability and achievement. The essays which follow explore aspects of the Revolution, the British culture of which it was a part, its debt to Europe, and its personalities.

(i) America and England, 1720–1820. The Fusion of Cultures

For an Englishman driving about New England, there is an acute sense of cultural confusion. It is not that Leicester is but a suburb of Worcester, or that Epping is only a stone's throw from Portsmouth which, itself, is impossibly close to Manchester, the feeling of confusion goes far deeper than the place names. The same is true strolling about Charleston or walking round Savannah. The broad avenue of Bull Street, leading from Johnson Square to Forsythe Square in Savannah is curiously disturbing. Again, it is not the occasional foreign names – Chippewa, Monterey, for most of the rest are English enough. Nor is it the iron lacework balconies and railings, although they are ornate by the standards of England. Like the place names of the squares and avenues a little off-centre, maybe, but not critically so. The trees in Savannah and Charleston, the live oaks, the Spanish moss, the free-standing magnolia grandifloras, are exotic, strange, disturbing, perhaps, like the heat and humidity to an Englishman. In Charleston, the houses themselves are not English, not truly English, with their vast balconies, and their setting of semi-tropical gardens. And the same is true of the churches of New England. There they are built in gleaming, white-painted wood which makes them odd. All of these things give a touch of fantasy, of difference, but they do not explain the fundamental disquiet. To go into a well-preserved house, full of furniture of its period, such as the Owens Thomas House in Savannah or the House of the Swords in Charleston, the sensation almost of anxiety becomes even more acute – beautiful, eighteenth-century furniture, some imported, some locally made: Wedgwood's creamware; Boulton and Watt's silver plate; but alongside these there are paintings, pottery, stools and chairs, bed-covers and curtains, curiously primitive and very American, bringing a powerful echo of an England long dead by 1800. The confusion arises, I think, not because of the superficial differences or the exoticisms created by climate or the inertia of fashion and taste caused by distance. One may be astonished to find a house, like the Isaiah Davenport House of Savannah, built in 1820, when it might have graced Salisbury, Wiltshire, in 1750, but it remains truly English. The explanation lies in the fact that New England, much of the South-East as far as Georgia, is so deeply English; at least in what remains of the houses and furniture of the eighteenth and early nineteenth centuries. The English eighteenth century lives as powerfully in Savannah and Charleston; in scores of towns, like Leicester and North Oxford in New England, as it does in Bath or Tunbridge Wells, or the great Georgian terraces of Edinburgh. But what is disturbing is that these powerful vestiges of eighteenth-century England live in what, for an Englishman, is the alien ambience of twentieth-century America, with the hideous, revolving, neon-flashing advertisements, and used-car lots, with their odd fluttering flags, like Tibetan prayerwheels.

American eighteenth-century buildings, furniture, even paintings, cannot be regarded as mere country cousins of Britain. In Copley and

West, America produced artists of European, let alone British, reputation. American craftsmen were of the highest distinction. Surely
America did not produce a Paul de Lamerie, or Thomas Chippendale,
but a silver coffee pot by Paul Revere or Jacob Hurd or Charles Le
Roux was every bit as fine as any by Thomas Whipham, E. Wakelin, or
Pézé Pillau, or any other first-class London silversmith. Chests of drawers
by Jonathan Gostelave or card-tables by Thomas Afleck were as good
as could be found in the warehouses of the best English cabinetmakers.
Of course, the further one got away from Boston, New York, Philadelphia or Charleston, the more clumsy were the decorative arts, but the
same is true of Britain; or, for that matter, France; they, too, had plenty
of provincial furnishings of moderate quality, even in the eighteenth
century.

The closeness of the artistic bond between America and England in
the eighteenth century was not, however, inevitable. In the seventeenth
century, the craftsmen of the American colonies had been touched by
changes of English fashion, but often very lightly, and they had persisted
with styles and forms for many generations, and by and large they had
satisfied their market. Only the very rich, and they were not numerous,
had imported works of art or decorative porcelain, silver and furniture
of high fashion. Nor in the seventeenth century had England itself been
swarming with silversmiths, cabinet-makers, painters and carvers, or
even china-makers of high distinction and genius. There was not, in fact,
a great deal in England to entice the guineas from an American middle-
class pocket. It was affluence in both England and America, and in
America a fantastic surge in the size of the middle class. that had so
profound an influence on the development of a common culture in the
eighteenth century.

The jump in the population of the American colonies was dramatic
between 1700 and 1770. As Thomas Malthus wrote years later, it was
'a rapidity of increase almost without parallel in history', from a mere
629,000 in 1700 to 2,148,000 in 1770; by 1800, 5,000,000. Of course,
this might seem a trivial population, considering the immensity of the
thirteen states, but the population was not unduly scattered, much of its
was highly concentrated. Philadelphia, in 1770, had become the second
largest city in the British Empire. And although the proportion of this
growing population which lived in the cities was actually falling, the
growth of the major cities was great enough and rapid enough to sustain
a prosperous and cultured society. Without cities, a highly sophisticated
culture is not possible. Nor, in eighteenth-century terms, was it possible
without a class rich enough to indulge in conspicuous consumption or
without the leisure to read, to watch the theatre, to listen to a concert,
or even to build their houses and adorn them, of which nothing is more

time-consuming. By 1750, the five major seaports – Boston, Newport, New York, Philadelphia and Charleston – already possessed a very prosperous class of commercial gentry, and it was a class which was growing fast and becoming richer. The wars against the French and the Indians of the 1740s and 1750s made many fortunes, as did the buoyant trade in tobacco, rice and indigo. Although he began as a bookseller and graduated to be a papermaker, the bulk of John Hancock's fortune was made out of supplying British forces in America, engaged in war against the French and the Indians, and it was Hancock who, in 1737, built on Beacon Hill the most distinguished house that Boston had seen, with its flanking pavilions to contain the ballroom and the domestic offices, the house was typically that of an English country-gentleman of moderate means. From London came Hancock's marble chimney pieces, his blue Delft tiles, his looking-glasses and his wallpaper; likewise he imported his fruit trees and his walnut trees and yews, but the rest of the house and its furnishings were by American craftsmen. With burgeoning population and wealth, there were never enough American craftsmen; or craftsmen sufficiently ahead of fashion to supply the needs of the rich middle class. Pattern books flew across the Atlantic and were rapidly reprinted. So buoyant a market became a magnet for young professional architects, or English master craftsmen who had too small resources for the severe competition of the London market. As always in colonial society, the goods imported from England, and to a lesser extent from Europe, possessed a cachet in American eyes that no similar home produced goods could rival. Also, as fashions changed in England with novel speed (the patterns of textiles every year), American craftsmen and manufacturers tended to be forever a step behind, thereby enhancing the *chic* of the imported goods and making quick copies of them a surer way to a profit than an attempt at originality. In England, the emphasis was on modernity; the pressure on men such as Josiah Wedgwood and Matthew Boulton to invent and explore new materials and new shapes in order to capture the market was intense. In America, therefore, a copy which could pass as just imported might have a readier sale, but it always proved exceptionally difficult to defeat the true imports. This is beautifully illustrated by the first porcelain produced in America, the soft-paste wares of Bonnin and Morris of Philadelphia. The few pieces that remain are all pastiches of English factories – Bow, Worcester, and the rest. Neither this firm nor Batchem in South Carolina survived for long. They could not secure sufficient skilled workmen, nor could they produce so economically as Wedgwood or other English potters who continued to dominate the china trade for decades and therefore were responsible for setting the style of American decorative arts.

The Revolution caused little break with the flow of fashion or the emigration of professional craftsmen from Britain to America; indeed, British culture remained dominant for the early decades of the nineteenth century. From 1830, however, America became more strongly influenced by European styles and also began to develop in literature, in painting, in the applied arts, a culture that was markedly her own. Nevertheless, the impress of Georgian England goes very deep. From Bar Harbour to Savannah, the Englishman today is constantly reminded, in one visual image after another, of the most beautiful age of British architecture and art.

But culture is more than art and to sustain a sophisticated way of life requires new attitudes, conscious commitment in men and women, as well as novel social institutions; in cultural activities there must be a sense of worth and of aspiration. In eighteenth-century Britain, there was a great expansion of cultural activity. Young aristocrats, like Horace Walpole, were bred to think of art and literature as the natural occupations of a gentleman, along with building, gardening, and the support of the theatre and music. The same passions, the same interests were seeping down through every gradation of the middle class. Much of this culture was sought after because of its self-improving nature – an aspect which quickly caught the attention of Benjamin Franklin. Indeed, in many of his interests, Franklin was as typical of the newly emerging British middle-class culture as he was of Philadelphia's. Both English and Americans were busy forming discussion clubs, founding book subscription libraries, schools and hospitals, and attending the lectures of itinerant lecturers on science – except here there was one startling difference between England and America. Franklin bought the scientific apparatus of Dr K. Spence, who visited Philadelphia, and made far better use of it than the lecturer! Nevertheless, the emerging culture of Philadelphia in which Franklin was so deeply involved was typical of many provincial towns of England, particularly the new manufacturing towns of Birmingham, Manchester and Leeds. But it was to London that the Philadelphian Subscription Library sent for its first consignment of books, and indeed it would be books written and published in London that would provide the bulk of the library's reading for the rest of the century and beyond. There was, of course, a growing range of publications of purely American origin, printed in Philadelphia, as well as a great deal of piracy of British books. Nevertheless, English publishers and English publications dominated the market. And that was true, too, of the subscription rooms and reading rooms such as that at Charleston, which so quickly followed Philadelphia's example. Books, itinerant science lecturers, flowed across the Atlantic; so, too, later in the century, did plays and actors, music and musicians. The traffic was, of course, not all one way, for Benjamin West came to be George III's favourite painter, and he acquired a dominant authority in the art world of London. And in many ways, some obvious, some obscure, America contributed to the culture of Britain. One influence that is often neglected is how America enriched the British flora in the eighteenth century. Englishmen developed a consuming passion for their gardens, and were soon ransacking America for new trees, new shrubs and new flowers. By the 1730s it was possible to buy, at the chief nurseries in England, tens of thousands of native American trees; plants of every kind from America had been acclimatised and often hybridised. And men such as John Hancock were quick to raid, in return, the British nurseries for their exotics: after all, the camellia, 'the Japanese rose', reached America via Britain at this time. At all cultural levels, from the breeding of flowers or horses to natural philosophy, literature, and the arts, the two countries were almost as one.

There were, however, deeper resonances than in art or literature or architecture or science, or in the planting of gardens or the furnishing of houses. England in the 1740s, 1750s and 1760s witnessed a mounting sense of political unease that quickly developed into active discontent. There was a great expansion of political comment in the daily newspapers, in the political press, in the pamphlets and broadsheets that festooned the taverns and coffee houses. Great issues of peace and war, and of taxation were violently debated, often with a satirical bitterness that included the royal family, as well as the chief ministers – a freedom of satire that astonished foreign observers. A new type of urban radicalism began to take root, first in London and then in the major provincial cities, particularly those which were concerned with commerce and industry. There was a growing feeling that the high hopes, bred by the success of Parliament in the seventeenth century against the Crown, for a society based on liberty and freedom had been betrayed; that the power, wealth and patronage had passed into the hands of a narrow oligarchy and that Parliament was no longer representative of the people, but an institution riddled with corruption and self-seeking, and one in which the deeper needs of the nation were ignored. It was a mood of incoherent distrust and criticism that knew what it was against, rather than what it was for, but it was a mood which resonated in Boston, in Philadelphia, in New York, which showed the same feelings of frustration, of exclusion from true power, of being used. It was a mood which was easy to ignite by a specific act of obvious injustice, as London, and then all England, was ignited by Wilkes, or America was inflamed by the Stamp Act. Although many Englishmen, like Americans, believed that their country enjoyed a degree of freedom unparalleled in history, nevertheless, many of the more sensitive and intelligent critics believed that freedom to be in jeopardy. From the 1720s, let alone the 1730s, an impressive literature of opposition grew up in Britain of which the most persuasively argued were *Cato's Letters* and *The Independent Whig* by John Trenchard and Thomas Gordon, and the essays of *The Craftsman*, many of which were written by Bolingbroke. These essays, either verbatim, paraphrased or just cribbed, were immediately published in American newspapers from Massachusetts to South Carolina. Once again it was as if America were but an extension of England, not, however, of official England, of the men of power and authority, but of their critics. As Bernard Bailyn has written,

> The political culture of colonial America – the assumptions, the expectations, patterns of responses, and clusters of information relevant to the conduct of public affairs – was thus British, but British with a peculiar emphasis. It was not simply a miscellaneous amalgam of ideas and beliefs common in eighteenth-century England, nor, most emphatically, was it simply a distillation of the thought of a few great minds, particularly Locke's. It was, rather, a pattern of ideas, assumptions, attitudes and beliefs given distinctive shape by the opposition elements in English politics.

And likewise when the great struggle was joined in the 1760s and 1770s, pamphlets attacking the ministerial actions, printed in Boston and Philadelphia, were rapidly reprinted and extensively sold in England, as, indeed, were those of the English defenders of American freedom, such as the pamphlets of Jonathan Shipley, of John Cartwright, and the rest, in America. Nor is it surprising that the most powerful of all propaganda weapons printed in America – Tom Paine's *Common Sense*, was the work of an Englishman. American discontents were English discontents, giving rise to a common rhetoric of political opposition. And America and England adopted common political heroes. John Wilkes, in gaol, received presents from Boston and from Virginia. All propaganda material, which with Wilkes amounted almost to an industry – the prints, the punch bowls, the mugs, the buttons, all proclaiming 'Wilkes and Liberty', had as ready a sale in the American colonies as in provincial England. After the Revolution, the political experience of America and England began to diverge. America developed its own patterns of political discourse, its own style of parties – nevertheless, vestiges remained of its ancient political attitudes. The substantial ghost of George III, King and tyrant, stalked through the school history books generation after generation; there was bred an immediate, instinctive, and often wrong-headed sympathy for all movements in the British Empire which could be dubbed anti-colonial, so deep was the memory, or so frequently refreshed was the memory, of its own struggle against monarchy and the British Parliament.

Although the paths of politics began to diverge most sharply after

1800, the institutions of government, created by the British, proved to be incredibly strong and completely acceptable to the American people. It is often forgotten that the pattern of local government in American states, as well as in American towns, stems directly from British practice. Even the township meetings of New England communities has much in common with the open vestry meeting of the English parish, whilst the county system is as undeniably British as the Grand Jury and the sheriff and his posse. Many of these institutions, such as the Grand Jury, long moribund in Britain, still enjoy a vigorous life in America. America's legal system which, of course, it shared with Britain in the eighteenth century, has, in many aspects, displayed an inertia, an avoidance of change that is in marked contrast to England. Even in the most funda-mental concept of all – namely democracy – America owes more to seventeenth- and eighteenth-century Britain than is commonly supposed. Few realise how very wide the county franchise was in England in the eighteenth century; that is, those who possessed the right to vote in the election of the Members of Parliament for the county seats. It embraced far more of the adult male population than had the right to vote *after* the Reform Bill of 1832. The forty-shilling freehold had become so trivial by 1700, that it was scarcely possible to question the vote of any adult male who turned up at the hustings. The same had been true of seventeenth-century America, when many of the states were creating the franchises for their own assemblies: the broad suffrages adopted by the states had their roots deep in the English tradition. And so did the methods of the management of the electorate. In neither country was it possible to dominate totally so broad an electorate and form it into a political machine, but that did not mean that influence lacked weight. In Virginia, as in Yorkshire, the gentry families – one has only to think of the Byrds – maintained a permanent political position generation after generation, as did the Fitzwilliams in Yorkshire. Again the method of patronage employed feebly, and not very successfully, by the royal gover-nors and officials in colonial days were not cast away by the Revolution. The use of the post office service as a source of political patronage was not an American invention. It was the common English practice of the eighteenth century. The irony of history lies in the fact that whilst England rejected many of its eighteenth-century political habits, America did not; rather was the system extended. Nor was the machine politics of Tammany Hall devoid of a British counterpart. They were a common-place of urban politics of eighteenth-century England, and particularly deeply embedded in the treacherous poverty-ridden suburbs of London, such as Stepney.

Even the American Constitution is indelibly English, rooted in what the opposition to the English political establishment of the eighteenth century believed to be the pure form of the English constitution, in which the separation of powers was the keystone. And it was this false interpretation to which Montesquieu had given a wider currency; false because English legislature and the executive had never been separated, only politicians out of office believed that they had been and should be. The Founding Fathers, however, adopted what they felt to be the pure form of the English constitution. Again the Senators – two from each State – reflected the English Knights of the Shire, always thought to be the wisest and most independent of Members of Parliament. Tiny Rutland has as many Knights of the Shire as vast Yorkshire, just as Rhode Island was to have as many Senators as New York State. And the powers of the President were those of an English monarch, deprived certainly of the capacity to give honours or create aristocrats, but in other ways more powerful, one might say more absolutist than the English King who, by 1782, could not choose even his junior ministers. Indeed, the American Constitution was the result of eighteenth-century British political attitudes and constitutional interpretations.

For more than two centuries, America and Britain enjoyed a common political and social culture. When divergence came, it was brought about by the vast immigrations of the nineteenth century, but two centuries of common culture cannot be obliterated, particularly when it was the foundation upon which subsequent generations had to build. And already this common culture had learned how to assimilate what might so easily have become symbiotic enclaves of alien cultures. The great German influx in the 1740s and 1750s into Pennsylvania, with its full complement of churches, schools, newspapers, had made Franklin aware of what might happen. Although the German language and traditions lingered, and small communities persisted in maintaining their German culture, the majority were within a generation or two absorbed into the Anglo-American culture of Philadelphia – for success in trade, in manufacture, in banking and finance was only possible through the English language, which ambitious young Germans quickly realised. And so, by 1820, it was already clear, come Germans, Dutch, Italians, Greeks, Russians and Armenians, the language of government, the language of commerce, the language of culture would be English. Just as there would be no balkanisation of government, so there would be no balkanisation due to language. And language remains the basis of culture – it is, and must remain, the foundation of that special relationship between America and Britain, making for a natural cultural interchange that no other European nation can enjoy with America.

(ii) The French Connection 1776–1782

Two great historic figures – men who have merged into myth – are almost the sole remains of the alliance between France and the revolutionary forces of America – Lafayette and Benjamin Franklin. And like most myths time has changed them, clothing the reality in a web of romance. The young Marquis de Lafayette, plunging ashore on North Island, North Carolina, is seen as the personification of those forces in France which yearned for liberty, for freedom from the oppressive hierarchical régime of an absolutist monarchy. These young French idealists found so much justification for their attitude in the simplicity, the honesty, the ruggedness and equality of American life – or so we are told. In contrast, Benjamin Franklin at Passy symbolised for the sophisticated Parisian *salons* the true philosopher – natural, unaffected, wise, free from all artifice. The textbooks tell us that the ease of his presence, the extraordinary sanity of his views, his undeviating patriotism, his strength and gravity, rallied all that was best and generous in French society to the American cause. Lafayette, back from America, transmuted warmth into action; and so, standing symbolically behind the serried ranks of Rochambeau's troops at Yorktown, is Lafayette, with his sword held aloft, and Franklin quietly smiling like a Chinese sage. Both men have left a profusion of papers behind, certain of their place in history and not at all unmindful of the image which they wished to display to posterity. Great men though both undeniably were, the writers of history, and so posterity, have been over-generous in their praise. Both men may not have had feet of clay, but there was certainly clay on their boots.

Their dazzling prominence has thrown a shadow on many men, particularly this is true of Lafayette, who was only one of many foreigners whose help was of great aid to the Revolution in the early stages. Who now thinks with gratitude of De Kalb, of Steuben, of Pulaski? Or of Lafayette's compatriots – Pontigibaud, Armand, Desportail, Vrigny, La Colombe, Fleury and the rest? And although both Arthur Lee and Silas Deane have been rescued from relative obscurity, it is the Franklin of the salon, the *cher Papa* of the witty, sophisticated middle-aged hostesses, who continues to steal the limelight. To understand the French connection in 1776, one must dig deeper than the simplicities symbolised by Lafayette and Franklin, important though they were.

Early in August 1775, a large coach rattled into Metz and deposited the Duke of Gloucester, the brother of George III, at the door of the military governor, the Comte de Broglie, with whom he was to dine. Gloucester was thirty-two years of age. He had outraged the Court, the government, and the King in particular, by first living with, then marrying, the bastard daughter of Sir Edward Walpole, the son of George II's great minister, Sir Robert. The bitterness of the Court, mountainous debts and ill-health, had driven him from England. And many politicians, as well as the Court, heaved a sigh of relief as Gloucester and his bourgeois bride left Dover, for he, at loggerheads with his brother, favoured the radicals and the firebrands, particularly John Wilkes, the most skilful agitator opposed to the King. Indeed, one of the reasons why the Comte de Broglie was so eager to be his host was that Gloucester could give him first-hand information about the support, or lack of it, that George III's American policy enjoyed in England. Like all of the Hanoverian royal family, Gloucester talked volubly and indiscreetly. Influential men in London, powerful men in the provinces, a great number of Members of Parliament, were bitterly opposed to his brother's policy and his brother's ministers, Gloucester informed Broglie, and the words were as sweet to Broglie's ears as they were soothing to Gloucester's bruised ego. Indeed, Gloucester painted so dramatic a picture of the divisions in England that he seemed to hint at a nation on the verge of civil war, the provinces in an uproar, and Ireland in turmoil. In later years, writing of this dinner, Lafayette recalls how he closely cross-examined the Duke and, realising how liberty and freedom were oppressed in England as well as America, he was fired by a desire to spring to America's aid. Alas, nothing is less likely to be true. Lafayette was a shy, reticent boy, eighteen years of age, young-looking for his years, who had recently been sent to Metz to do garrison duty under his relative, Broglie. He was a naïve young aristocrat of small experience of the world. Doubtless he sat silent amongst the equerries, but certainly his imagination was fired, and this was the starting point of Lafayette's journey to fame.

The dinner, however, had far more important consequences than stirring the warm and passionate heart of a young adolescent. Broglie was a man of the greatest consequence, banished to Metz in semi-disgrace because of the defeats he had suffered at the hands of the British and, like so many men of his class – the élite aristocratic generals of the French Army – he longed for revenge for the humiliations inflicted on France by England during the Seven Years War (1756–63). What rankled most was the Treaty of Paris. They loathed the arrogance of the British Commissioner installed at Dunkirk, who made certain that the moles and ramparts remained destroyed so that this superb naval base could not be put into a state of readiness. The swift French corsairs based there had preyed happily on the slow, rich British convoys beating their way up the Channel or across the North Sea from the Baltic. Even more bitter were the memories of what they had lost – Canada, the earliest of all French colonies, along with France's commercial posts in India,

its trading forts in Senegal, but worst of all, as Vergennes, the French
Foreign Minister, wrote to Louis XVI at his accession, was the humiliation, the shame of defeat. As Vergennes gloomily noted, the French
government, which used to be the greatest of European powers, was no
longer consulted. It had become a mere spectator of great events. French
pride had been dipped in gall.

The humiliation, the shame of the defeat, bore so heavily on France
for reasons not commonly realised. France possessed men, money and
materials in a profusion that totally outstripped England. France's population was some twenty-six million to England's eight or nine million,
but the close alliance with Spain (the Family Compact) weighted France's
favourable balance by another ten million. Furthermore, France had on
call some 300,000 military men and a professional standing army of
about 140,000, very well equipped and excellently trained, whereas the
British standing army, loathed by Englishmen and constantly under
attack by Parliament, numbered about 35,000. Although near to equality
in naval affairs, England was, of course, seriously outnumbered by the
combined fleets of France and Spain, and it was for this reason that the
British always dreaded a war against France without the support of
the Dutch. The material riches of France were commensurate with its
population – it possessed excellent armament industries, indeed, the best
in the world, backed by great financial resources. But here, at least,
England could look eye to eye with France, for England had developed
a sophisticated and stable financial system that bred confidence not only
in the British people, but also the Dutch, who invested heavily in British
funds. Without great financial resources England could never have hoped
to defeat the Goliath of France, but money bought mercenary soldiers,
notably the Hessians, whose discipline and accuracy of fire the Americans were soon to taste. Even so, the British politicians feared France;
indeed they had been scared by their own victories in the Seven Years
War – especially in 1759, the great *annus mirabilis*, Wolfe stormed
Quebec, the French fleets were humiliated at Lagos and Quiberon Bay,
and even the British army scored one of its rare victories in Europe – at
Minden – the first for fifteen years. Chatham, the architect of these
victories, had wanted to smash France and Spain for good, but his
colleagues were appalled by the enormity of his vision of Europe. They
backtracked. And the Treaty of Paris, in 1763, loathed and hated by
the French, was, in fact, an extraordinarily generous treaty, giving back
to France almost all, except Canada, that Britain had conquered. This
was done quite deliberately in the hope of avoiding another war with
France. A severe settlement, many argued, must lead to renewed wars,
and the British did not in their hearts believe that they could go on
defeating the greatest military power in Europe over and over again.

Smug in their own generosity, few English statesmen appreciated the deep sense of ignominy and shame that gnawed at the hearts of Frenchmen such as the Comte de Broglie – for so great a power as France to be humiliated by a small nation of shopkeepers was too bitter.

The Treaty of Paris naturally affected the destiny of America – the expulsion of the French from Canada which, at that time, reached down to the headwaters of the Mississippi, freed the West; indeed, one of the reasons that influenced the British government in choosing to take Canada, rather than the rich sugar islands of Guadaloupe and Marti-nique, was that military pressure on the frontiers of the American colonies would be relieved. Whether Britain was wise can be endlessly debated. The sugar isles gave the French not only commercial riches, but superb naval bases from where its fleets could threaten not only Jamaica and the West Indies trade, but also the coasts of the southern states. Chatham would have seized both possessions – Canada and the West India Isles – from France, for he felt that the policy of compromise was bound to leave a French dagger pointing at British colonies. He was right, for that dagger was to become the executioner's axe at Yorktown. The American colonies, therefore, either at peace or at war with England, lay at the very heart of the strategic confrontation between England and France.

There was a soldier of fortune present at that dinner at Metz, who knew the importance and the intricacy of this strategic situation – de Kalb, a Prussian soldier long in the service of France, a man of great experience in all the arts of war, specialising in logistics and fortification, who had already spent time in America reconnoitering the situation. A tough professional of excellent judgement, he was as confident of France's opportunities as de Broglie, and as eager for action as young Lafayette.

And there were scores of soldiers, aristocrats like de Broglie, scattered throughout the garrisons of France, longing, praying, for revenge, and rejoicing in the American opportunity. England's espionage system was admirable, and her diplomats were alive to the threats, but what should French policy be? Vergennes, the Foreign Minister, wanted war so long as Spain was a committed ally, but Spain was vulnerable both in America and in the West Indies, and to persuade Spain took time. In any case France needed time to reflect. Also, in the early stages of the conflict, Louis XV, an ageing *roué*, gave his ministers little encouragement; his death in 1774, however, revitalised the Administration and strengthened its resolve. Nevertheless, for many years the French government had been playing its own war game – plotting and planning how to get a military advantage over Britain. It had sent its master-spies and agents to London, the bisexual Charles d'Eon, who dressed and lived as a woman, and Beaumarchais, the creator of *Figaro*, whose contacts were complex and far-ranging. They planned possible invasions of England. They listened to the radicals and tested the opposition to Lord North's policy. They learned of the weakness of the British army, the unpreparedness of the navy. The troubles in America were music to their ears. Their reports, always optimistic and eager for conflict, flowed into the Quai d'Orsay. Aware of their activities in general, if not always apprised of their detailed information, the British government, through its Ambassador Stormont in Paris, thrust out its jaw, telling the French bluntly that aid to the American rebels would mean war. By the accession of Louis XVI the momentum of involvement was mounting, although Louis XVI and his advisers still hoped to avoid a direct confronation with Britain. They were no longer complete masters of the situation. Games became realities.

As soon as it became a shooting war, the Americans needed France desperately – they could manufacture gunpowder, but nothing else. And their financial resources were ludicrously small. America's urgent needs at first made the French Government even more reluctant, for they did not wish to commit themselves to a lost cause and have to confront an armed Britain who might take a quick revenge. And, as great nations are wont to do in such circumstances, they tried to make the best of both worlds – give large-scale succour to the colonists, but protest their neutrality to Britain. What could the King do if idealistic boys like Lafayette chartered a boat and sailed as knight-errants to America? What could the King do if his subjects sold arms, ammunition, or even made loans to the colonists? How could he prevent soldiers of fortune, such as de Kalb – after all, a Prussian – seeking fame, glory and riches with Washington's army?

These were wonderfully muddied waters for shark-toothed men to fish in. Naturally armaments were the first necessity and the prime preoccupation, not only of Silas Deane and Benjamin Franklin, but also Beaumarchais, who was as creative in action as in writing. He saw a golden opportunity to aid himself as well as America. Two million francs were to be given by the government to his cover company Hortalez. This money was to be used to buy up-to-date weapons from the royal arsenals which were to be shipped to America, a free gift, suitably disguised, from the French Court to the American people. After the Government had paid over the money, the waters became muddier and muddier. Beaumarchais realised that his Government would have to conceal its interest. Such a golden opportunity for fraud was irresistible. Deane was himself involved in these murky dealings, Beaumarchais sent an agent to deal with Congress who did not discover for some years that the French Government had intended these armaments as a free gift. Fortunately, they had not been quick to pay Beaumarchais, whose descendants were still suing for payment long after his death. Like many a golden dream, it proved a mirage. Deane and Beaumarchais were not alone in dabbling in armaments: Benjamin Franklin was also involved for personal profit as well as through patriotic zeal. So complex a situation in which the French Government had to act in the dark through agents who were far from scrupulous, made wheeling and dealing easy. Some armaments, too, proved wretched when brought, yet essential supplies got to America – the rifles, the guns, the shells, without which there could have been no victory. Deane may have been a British agent, Franklin was careless about secrecy, and Beaumarchais' ebullient exhibitionism bordered on the suicidal. At Le Havre, *incognito* in order to expedite a ship loaded with armaments, he appeared at its theatre to rehearse his play, *The Barber of Seville*. It is not surprising that the British knew exactly what aid was being sent to America. But so slow were communications, so leisurely the reaction to military intelligence, that Beaumarchais' boats mostly got through.

As with armaments, so with men. The Court was forced by its official policy of neutrality to show disapproval, particularly of Lafayette and the young Noailles, who showed no discretion whatsoever – who dies at nineteen – about their intentions. Naturally, they were ardent proselytisers amongst their young aristocratic friends. Noailles' family checked their knight-errant, but Lafayette, who enjoyed the control of his own immense fortune, could not be stopped by his family, and the Court's measures to stop him were always half-hearted and always too late. Also they were eager to get de Kalb into America – on his judgement and military intelligence they could wholly rely, and Lafayette's boat was most convenient. It is not surprising that the order to arrest Lafayette arrived too late. When de Kalb reached America with young Lafayette, they found plenty of foreign military adventurers swarming around Congress demanding the highest commissions, and most of them with supporting letters from Silas Deane. Most American commanders were naturally irritated to see Frenchmen promoted above them. Congress itself was growing restive yet the importance, the need for France was so great, that most of them got what they wanted and Lafayette himself became a general under the avuncular care of George Washington.

The early days of the French connection need not be told – most of the French fought well, most of them took a gloomy view of American fighting ability, generalship and capacity to survive. De Kalb formed a low opinion of Washington's abilities that was only dispelled by Valley Forge. At times even Lafayette's enthusiasm wilted. But his dreams sustained him – the reconquest of Canada, a descent on India, the expulsion of the British from the West Indies – there was nothing mean about Lafayette's hopes and fantasies.

It was England's inability to make the kill which finally convinced the government of France that outright support should not be withheld. This was strategically right, it always had been, but now it was tactically correct. Yet, as Louis XVI's advisers well knew, such a course of action meant war with England. England's control of the Atlantic had to be broken or evaded if first-class French troops were to be landed in America, and without French troops, stalemate or compromise was a more likely end to the war than American victory. But the only hope of overcoming the English navy was with a combined Franco-Spanish naval force. France could not commit herself openly, therefore, to the American cause without Spain.

Spain was slow to move. Spain claimed vast unmapped territories in the West and South-West of America. Louisiana belonged to Spain, and the Mississippi she thought of as a Spanish river. Florida, now British, had been Spanish, and Spain wanted it back. Would a victorious America respect her territorial rights? Her government doubted it. Also the Spaniards thought that one successful revolution might lead to another – and next time in their possessions in South America. The Spanish ministers might be dilatory, but they enjoyed clarity of vision.

Had this been all, Spain would have been impossible to move, but Spain, too, had suffered searing humiliations. Gibraltar, a part of the Spanish homeland, was in British possession; Jamaica, in Spanish eyes a nest of detestable mercantile pirates who preyed on her colonies, was almost as bad. To get Gibraltar back, to win Jamaica, and to have Florida restored made the American gamble seem just worthwhile. It was hard going for France's diplomats, but they knew from long experience how to handle Spain but, alas for England, they had more surprising and unusual success elsewhere. Britain's imperious handling of neutral shipping had irritated and outraged the Dutch – their age-long allies. And so French diplomats were able to persuade the Dutch to keep out of the conflict, to declare their neutrality, which was a bitter blow for England, who needed the Dutch navy to counter-balance France's acquisition of the Spanish.

And so, finally, in 1780, the American revolt became a global war, the third act of the great imperial conflict between France and Britain, and it spelt the end of the possibility of Anglo-American compromise. There had been great sympathy in England for the American cause; once France and Spain were allied with America, that sympathy died, drowned in a surge of patriotism. The City of Bristol, which had been ardently pro-American, turned round completely and supported Lord North. Until the entry of the French, complete victory, although desirable, was not necessary for the British. Stalemate, combined with soaring inflation and an unpaid army on the brink of dissolution, might still have strengthened the powerful loyalist party sufficiently to secure peace. Time, therefore, so long as help from Europe was kept to a minimum, was on England's side. With France and Spain as belligerents, victories became essential; victories over the colonists and victories over Spain and France. The British knew that Gibraltar would be invested, France's allies in India would take the offensive, Jamaica become a target, English commerce throughout the world a convenient and easy prey for privateers. And England had *no* allies. Without the Dutch her navy was outnumbered and her army always had been pitifully small. Quick victories were essential, and quick victories eluded England.

French tactics were simple – to threaten England's possessions in the West Indies, to draw off the British navy so that seasoned French troops could be landed in America. The plan was easy, the accomplishment difficult and muddled. The Americans asked prudently for 4000 men – sufficient to help, yet unlikely to be regarded as *the* decisive army. A point rapidly taken by the French, who elected to send 8000 men, including some cavalry with horses. Supplies, of course, for the 8000 men had to go with them. Almost incredibly quickly, by eighteenth-century standards, 7500 men were assembled at Brest. Alas, there were no boats to take them across the Atlantic. The Spaniards, already myopically preoccupied with Gibraltar, could send none. The Spaniards also were huffed because the French refused to send their army to recover Florida. So in the end only 5500 sailed, and not a single horse – not even the Commander-in-Chief's. The decision was a tough one, for Rochambeau parted with two tried war-horses which he could never replace, but it was two horses or twenty men. Rochambeau chose the men.

A typical decision, easy maybe for Rochambeau, but it would have been almost impossible for most European generals, conscious of their status and dignity. But Rochambeau possessed great qualities and great integrity. A professional soldier for all of his life, he had steadily risen through ability, sound judgement, and honesty – qualities which he was now to display at their best.

Excepting horses, the logistics of the expedition were admirable. Everything went with it – clothes and tents, as well as guns and bullets. And most important of all, money. Rochambeau was well aware of the dangers for a French army in America. After all, the French alliance had created considerable distaste; many Americans were still English enough to hate the French and to suspect France's motives. There was quite a strong anti-French party in Congress, led by the Lees. A few rapes, a little pillaging, demands to Congress for money, and the French would be hated more than the British and as much as the Hessians. Rochambeau resolved to pay for everything that his army required, and his experience told him that he would have to pay grossly inflated prices – that was the nature of war. He demanded and got eight million livres for the expedition, a vast sum by eighteenth-century standards. The army was of high quality, and, as if to impress the Americans with the sincerity of their intentions, some of the great aristocratic families were with it: the Duc de Lauzun, with six hundred men of his own family corps, the Légion de Lauzun; the Marquis de Laval-Montmorency was there; and, at last, the Vicomte de Noailles, the ardent friend of Lafayette, among scores of others, eager to revenge the ignominy of France.

All of these aristocrats were young, rich, extravagant, brilliantly dressed, and exquisitely mannered, used to the gardens and sophistications of Versailles and Paris. They found colonial America a primitive place, but they were fascinated by it. They loathed the food but loved the girls, whose freedom in society amazed them as much as their beauty attracted them. The setting, in terms of houses and furniture, they regarded as unnecessarily crude, but the style of life – its ease, its freedom – won their hearts. But what amazed them most of all was the absence of grinding poverty, at that time the dark background to their gilded lives.

They were ardent, confident men, yet at first it looked to them as if the ignominy might never be obliterated, but only strengthened. Before landing at Newport, Rhode Island, on 10 July 1780, Rochambeau had heard of the fall of Charleston. He found the American forces dispirited, ill-equipped, and unpaid. Inflation was rampant, and the English stranglehold on Charleston and also New York encouraged defeatism and strengthened those drawn to compromise. In October he sent his son, Vicomte Rochambeau back to France, requesting a second division, more supplies, and enough cash for George Washington to pay his army. The young Rochambeau exchanged the gloom of New England for the gloom of Versailles. The Spanish were obsessed with Gibraltar and reluctant to commit any forces except in Florida. The loss of Charleston depressed Louis XVI, and neither he nor his ministers were relieved by what they heard of the American army: the news of the Pennsylvania mutinies had already reached them. Another British victory and the end would be in sight. France would then be mercilessly savaged in the Caribbean. Another long war seemed to be in prospect, and France's treasury was on the point of exhaustion. Tough decisions were made – no more troops were to go to America. Rochambeau must win or lose with what he had. But six million livres, enough for Washington's army, were scraped together. Rochambeau was told that if opportunity and his own tactical situation allowed, de Grasse would be permitted to leave his West Indian station to help in a combined attack on the British during the next campaigning session. Nevertheless de Grasse's main purpose – to attack Jamaica with Spain – was his first priority.

Victory in 1781 sprang mainly from de Grasse's judgement. De Grasse had long served in the French navy but in subordinate capacities. Now in his late fifties, he was a most experienced professional sailor. But he was more than that. His ancestry went straight back to the Prince d'Antibes of the tenth century. His birth, his education, his inherited assumptions about his role in life, bred in him a supreme self-confidence. He made decisions easily but never foolishly. The arrogance of his temperament enabled him to ignore instructions that hobbled his actions. Like his ancestors he pursued *gloire*. Very quickly he realised there was little to be gained in the Caribbean. Taking a minor island here and there was unlikely to make his name memorable to posterity, and in any case the English fleet, strong but elusive, did not wish to engage in a decisive battle.

This de Grasse had realised before he crossed the Atlantic. From the very earliest days of his command he had longed to perform a bold and decisive stroke against England in America. He had written at once to Rochambeau to ask what he might do to help.

Rochambeau, as clear-sighted as ever, knew exactly what he wanted. He wanted de Grasse's fleet to contain or destroy the British ships that were sustaining their troops and he wanted more French soldiers and, equally important, more French money. But the point of attack – New York or Virginia – was not Rochambeau's to decide, and de Grasse was not to leave the West Indies without the concurrence of his Spanish ally.

In war luck helps, although it rarely decides the outcome. Perhaps luck, however, was more decisive in the last year of the Revolutionary War than in most. At first the dice fell badly. Washington decided to attack New York. Washington and Rochambeau's armies met outside New York amid much mutual admiration of the differing qualities of each – the splendour, the discipline, the professional efficiency of the French striking the Americans and the simplicity, toughness and dedication of the Americans surprising the French. Nevertheless Rochambeau had little hope of victory. In his judgement it was hopeless to attempt to take New York. It was doubtful if de Grasse could get his fleet over the harbour bar in order to be of material help, and Sir Henry Clinton's forces were too strong. And more than half the burning summer passed before Washington began to realise that he was wrong and Rochambeau's strategic sense was correct, and that the right British army to attack was Cornwallis', in Virginia. De Grasse settled that question, as indeed he was to settle the war.

De Grasse saw his opportunity for enduring fame. His Spanish counterpart in the West Indies was, as Spanish admirals tended to be, slow, very slow in his preparations for the attack in Jamaica. Closing one eye like a Nelson, de Grasse exceeded his instructions and left his Spanish ally for two months, taking with him nearly 4000 soldiers and, better still, a million livres raised for him by the Governor of Havana. Rochambeau had informed de Grasse that he would be wanted at either Chesapeake or New York. De Grasse signalled Rochambeau that Chesapeake was his goal: he only had eight weeks to spare; every day was vital, and he, too, feared the harbour bar at New York. So he was *en route* to Chesapeake. Clinton saw the American and French armies strike camp and march south, but he did not follow, for he still believed that New York would be the ultimate target. And miracle followed miracle. De Grasse landed his troops on the James River without resistance, the American and French armies arrived there unmolested by the British, and the French fleet from Rhode Island made a successful rendezvous with de Grasse's ships of the line. Three armies and two navies spread over 1600 miles of land and ocean came neatly together – considering the logistic difficulties and the casualness of eighteenth-century communications, it borders on the incredible. As in an elaborate but deadly game of chess, the outcome was so clear to Cornwallis that he rapidly threw in his hand. There was not much battle and singularly little bloodshed at Yorktown, but what there was fell mainly on the French, whose casualties were twice those of the American forces. Even so they were tiny – 52 killed, 134 wounded. And everyone spoke glowingly of the dash and *élan* of Lafayette and his young aristocratic friends. But it was de Grasse's fleet in the river that had sealed Cornwallis' fate.

De Grasse had had the luck – for complex reasons that included bad British judgement – to hold temporary command of the sea and so secured the fame he pursued. Alas, fame proved fickle, for the man who made Yorktown possible was, within six months, defeated and taken prisoner at the Battle of the Saints. But for Rochambeau and Lafayette and the glittering army of the French aristocrats the next year was a delightful round of dinners, balls and enthusiastic girls. The French army was meticulously correct, paying stiff, usually outrageous prices for all that it needed; so mutual happiness abounded. The diplomats took over, for Britain had conceded defeat – surprisingly so, but Parliament was restive. The country-gentlemen who sat there could not face the cost of a long global war. And the French, too, with an empty treasury, were as eager as the British to extricate themselves from America, especially after de Grasse's defeat in 1782.

Yet peace, like war, has its capacity to surprise. The Jeremiahs in England had bemoaned the possible loss of the American colonies for over a decade. It would, they said, be the economic ruin of Britain. They echoed Chatham's immortal words that America was 'the fountain of our wealth'. They forecast that France would be there, drinking deeply. There would be no drop left for Britain. Yet in fact British trade to America sped to dizzying heights after peace was signed. If the French did not gain America's trust, at least they won back not only a few islands in the Caribbean but also, and much more important, their self-respect, though at the cost of an empty treasury and the certainty that sooner or later Britain would seek her revenge – as she did, a revenge that culminated in the shattering French defeat at Waterloo.

The reluctant warriors, the Spaniards, did better in territory by regaining Florida, east and west, and securing Louisiana; but, alas, they did not recover their self-respect, for Gibraltar remained firmly British. Neither France nor Frenchmen gained much from their expensive American alliance. Mr Du Pont de Nemours, perhaps, fared best with his huge fortune made from gunpowder. Lafayette, as few adolescents do, realised his dreams of glory. Beaumarchais got nothing but years of litigation, Rochambeau only a statue outside the White House. The rest of the glittering cavalcade, the like of which America was never to see again, took back little but the memory of American girls. The Prince de Broglie could never forget the sparkling eyes of Betsy Brown of Providence. The Comte de Ségur, however, took a deeper, if no more lasting, impression with him – but one, too, shared by many of his young artistocratic companions. 'I leave,' he wrote, 'a country where one follows a simple code of simple laws, and respecting good morals, one is happy and tranquil . . . I was treated as a brother everywhere in America. I saw only public confidence, hospitality and cordiality . . . I know a country cannot long preserve morals as pure as this, but if it keeps them for a century, is a century of happiness nothing?'

The revolutionary generations in America and France died away; and most remarkable, most ironic of all, when in the nineteenth century all the countries of Europe were pouring into America, scarcely a Frenchman came.

(iii) The Peacemakers

America may be accomplished in the arts and sciences of mankind, but peace-making has never been her *forte*. After both World Wars opportunites were lost and complexities created that could easily have been avoided; suspicion and naïveté both contributed their quota of mistakes, yet by Yalta the American Government had over a century of diplomatic experience, time enough one might have thought to build up a formidable and confident diplomatic machine. The Founding Fathers, lacking all experience of the diplomatic complexities of Europe, did far better; but then they were guided by principle rather than the pursuit of principle *and power*, often a poisonous and dangerous mixture that needs a professional sense of historical processes to exploit with any hope of success. Wilson, Roosevelt and their State Departments lacked historical *nous*. Fortunately the Founding Fathers did not require an historical sense, for their purpose was both limited and, as political situations go, pure. America wanted to be free; to decide its own fate; to rule itself by institutions of its own devising. For this, Americans had fought and died in the fields, woods and creeks against the most formidable military power the world then knew, a power which had only recently broken France and wrested from her a commercial empire that stretched across the world. To contemporaries it seemed absurd that the Americans might one day win; sooner or later British might must prevail. And America's allies, France and Spain, cared little as to whether America remained free or not, once they had achieved their own aims.

So the cards were stacked against Adams, Franklin and Jay. To the arrogant French or Spaniards they were insignificant pawns in an elaborate diplomatic game that had been adroitly played for centuries; of use perhaps to check Britain or to wring concessions from her. Indeed, neither Spanish nor French ministers hid their contempt for the American representatives. Jay was kept waiting in Cadiz, and when he reached Madrid he was given no recognition at all, whilst Aranda and Floridablanca explored every hypothetical peacefeeler put forward by spies, double agents or diplomatic pirates out for a quick guinea: underworld types which abounded in Europe.

Indeed, one of the most baffling aspects of the world into which Jay was plunged must have been the weird assortment of agents, official and unofficial, who flitted like bats across the diplomatic scene, from the devious Roman Catholic priest Thomas Hussey to the mysterious Montague Fox, whose extravagant forgeries laid the French and Spanish Chancelleries by the ears for months. What his purpose was is as mysterious as his name and Professor Morris has probably got as near to the truth about this strange efflorescence of the diplomatic underworld as one can ever get. Montague Fox, however, is typical of the slimey web of chicanery that entangled the diplomatic relationships of the great powers. A cog in the British government's espionage system, Montague Fox's purpose was, Professor Morris thinks, partly to sow suspicion between France and Spain, who were about as happy together as allies of America as China and Russia are as supporters of Viet Cong, and partly to discredit the opposition to George III's Government by supplying to France fictitious but treasonable documents, purporting to come from Shelburne, Fox, Richmond and Barré (rather as if the State

Department were selling letters to Russia, purporting to come from Robert Lowell and others, describing their contacts with Ho-Chi-Minh in the hopes that Russia would publish). Is it surprising that in a world of such deceit, hypocrisy and corruption that either Jay or Adams should feel first bewildered and lost and then utterly determined not to lose one scrap of America's moral or military advantage at the council table. It proved a hard fight and the American peace commissioners learned a lifetime's diplomacy in a few months.

The Spanish Government viewed the prospect of America's independence with distrust, well realising that a strong and powerful neighbour to the north of her colonies could do her no good. Spain wanted Gibraltar and, if possible, a constant thorn in Britain's flesh. For the former she would have deserted her ally promptly, for the latter her idea was that each State of America should enjoy the same independence that the Electors or Free Cities of the Empire did in relation to the Holy Roman Emperor. If only that could be achieved, the Spanish ministers believed that constant bickerings, turmoil and revolts might be confidently expected, and so Britain weakened.

Naturally once they heard of such ideas, Adams and Jay regarded them as bordering on lunacy, but it gave them a healthy idea of the nature of European alliances. France was more subtle but no more dependable. Republican sentiments and revolting colonies were not Louis XVI's idea of the natural order, nor his minister Vergennes'. And France viewed with approval a Spanish scheme to exclude Americans from the Mississippi valley and confine the States to the Eastern seaboard, preferably with an odd State such as Georgia detached and left in British hands in order to make mischief. Naturally the British were not slow to fish in such troubled waters, but fishing got them nowhere. Unlike the Spaniards and the French they had an intractable lump of reality to face – the military situation. They had lost battles and they had won battles, whichever happened they continued to be defeated. Military advantages and naval advantages slipped from their hands. Their vast financial resources proved useless even against the States teetering on the edge of bankruptcy. They had to learn the bitter lesson, so hard it would seem to learn, that against a nation in revolt you can hold all the advantages and lose. By 1782, however, the British ministers knew that America must be free: the question only remained to avoid too acute a humiliation for George III and to try to keep the boundaries, at least in the North, to Britain's advantage, and exclude, if possible, the Yankees from the Newfoundland fisheries.

By this time Jay, if not Franklin, was beginning to move about the diplomatic chessboard with the skill of a master. He appreciated more quickly than anyone that the prospect of commercial advantages – free trade on the Mississippi as well as with the sea-board States – would entice Britain: as a *sine qua non* of that enticement, he demanded a prior recognition of America's independence whatever effect it might have on George III's head or heart. This was essential, far more so than Franklin realised, not only because it was what America had been fighting for, but also without independence it was impossible to loosen the ties he still had with France and Spain. America had to sit at the conference table as an equal not as a protégé of powers wishing to sell her short.

Once that was done – for Jay got his way, George III notwithstanding – the in-fighting started and here Britain proved something of a match for the American commissioners, but even so concessions were few and America's peacemakers emerged triumphant: recognition, no dismemberment, the West wide open; a puny David had slain a Goliath.

It is an astonishing story and Professor Morris makes the most of it. His knowledge of the sources is remarkably thorough. He has been everywhere and read everything. He handles the massive detail with panache and his characterisation is astute. His book ought to be compulsory reading from the President downwards for it illuminates the present as well as the past. It is full of overtones and ominous echoes. And when the Viet Cong sit down at the conference table, it will be tough going if their commissioners possess the skill and vision of Jay and Adams. That they will match them in dedication and integrity few can doubt. But there are other lessons too: America, after independence was secured, had little use for her erstwhile allies; and trade flourished with her old enemy as never before. The acknowledgement of defeat is often far less disastrous morally or economically than the leaders of nations imagine.

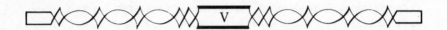
The Men of the Revolution

I had always been fascinated by people, especially people of the past – their similarities, their differences to ourselves – but, above all, their deeper human qualities which would have been the same in any century. As all great historical traumas do, the American Revolution had given opportunities to bold, active, complex men. And three interested me most of all – Washington, Franklin, Jefferson – Adams nearly, alone he did not quite make it – with Abigail, that remarkable woman, he did. They were joined by a man, so martyred, so castigated that I did not consider him, until Bernard Bailyn's *Life* illuminated that complex, sad, baffled and defeated man, Governor Thomas Hutchinson. Bailyn's biography is a remarkable work – one of the most sensitive biographies of a man of power ever written.

The deification of Washington was as interesting as the man himself, starting even before Parson Weems came along with the cherry tree. More than a century later, warts were being cauterised and new skin grafted. J. P. Morgan, a bibliophile, a collector hungry for the rare and the unique, destroyed some of his Washington letters because of Washington's indulgence in obscenities and lecheries; a tiny facet of Washington's character was obliterated for ever. Doubtless other evidence has vanished too, so that now it is difficult to get behind that marmoreal gaze, that heroic stance, the God-like sense of destiny that oozes from his portraits. Not that Franklin's character in spite of an autobiography and millions of words in letters and print, is much easier.

Jefferson is, of course, much more straightforward – faults as well as virtues – with Jefferson the problem is the quasi-miracle of his success – such gifted, intelligent, reasonable men as Jefferson rarely get anywhere in the trauma of revolution, let alone mould it to their liking. Jefferson's success is highlighted by Hutchinson's abysmal failure. A liberal-minded man, given to compromise, eager to find solutions, believing in the rationality of man, was utterly destroyed by what seemed to him the unprincipled violence of the gutter.

And, of course, there were dozens of others worthy of the closest study, a study now made possible by the publication of huge archives that many of the Founding Fathers left behind. One of the glories of the more pedestrian side of American historical activity has been the development of well-funded editorial factories which produce volumes of their letters and papers. Only a very rich society could have funded such activity. I was told that a single volume of Franklin's letters cost $200,000 before it reached the press. In the end, of course, such profusion is self-defeating. No one can read all the printed material available from the leading figures of the American Revolution. In this situation it becomes safer for the professional scholar to take refuge in the editor's chair.

Fortunately the losers have gone on losing – often like Thomas Hutchinson they lost great parts of their own archive and what they did leave was ignored for decades after their deaths. So Hutchinson was a manageable problem when Bernard Bailyn first became interested in him. He had not been buried under a pyramid of his own detritus. In consequence, he provided an excellent subject for Bailyn's exceptional powers, and The Ordeal of Thomas Hutchinson confirmed what I had begun to feel at Columbia – that there was a generation of young American scholars some ten to twenty years younger than myself who would revolutionise the quality of American History. Of that generation Bailyn is now one of its practitioners but I doubt whether he will ever write a better book than Hutchinson. His appetite for size had grown with the years. His Origins of American Democracy was short and brilliant; his other books on the Ideology of the American Revolution and Education in the Forming of American Society were solid but not over-large monographs but the project to which he has devoted the years in which his abilities are at the most developed is a gigantic multi-volume work, The Voyagers to the West which deals at an extraordinary level of detail with emigration to America. Once again it would seem that bigness in scholarship (a disease that the huge grants available for American scholars must encourage) is going to secure its most distinguished victim. The trouble is that the theme is simple in concept and the factual matter vast if basically repetitive. Of course Bailyn's skills are there, brilliant prose, immense human understanding, but boredom sets in early. Butterfield once said to me that you could write the life of Napoleon on a postage stamp or in ten million words and the test of an historian was the choice of the point on that scale commensurate with his powers and the capacity of his audience. But back to the Founding Fathers.

1. BENJAMIN FRANKLIN

(i) *In Search of Benjamin Franklin*

For over twelve months now I have been in pursuit of Benjamin Franklin – re-reading his autobiography, ploughing systematically through his letters and essays, sampling the deluge of Franklin books that flow from the presses. Franklin is still, I suspect, a million dollar a year industry, possibly more. Who buys, who reads, who believes? Why has Franklin resonated down the centuries; does he still ring loud and clear to the present generation? Why, again, were his talents so appropriate to his age? Is he, above all, a man whose depths of character combined with genius puts him into that category of great men that time and change in society and politics can never topple? And that, oddly enough, is the easiest question to answer. No. He does not belong with Shakespeare, Newton, Washington, Beethoven, Darwin, Marx, Freud, and the rest of the indubitably great. He obviously lacked in science, in politics, in life a quality hard to define – passion, vision, penetration, call it what you will, but that mysterious quality which transforms great capacities into towering genius. He changed neither politics nor science in any fundamental sense. Having lived with Franklin for twelve months I no longer, however, doubt his capacities; I do not underestimate the power or force of his character; or even at times his originality and at others his daring. He was a very great man ravaged by common sense, and perhaps ultimately defeated by those very controls of his temperament that led him to immediate success.

I did not think this at first. Renewing acquaintance with him in depth, I felt initially a growing distaste for Franklin. And when I re-read D. H. Lawrence's article on him in *Studies in Classical American Literature* I thought how penetrating, how wise. Of course, it was written in the most repellent form of Lawrentian prose. 'All the qualities of a great man, and never more than a great citizen. Middle-sized, sturdy, snuff-coloured Doctor Franklin, one of the sound citizens that ever tried or "used venery".' That rankled with Lawrence, 'used venery'; the dark animal forces were unlikely to be a subject of common sense, and Lawrence abhorred Franklin's wise advice to the incontinent young man to take an old not a young mistress, pointing out that the trunk might still be succulent though the limbs were ageing. 'And that, as in any craft, there was a knack in making love, more likely to be known to the old practitioner than the young novice.' Naturally such bland common sense was an anathema to Lawrence, and for him it indicated an absence of passion, an absence of those deep primeval drives, not merely sexual, that, had he possessed them, would have lifted a man of Franklin's qualities into true greatness. However, Franklin for Lawrence was never more than a great citizen. Certainly this is perceptive, certainly it touches the heart of the matter as Lawrence so often could in a few near hysterical personal sentences that read like Carlyle at his worst. And because of the scream in the prose, Lawrence's sound perception is often overlooked. The essay on Franklin, like the rest of his studies of American literature, bears reading and re-reading.

But it is not enough. Snuff-coloured in soul as well as clothes, Franklin might be, but his achievement was indubitably there. After all he *was* the mainspring of cultural growth in Philadelphia. And Franklin's powerful journalism began to create for the Northern colonists a sense of their own identity. He made them aware of what they felt, as Americans, should be their social attitude, and how to conduct their personal relationships. His positive contributions to science cannot be denied, nor, too, the cool-headed statesmanship, nor his effectiveness as a gracious ambassador. Franklin's achievements are as undeniable as they are permanent. For anyone who doubts it, look at *Benjamin Franklin, A Biography of His Own Words*, edited by Thomas Fleming, for it deserves looking at as well as reading and pondering, as it is beautifully and pertinently illustrated. In this book his life is told as plainly as one could expect in his own words. And like all else that he did, Franklin wrote well – always to the point, usually unadorned but never over-plain, for his clarity possesses a remarkable radiance. Franklin learned quite early the value of irony and at times he permitted himself a sardonic humour. And yet, taken in bulk, he is not compulsively readable, the clarity is so unrelieved that, like white light, it tires the eyes as much as his devastating common sense bores the mind. Even his *Autobiography* (the best and most beautiful edition is the one edited by Leonard W. Labaree, Ralph L. Ketcham, Helen C. Boatfield and Helene M. Fineman for the Yale University Press; in consequence it is exquisitely printed), is hard to get through in one sitting, although it is a mere 20,000 words. About it there is a strange opacity, an odd lack of variety, rather as if Franklin's mind could only take a photograph and never paint a picture. There is a total absence of any sensitivity to the external world. Franklin describes accurately and clearly the violent squall he encountered off Long Island on his first voyage from Boston. And yet we never hear the wind nor feel the rage of the sea. We enter New York and Philadelphia with him; of their sights and sounds we learn nothing. We are told that Collins drank, but never what he looked like. We should never have heard of Keimer's beard except that it arose from his religious principles and so became an object of Franklin's interest. Although he mentioned with self-satisfaction the genteel new suit in which he visited his brother, we remain ignorant of its colour – brown, black or grey. And yet Franklin was a man of extraordinary curiosity and a most acute observer of all external phenomena. Perhaps his intensity of observation and his accuracy were greater because of the almost total absence of aesthetic and emotional response. Noticing but not troubled by the ravages of age in a woman's face, one could see what others might not – the firmness and succulence of the trunk. Unmoved by lightning, one watched it. Imagination had no place in Franklin's world, and his intuitions were entirely intellectual.

This absence of self-involvement with nature is, I think, an exceptionally powerful force in Franklin's early success. Distance and detachment from the world about him would have been a useful social asset at most times in human history – at least at the level of personal rather than public achievement, for these qualities make for a good merchant, a good steward, a sensible administrator, but Franklin's personality fitted his time and the milieu into which he was born like a key to a complex lock.

The spirit of enlightenment in the eighteenth century flourished and grew most vigorously not where we might have expected it – in England or the Netherlands where intellectual freedom was greatest and press censorship the least, considerable though the contributions of both countries were. The spirit of enlightenment developed most strongly where there was severe tension between a powerful, ideologically committed Church, either Calvinist or Catholic, and the new spreading of secularism. The gradual contraction of the area of social and personal life which the Church could dominate had begun to contract, in Boston as well as in Paris, before the end of the seventeenth century. In the 1690s there was a growth of scientific speculation and activity at Harvard. In religion, too, there was a slackening of hostility to associated religious sects – the latitudinarian Tillotson's sermons, the works of the Cambridge neo-platonists were recommended reading by Brattle and Leverett. Not only was scientific activity pursued, but also French – that language of radicalism as well as sin. Addison and Steele's *Spectator*, the early works of Voltaire, circulated widely and so strengthened an attitude towards religon that was becoming widespread in Europe, namely Christianity, that was not grievous, that right behaviour, a decent charity towards one's fellow men were the fundamentals of a Christian life. That was rational enough for Franklin. Even better, the view that riches, the world's goods, even places of profit, were not inherently wicked in themselves, gained ever increasing currency. This new social attitude towards religion spread like a prairie fire, not only in England at the turn of the seventeenth century, but also in Catholic France; and its growing presence in America had, of course, scared the active New England puritans, creating tension in Boston and elsewhere. Yet, like the on-coming of permissive societies in our generation, change of religious style could not be stopped. It was the mood which fitted the enterprising businessman, the complacent well-to-do, the ambitious and the successful. The outward clothes were prudence, modesty, hard work and charity; the inward dynamism was a lust for worldly success, a hunger for power, above all – acquisition. No emergent ideology could have been more appropriate for young Benjamin Franklin, or Poor Richard. This new social attitude to religion fitted this cool man like a glove. It removed the agony of a spirit tortured by good and evil, and replaced it by an aphoristic Confucianism that judged godliness by social behaviour. America was particularly ripe for an easement of the rigours of doctrinaire Calvinism. And, once the immediate purposeful hand of Providence was removed from daily life, it left so much of the visible world open to secular explanation. Once lightning was no longer God's wrath directed at particular people and places, to remind them of their sins or to punish them, it could be investigated, explained, and may be controlled. Franklin, his cool observant nature, and the blossoming spirit of his age fertilised and nurtured each other, a fact of which Franklin himself was acutely aware, and he did all he could to foster common sense, prudence, conciliation and rational acts based on rational grounds. Franklin could coolly assess the contingencies of politics; time and time again he projects this cool, reasonable image of himself for posterity's sake.

At which point it is prudent to turn again to Cecil B. Currey's *Road to Revolution: Benjamin Franklin in England, 1765–1775*, which attempts to depict Franklin as a devious, self-seeking politician, who became radical more through frustration of his private enterprises by British officials than through commitment to the American independence. It seems plausible, but is not. And yet one can admit straight away that Franklin was devious; so was Voltaire. Both liked money, both enjoyed social success, both were avid in old age for female flattery, yet both could separate these things easily enough from politics. A cool temperament does not imply lack of greed, only a lack of passionate involvement in people, in events, in beliefs. True enough, some of Franklin's complex manoeuvres to make a fortune out of land speculation are as involved as any of Voltaire's financial enterprises. Franklin certainly enjoyed money – getting it, spending it, and used most of his considerable cunning to get it. Money and fame were certainly deep driving forces in Franklin's nature, but, as he well knew, dangerous to success if too candidly admitted. Guile, discretion, surely were a part of Franklin's common sense. But frustration of his economic hopes does not explain Franklin's commitment to the American cause. True, in 1760 he approved highly of George III, probably he toyed with the idea of settling in England. But remember the early 1760s. British arms had never been so successful; the French were thoroughly beaten, in Canada as well as the West, and so the American situation had scarcely looked brighter. Problems about finance, taxation, commercial relations with Britain were neither worse nor better than they had been for a generation. But as soon as Franklin realised the note of intransigence, as soon as he grasped the likely magnitude of the impending conflict between Britain and America and the possibility of independence, then he saw the potentiality for himself as well as his country. It was a typical cool assessment, and one suitable to his social and political attitudes, and easier to exploit in his own interests than the frustrating rigidities of English oligarchy and bureaucracy. The best opportunists are not warm men; and no one seized their chances more adroitly than Franklin did between 1765 and 1775. After all, these were the years when he transformed himself from a successful colonial to a man of his time. That he should at the same time have been working with highly placed British politicians and officials to grab a huge territory in Ohio for a pittance is in no way contradictory. It was another opportunity.

A sympathetic social environment combined with a cool temperament, practical intelligence, driving ambition, hunger for work, a capacity for secrecy and guile, are these sufficient to explain Franklin's growing public fame, and one which overrode the bitter and critical attitudes of his enemies, many of them men of distinction and ability? Yet against the dislike of John Adams, Arthur Lee or Lord Hillsborough, there were scores of Franklin admirers from Philadelphia to Paris. In this struggle for public acceptance, Franklin won handsomely. Few men have exploited both themselves and their opportunity with such skill.

One of the most difficult problems for an historian dealing with individual personalities is to get an idea of the physical impression that a man such as Franklin had on his contemporaries, on the men with whom he plotted and negotiated, for as anyone who has ever sat on a committee knows, physical impact is important, as is the voice – its warmth, its timbre, its speed. Some men by their very physical presence disturb others; some create a sense of authority, others exude charm. Often men are disturbed by the suspicion of a rich instinctive life in others beyond their own hopes; sexual envy and malice can find their outlets in the dreariest committee. And so it is as well to ponder on Franklin's face as well as his letters, pamphlets and autobiography, and there is Charles Coleman Sellers' magnificent *Benjamin Franklin in Portraiture* to do it with. From earliest to latest we witness, of course, the ravages of time, but even so the same basic notes are struck. Franklin's face was neither sensual nor virile: it lacked vivacity. Certainly it was a strange, unusual face, with its thin, tight lips, heavy chin, cold eyes and huge domed forehead, but one that was basically plain and charmless; powerful, but unlikely to stir sexual envy. The most impressive fact about it is the sense of controlled power and watchfulness that comes through even in the worst of sketches. A man, one feels, who had little difficulty, but considerable desire to control his emotions. Compared, say, with Rousseau's, or even Voltaire's, it is an exceedingly passionless face. Although many may disagree, I feel that Franklin's face helps us to grasp some of the reasons for his swift success, the ease with which, during his early days in Philadelphia, he could cajole men to fall in with his schemes. Franklin's face is a tranquil face; intelligent, quizzical, but not emotion-ridden, not flamboyantly handsome, not full of suspect charm. It is the face that might have been designed by a public relations expert for his *Autobiography*. The face, indeed, that one can imagine arousing D. H. Lawrence's ire, but few girls' hopes.

Quite early in life, Franklin had his eye cocked on posterity. Throughout his life he was busy manufacturing a *persona* which he hoped would appeal not only to his own time and generation, but also to the future. And this needs to be grasped, otherwise his huge bulk of papers can so easily mislead. These are now being magnificently edited from Yale by a skilful team, now headed by William B. Willcox, and beautifully produced by the Yale Press. But there is more than enough, like the portraits, to see the man at work. How rarely is there any rage or passion; indeed never. Even when he writes to his wife about her extravagance and the need for retrenchment, he is all benevolence and generosity; in the evening of life his letters to his grandson betray the same model equanimity and kindness. True, such severity, such sweet reasonableness, makes him at times almost a bore to read. However, it is well to remember that every letter Franklin wrote was written in the awareness that it might be one day printed. Their composition was influenced by the way Franklin wished to be regarded as much as the *Autobiography* itself. Franklin was as avid for greatness in the future as the present. He realised that he would be a public man, an historic figure, long before it can have seemed possible to others, and took the necessary actions to construct a durable image of himself. And Franklin successfully projected himself for the best part of two hundred years – projected an image which America could accept as symbolic of its own qualities – frugal, prudent, kind, above all *practical*, all leading to worldly success and the esteem of one's fellows. And this image, created by Franklin, has been sold to the historians. And, of course, it embodies some elements of the truth. But increasingly it seems too simple, too cool, too contrived, and Lawrence's criticism would today find far greater acceptance, indeed the mask and the man are coming apart. So long as the bourgeois world continued to expand in America, Franklin's name, career and writings resonated in the classroom and remained a substantial myth in America's past. But increasingly his aphorisms, his autobiography and his letters create a sense of distaste as the mechanics of the projection of his personality become steadily more obvious.

Franklin made a vast success of his life and so made certain of his immortality which always controlled both the tactics and strategy of his actions. From adolescence his eye was glued both to his image and to posterity. And yet his fame would have been greater, and in the present day less at risk, had his candour been greater. Cool temperaments, however, are rarely candid. The bitter anger towards his brother, the sexual hunger of a plain-faced youth, the longing for intellectual and social acceptance, the unassuageable thrust of ambition, the rage against the world, that any man of great powers must feel at times of frustration, were these things repressed into the deep recesses of his being, or were they always lacking in intensity? Was he one of the true spectators of the life of the heart, sitting quietly behind the plateglass window of his temperament? Here is the enigma of Franklin. But we should remember that often cool temperaments are not repressed temperaments; anger, lust, longing may not have stirred the depths of Franklin. Of one thing only can we be certain, that he craved distinction, hungered for success and used all his resources – guile, intelligence and above all, the opportunities of his age to achieve it – but perhaps at the cost of the richness of his instinctive life.

(ii) Franklin Unbuttoned

An English historian must tiptoe as he draws near the American Pantheon, stuffed as it is with white marmoreal figures – austere, virtuous, dedicated. No virago here, like Elizabeth I, whose language could rival the porters at Billingsgate and was not above a bedroom tussle with her courtier favourites even though none of them ever sighted the promised land; no homosexual buffoon like James I; no dolt like George III. Indeed no avaricious Burleigh, no power-hungry Walpole, no manic Chatham or drunken Pitt, no weird Dizzy or lecherous Lloyd George. Instead, Washington, Jefferson, Adams, Madison, Franklin, who shine and gleam with virtue. Here even Lincoln's dirty stories are forgotten or forgiven. These Founding Fathers in the central hall are lofty with purpose; it seems almost indecent to think of Washington scratching his backside or Jefferson picking his nose. And now we have Franklin thoroughly unbuttoned, although not nearly so unbuttoned as he wished to be. Yet we must be very grateful to Claude-Anne Lopez. She has written a book of exceptional perception: scholarly, tender, full of style. And the Yale University has added another book of exceptional physical beauty to its lengthening list.

At seventy Franklin loved to have his neighbour's wife on his lap and cover her with kisses. He pined for more, begged for more, railed at the Seventh Commandment, but Madame Brillon handled him with such skill that he subsided into a mildly indecorous 'Papa' while she rioted in the role of a highly emotional but loving daughter. The hint of incest may have been spice to Madame Brillon but, obviously, for Franklin it proved a tedious game, made tolerable only by his age, which had weakened, although not obliterated, the fires of the flesh. So they poured out tender effusions in the best eighteenth-century pastoral style. Madame Brillon, neurotic, self-involved, delicate in health as she was steel-like in will (her husband's mistress, once discovered, never stood a chance; she was kicked out of the household and Brillon locked firmly to his wife's side) revelled in Franklin's greatness as much as in his devotion. It is hard to know just how genuine were the emotions of these tender yet teasing lovers, one elderly, the other middle-aged. Genuine concern was certainly there on Franklin's side, plus a definite eroticism that expressed itself in endless kisses or the hope of kisses. For Madame Brillon the kisses were a tribute to her power, and Franklin's affection a splendid social asset. Even so, she played the game with delicacy, wit and skill; and their days at Passy possess a Watteau-like quality until one realises that the gallant has gout, thin grey hair, and teeth 'like cloves', and the girl is a grandmother at the menopause.

Salutary to remember. Men and women of the eighteenth century possessed no false attitudes to age – love, romance, the ardours of the flesh among the elderly were not comic to them, no more, no less than the fumblings and excesses of youth. There was nothing exceptional in the agony of Madame du Deffand's burning passion for the young Horace Walpole, nothing comic in the transports of unrequited passion of two middle-aged lovers – Rousseau and Madame d'Houdetot disturbed by the wagoner, as she was about to succumb under the famous acacia tree. Indeed, the tree became the object of romantic pilgrimage. These men and women were wise enough to know that the winds of love never cease to blow and that even in age they could swell into a gale. One of the best-loved stories of the century was that of Fontenelle approaching a hundred, discovering Madame Helvétius in déshabillé and exclaiming, 'Ah, Madame, would I were seventy.' And so, for Franklin to be kissing, stroking, imploring – fifteen-year-old girls, middle-aged women, and matrons of advancing years – was nothing untoward. It was a part of his charm, of his gallantry, of his devotion to the demigod of the eighteenth-century *haute-monde*. Eros: sex, love, affection – these were the essences of life.

And Franklin revelled in them. He was always lusty, and female grace gave a sweetness to his old age that he found quite irresistible, much to the fury of Adams, who loathed his dissipation and hated his women friends. Somehow Franklin got through his toilsome diplomatic work, never quickly, nor indeed expeditiously, and it was a rare day that work was allowed to thrust aside all pleasure. Plain by French standards his style of living might be, but it was deeply self-indulgent. Franklin understood his own nature well enough, and certainly did not disapprove of what he found within his heart and mind. Assured of his place in history, certain of the rectitude of his beliefs and hopes, he acquired an almost immutable dignity and grace, even with a woman of fifty or a girl of fourteen on his knees. In his quiet way he loved praise, which he elicited with unobtrusive but consummate skill. No wonder he thought of Passy as paradise.

Franklin was first and foremost an artist – his imagination played successfully with many ideas – scientific, technological, political, economic – but words were his abiding passion. He used them to project his image into posterity: an image carefully cultivated visually as well as verbally, so that the portraits of Franklin fit his autobiography like a glove. And, of course, it was this innate literary skill that made him such a cherished member of one of the most highly articulate societies Europe has known. Light verse, epistles in alexandrines, and mock-heroic odes flew endlessly back and forth – if Madame d'Houdetot received a melon from a neighbour it came with a poem, and thanks went back in verse. Her reception of Franklin with triumphant arches, sententiously decorated with philosophic aphorism, and declamatory verses on liberty and moral simplicity, struck no false note in his verbal paradise. So artificial and mannered to us, for them it was as natural as the telephone.

And it was a world more than mere words. Naturally it contained much human diversity – the satirical, the cruel, the oafish, the self-indulgent were all to be found as frequently as in any other society, but they never dominated its ethos. Its ideology was one of benevolence, hope and charity. Even if children of the Enlightenment failed, they aspired to be good. They might ignore the hunger and poverty at their palace gates, but they believed passionately in equity and justice and within their limited capacities worked for them. When greater social injustice came, many of them, ironically enough, finished in the tumbrils. Above all, they were, most of them, immensely tolerant: naturally much more so than the revolutionary bourgeois who were to replace them.

This society in which Franklin moved with such delight has many curious overtones with present-day America. In a sense America has produced an aristocratic bourgeoisie and, in consequence, many intellectual, social and artistic attitudes of the *ancien régime* have their counterparts today. The French aristocracy were sharply divided and so is the American middle class. In France an entrenched right wing was passionately concerned to maintain traditional institutions in Church and State, rigorously opposed to new ideas in sex, education, in social thinking, yet it never had the confidence to impose its ancient ideals with the ferocity that the times required. They sensed defeat and so were half-defeated, and I suspect that is true of our Goldwaters and their followers. In their bones they know the future cannot be theirs, nor the past perpetuated.

As with the right, so with the left. There were plenty of rich Frenchmen willing to play with advanced ideas, who, like our own liberal middle class, were tolerant of change, easy in morals, speculative, articulate and not without hope for mankind yet, perhaps, somewhat blind to the future that beckoned them. The French liberals, like many of ours, were not very perceptive about the contradictions between their economic situation and the intellectual ideas with which they played. And there are other similarities between the two societies – the *ancien régime* of Louis XV and LBJ, especially in their artistic, literary and philosophical preoccupations. Both societies show a preference for architecture and the decorative side of art, both are wedded to physical elegance, to the *objet d'art*, both are very chary of grandeur, passion and tragedy in artistic expression. Yet both can be regarded as periods of enlightenment, possessing a keen relish for intellectual comment on society and the individual. On the other hand, both are bored with religion, myth and convention; both have found excitement in technological ingenuity and scientific progress. The most enlightened spirits of each age show an acute awareness of the brittle nature of their privileges, aware too of the desperate poverty and hunger of the world outside their gates, but for whom awareness could never be, and perhaps may never be, translated into action. We are poised, like them, on the edge of revolutionary social change; is the *déluge*, therefore, just around the corner for us too? Are Robespierre, Danton, Marat and the rest growing up in San Francisco and New York?

Franklin would have appreciated the irony. Certainly he would have been at home in the most luxurious apartments of Fifth Avenue, glad to find good claret at last in his own country, and certainly wholly appreciative of the Renoirs, happy to enjoy what he had and to miss what might be coming. But I suspect that in our more prudish age neither girls of fifteen nor matrons of fifty would sit on his knee, shower him with kisses, and call him 'Cher Papa'.

(iii) A Little Revenge

Benjamin Franklin has not attracted, curiously enough, as many biographers as one might expect – in his life so multifarious and complex – scientist, journalist, diplomat, politician, entrepreneur and some would have us believe double-agent – that would-be biographers shy away. To make matters worse, the great man shifted territory for long periods and settled chameleon-like into new worlds of fashion, culture and politics with surprising ease. Compare, for example, the ambivalence of John Adams in London, Paris or the Netherlands with Franklin's easy acceptance. Franklin sinks into London, or Edinburgh for that matter, as into a comfortable, well-loved armchair; Adams is ill-at-ease, perched on the edge of his chair, waiting to get angry. And yet their social origins and early experiences were not so very different. Such easy transferences makes Franklin's life difficult for a biographer and much harder work. Franklin's life abroad requires a much deeper and more sensitive knowledge of British and French politics and society than is posed by any other American of his time. And the private man is as difficult and as complex as the public figure. Franklin has a curious capacity to slide around his own self – at one time secretive and devious, at another almost shockingly exposing his deepest compulsions whether in sexual behaviour or in hunger for riches and power. Add to this his capacity for ironic detachment, his social charm and vanity, his furious capacity for work, combined with powers of exceptional indolence, and the still deeper problem of the absence or presence of passion in him for people as well as ideas, then the problems of writing a biography of Franklin become as difficult as scaling the north face of Everest in a blizzard. And so historians who get involved in Franklin usually take an aspect – his work as a scientist, his social life in Paris, his role in London as Pennsylvania's agent; often these books have been illuminating but rarely of the whole Franklin.

And this is true of Randall's book whose central theme is the relationship between Franklin and his bastard son, William; a subject rarely explored in depth or made so central in Franklin's life as Mr Randall posits. Unfortunately, Mr Randall lacked material as the great majority of William Franklin's papers were destroyed. The early years of William's career which he spent involved almost entirely in his father's complex political, publishing and scientific worlds in Philadelphia lack sources of depth and weight. Benjamin Franklin's references to his son are often laconic, at times almost dismissive, so Randall also feels it necessary to paint the historical, political and social background in order to give depth and colour to his picture. Alas, the effect is of great shallowness and naïveté. The Franklins were in London when George III ascended the throne in 1760. Several ministerial changes followed, but Randall's description might have been taken for an American school textbook of 1850 although the works of Sir Lewis Namier are listed in his bibliography. Randall writes:

> In the eleven months before he was crowned [i.e. George III]. he not only dismissed his grandfather's ministers, but took into his own hands the immense treasury and used it to buy control of Parliament.

Later he refers to 'Tory society, now restored to power'. All of George III's leading ministers, like his grandfather George II's, were Whigs. As long ago as 1929 in *Politics at the Accession of George III* Namier exploded this myth of Tory takeover and the wholesale buying of parliamentary boroughs by the Crown. It was Whigs who made peace with France in 1763, who suppressed John Wilkes, who drove the American colonies to rebellion and to whom William Franklin stayed loyal. Tories in America and Tories in Britain are not of the same ilk.

As in large matters, so in smaller one, carelessness seems to combine with ignorance. 'Built of stone in the Flemish style of the seventeenth century Prestonfield was known to be the most fashionable House in Scotland.' Has Mr Randall heard of Thirlstane, Dalkeith, Drumlanrig, etc? He thinks that the Great North Road goes through Derby, Manchester and Lancaster, that Northamptonshire possesses 'moors', and so on.

None of these errors is very heinous but there are too many of them and they are likely to put off a knowledgeable reader which would be a pity. However we must forgive, alas, more than errors of fact. There is far too much inference from little or no evidence. Here one example must suffice. In 1766, both Franklins, father and son, were given honorary degrees at Oxford which 'thrilled' them. However that enjoyment in each other proved brief; according to Randall, Benjamin was growing deeply dissatisfied with William's aristocratic tendencies and jealous of his ease in society. Whether or not there was an actual showdown between the two men, Benjamin, according to Randall, obviously did not approve of his son's choice of a career, a wife or a political party. There is no evidence for this speculation and Randall begs the question. He could be right, he could just as easily be wrong, for it is difficult to see why William's choice of career – the youngest Governor of a Royal colony (New Jersey) and the first appointed by George III – could have earned Franklin's disapproval at that stage. Great influence for himself or his family was positively pursued by Franklin.

Overwritten, rather insecurely tethered to evidence and freckled with errors of fact, nevertheless this book deserves to be read. The uncritical reader will probably enjoy it, for it has considerable verve, an excellent story and one outstanding skill – a sense of character – and because of this, eighteenth-century scholars, if they are patient with the errors, can derive much from it. It helps us understand a little more thoroughly the enigma that was Franklin.

Few of Benjamin Franklin's relationships with other people had such depth. Because they were not entangled in ambivalent emotional demands, he could treat people with a detached kindness or just ignore them. His parents from whom Benjamin Franklin had escaped as soon as he could; his wife whom he neglected for years on end, often hardly bothering to write to her: all this indicates a cool temperament, for he never hated them and loathed quarrelling with them and, indeed, liked them after his fashion.

His strongest emotions were probably stirred by the conflicts of politics and power where vanity could be deeply wounded and hopes crushed. And yet even this cool temperament, as Randall shows, was warmed if not to fierce heat at least beyond the tepid by his son. William was brave, handsome, intelligent and through adolescence and early manhood very amenable to his father's hopes and plans. Whether in science or politics or war, William worked with skill, intelligence and dedication for his father. Indeed his contribution to the scientific experiments was crucial. Randall points out how very casual, almost dismissive, Franklin was about his son's help: on the other hand, William would have never received an honorary degree at St Andrews or Oxford University had not Benjamin stressed that his son's contribution was an essential part of his success.

Benjamin showed a lot of pride in William's success: of that there can be little doubt. Randall overstresses the importance of Benjamin leaving England just before his son's induction into the Governorship of New Jersey. Nothing on earth would have stopped Franklin's decision to return at once when he learnt that his powerbase in Philadelphia was in danger. Indeed I suspect Benjamin encouraged William's 'Tory' inclinations and drift: at least in the early stages, for it is unlikely that Franklin himself had much idea as to where the irritations and conflicts with the Penns and with the English might lead in 1762. Although old certainties were dissolving, new directions were not yet clearly visible. Who, even in 1765, could have believed that America would be an independent country by 1783? I suspect none, although a few may have had secret dreams.

In such circumstances the final split between father and son should not be traced back to the normal tensions between a father and his son. In general, Benjamin was quite exceptionally supportive and generous, especially when the stigma of William's birth was the reverse of a social asset. Temperamentally they had much in common – Franklin might pontificate in private about the desirability of breakfasting on gruel but he never showed himself too averse to luxury when it came his way nor indeed to public pomp so long as it was organised for him. Benjamin's pride in William lasted as long as his usefulness in politics.

The great merit of this book is that it does bring alive very vividly this initial closeness of father and son; and that William possessed many of the high qualities of his father. Perhaps Benjamin came near to total emotional commitment to his son, near but not close.

One day some well-trained professional historian with a passionate interest in human psychology should attempt a one-volume biography of Franklin. It is the most difficult task presented by an eighteenth-century personality, European or American. The documentation, difficult and complex, is there but to catch that multi-faceted man in a steady light would require a pen of genius. Nevertheless this book is worth reading and not without its illumination of two extraordinary men.

2. THOMAS JEFFERSON

(i) Inventing America

Another book on Thomas Jefferson! Already his life and work occupy yards and yards of shelving. And worse, the Declaration of Independence again! Surely *that* document has been so worked over that there is nothing more to say. Not so, for Garry Wills has produced an original, subtle and brilliant book on Jefferson and his Declaration. The only pity is the title, which neither expresses Jefferson's intentions nor encapsulates the contents of the book. Wills explores, through the language of the Declaration (the draft as well as the accepted version), Jefferson's political, social and scientific attitudes, and in particular his views on man as a social animal for whom happiness is a necessary goal. Wills is fascinating on Jefferson's intellectual debts, stressing the importance of the Scottish and Italian Enlightenments as well as the French.

First, however, he sets Congress, its leaders and the Declaration in their historical context. In one very acute chapter he demonstrates how Virginians, New Yorkers, Philadelphians and Bostonians were more familiar with London, its politics and its culture, than they were with each other, and that they were, therefore, concerned to work within the traditional framework of English parliamentary protest. For the Founding Fathers the Declaration had not the importance that future generations attached to it. It was the end of a process of petitioning about grievances, not an exposition of philosophic ideas.

Alterations made by Congress to the draft of the Declaration can only be understood in the context of its political strategy. Within that strategy the decisions of Congress were wise and sensible but they hamstrung Jefferson's argument, and in his eyes the Declaration that was signed was deformed – some theory and much emotion was excised.

Wills then sets out to analyse the philosophy of Jefferson's draft. This is the heart of the book, and a most significant achievement. Wills proceeds to investigate Jefferson's use of language and to assess the phrases of the draft. He understands, as few do, the way men of the eighteenth century used words which since their day have subtly changed their meaning. All too frequently this has led historians of ideas to miss the subtlety of eighteenth-century arguments – particularly Jefferson's. Wills makes no such mistake.

The Declaration can only be understood, also, in the context of British constitutional experience, particularly the Whig Revolution of 1688. Wills writes, 'As it stands the official document is a restatement of Whig theory vindicated in the 1688 Revolution.' He could have gone further. The form of the Declaration follows closely the Bill of Rights passed by the English Parliament in 1689. In that document there was a mounting indictment, clause by clause, of the rule of James II, stressing its innate illegality by its violation of constitutional rights, and also attempting to demonstrate how these actions of James II freed Englishmen from allegiance to their monarch. Only the closeness of this parallel can explain the excessive indictment of George III. Indeed, this context alone explains the weight placed by Jefferson on the final arguments about 'agonizing affection' which were cut from the draft. Wills does not fully grasp the importance of this parallel. Wills is, indeed, often insecure when he deals with the British background – thinking erroneously, for example, that Lord Bute was dispensing patronage in the 1750s and that there were no Catholic masses in London in the 1770s.

But these are small blemishes on an absorbing book; one that is luminous with intelligence. The most important part is that which analyses influences on Jefferson's thought: his commitment to a scientific attitude, his debt to Francis Hutcheson, to Beccaria as well as to giants of the French Enlightenment. Although Jefferson believed passionately in reason, in explanation, in the world of Newton and David Rittenhouse, like all other *philosophes* he was concerned to extend – by rational means if possible – happiness. Indeed, he was as much committed to the religion of the heart as Voltaire, but thought that reason was its best witness. (It is not surprising that Jefferson's favourite novelist was Laurence Sterne.) But throughout Jefferson's thought, the

desires of the heart are illuminated – even aided – by the decisions of
the head.

Jefferson possessed a mind of exceptional clarity which made him a
better philosopher than politician. He realised the philosophic problem
of declaring American independence. In spite of the enormities of George
III, 'a tyrant might be the ruler of a people', and the British showed no
signs of getting rid of him. So how did one part of a people – and a
minor part, i.e. the Americans – take, as it were, unilateral action? What
could justify such a breach? The accepted Declaration skates quickly
over this issue, mentions the warnings given to 'the British brethren',
and immediately declares independence. Jefferson's draft is more
complex, more concerned to stress why the British people as well as
George III had forfeited the right to American allegiance. In establishing,
however, the unfeeling nature of the British, Jefferson uses politically
dangerous arguments. The British people had established George III's
measures 'by free election', yet one of the great arguments of the colonists
had been the unrepresentative nature of the British Parliament. As the
astute leaders of Congress realised, it was better not to stress that the
political nation in Britain had supported George III.

Wills ends as well as he begins – with an admirable account of what
happened to the Declaration after 1776. An exciting book, this.

3. GEORGE WASHINGTON

(i) Man and Monument

Parson Weems realised almost as soon as Washington – gentleman,
Christian, patriot and statesman – was dead, that his life was a model
for the sober, thrifty, virtuous, successful, God-destined American. His
fertile mind quickly invented the myths that were needed to adorn a
folk-hero – the cherry-tree, the Indian who could not shoot him, the
prayer at Valley Forge. And so Washington who could not lie joined
the band of Anglo-Saxon nursery heroes – Alfred with his cakes, Sidney
with his cup, Raleigh and his cloak.

Publicists and historians have done Parson Weems's work in a
different key, and usually at infinitely greater length and infinitely greater
tedium. The obtuse, platitudinous reverence which infuses the six
massive volumes of Douglas Southall Freeman's recent *Life* cannot be
imagined by anyone – not even the most cynical – who has not read
them. It is as if all the headmasters of America, drunk with what they
had heard at their own speech-days, had drafted a copy-book hero's life
in committee.

From time to time a lonely, disgruntled figure has raised a sneer: debunking Washington, however, has never been popular. The materials are scant. J. P. Morgan burnt his Washington letters because they contained smut, the revelation of which he thought might tarnish his reputation. Nothing could. He has grown larger than life; as impervious to changing trends of fashion as the marble of his monument.

In this short, brilliant and dextrously contrived book, Mr Marcus Cunliffe attempts to tell simply and directly the story of Washington's life as it happened and without foreknowledge. He refrains from detailed investigation, eschews long quotations, and presents the bare bones of each of the phases of Washington's career – the early years as a Colonel of Militia, the middle years as Commander-in-Chief, and the consummation of his life as President. In the end, he concludes that Washington 'has become so merged with America that his is one of the names of the land, the presences in the air. Useless for his biographers to try to separate Washington from the myths and images surrounding him . . . None can. The man *is* the monument.' Yet on the way to this conclusion, Mr Cunliffe has protrayed a more human and credible Washington than will be found in a score of other biographies.

He stresses Washington's concept of himself – a gentleman formed in a classical mould – a Virginian Cincinnatus who could only find satisfaction in a life dominated by stern Roman virtues – *gravitas, pietas, simplicitas, integritas, gloria.* He shows time and time again how contemporaries found in Washington these virtues which he himself so much advocated. His cool, seemingly unself-seeking approach to all problems and to all authority, made his quiet acceptance of fame seem to derive from a sense of public duty and not from personal ambition.

Neither a very good general nor a very good statesman, Washington, by the sheer force of his character, nevertheless gave to America and Americans a sense of themselves as a nation with a destiny. His life and energies were spent in constant service to his ideal of America. Only a man of monumental character – cold, austere, marmoreal – could have achieved and imposed a sense of greatness on so young, so confused, so untried a people.

Mr Cunliffe is quite fair – he appreciates Washington's luck; time and time again his career could have ended in disaster: he realises that there were one or two other men who might have projected their personalities with equal force; he notices Washington's shortcomings: his stiffness, his lack of generosity, his incapacity for friendship, his snobbish sense of caste. Yet in the end he has almost unqualified admiration for this man who was so much greater than his life.

Admirable as Mr Cunliffe is in the structure of Washington's character, and brilliant as he is on its effects, the mainspring, I think, eludes him. Profound narcissistic vanity would seem to be the answer. Yet in the end if vanity were proved to be the mainspring, the monument would remain, for what Washington contemplated with such pleasure, other men could view with respect.

(ii) George Washington's Chinaware

We are so used to invention, to novelty, to the spinning world of fashion that we find it difficult to imagine a time in which the style of furniture, or clothing, or utensils changed so very slowly that it was almost imperceptible. This was never quite true for the aristocracy and the courtiers who circulated about the royal courts of Europe, for they hankered after novelty, but it was true not only of the labouring people – peasants, servants and craftsmen – but also of country gentry, doctors, lawyers, professionals of all kinds. Were we able to peer into our seventeenth-century ancestors' houses, rich or poor, we should be amazed by their emptiness – no carpets on the floors; a few chairs set along a wall; occasionally a hard wooden armchair, a few primitive family portraits; mainly walls without pictures, no wallpaper, very few vases if any, little or no glass that was not utilitarian. And for most people, no mirrors. Most furniture was solid and heavy, immensely durable oak, carved, occasionally richly, mainly badly. And, of course, there was no china, no china at all. Before the eighteenth century Europeans could not make it, try as they might.

A German chemist, Böttger, found kaolin at Meissen near Dresden and started the first china factory under the patronage of Augustus of Saxony. It took Europe by storm. Naturally Böttger and his patron tried desperately to keep the process secret and for many years they succeeded. The success at Meissen had two important effects. The demand for porcelain could not be met by Meissen alone, so larger and larger quantities of Chinese porcelain were imported – some had been in the seventeenth century – but now imports increased enormously. This china was also frequently designed not only for the European market but for particular customers there, and decorated with their coats of arms. The other effect of Meissen's success was to encourage entrepreneurs everywhere in Europe to try to make china, and to bribe workmen to leave Meissen to help them. They succeeded, particularly with bribes, and by 1750 Europe was studded with china factories, most of them under the patronage of kings and princes. Louis XV of France and his mistress, Madame de Pompadour, were deeply involved in the Royal Factory at Vincennes (afterwards Sèvres). His monogram adorned the wares and indeed once a year he personally conducted a sale of the china at Versailles. As with most new industries, more factories failed than succeeded. Amongst the china factories in England, Chelsea, Bristol, Plymouth, Derby, Longton Hall and Bow all failed, only Worcester succeeded. The success of porcelain also stimulated the makers of pottery. This was particularly true of England, and of that great genius, Josiah Wedgwood, who proclaimed that he wanted to become 'Vase Maker of the Universe'.

It is hard for us to imagine the excitement that these new luxurious chinawares created, especially amongst those who were entranced by the new world of spending that the eighteenth century produced, for, along with china, there were other excitements – wallpapers, chintzes and textiles, exotic garden plants and new varieties of old ones. All of these new objects and new fashions created a *joie de vivre* – indeed they did more than that, they engendered confidence and a sense of belonging to the future.

Certainly it was a world which fascinated George Washington, and one that attracted him very strongly after his marriage in 1759 to Martha Custis, who brought him the wealth which allowed him to emulate, albeit modestly, his neighbours. His expensive tastes, his desire for distinction in clothing as well as domestic furnishings, had been enhanced by his association with his relatives and neighbours, the Fairfaxes who belonged to the British aristocracy: indeed male Fairfaxes were educated in England and were accustomed to high fashion in London. And then beyond the Fairfaxes, further down the Potomac, was Gunston Hall, where George Mason had built and furnished a house of great magnificence that would have passed muster for the country house of a rich merchant of London. Also, of course, there was Williamsburg, where the Governor's Palace glittered with the luxury goods of Britain and, indeed, during Lord Botetourt's term of office it had a splendid display of Chelsea figures.

Fortunately, Washington was a meticulous man who kept exact records – a habit partly forced on him because trade with London was erratic as well as lengthy but also because precision was very conformable to his own nature. And it is these accounts, together with the pieces of china that still remain either with Washington's descendants, or have been assembled at Mount Vernon, or donated to other museums that form the basic material of this handsome and scholarly book.

Quite clearly these records show that Washington had a passion for china. His taste was not idiosyncratic but very similar to that of other rich men of his time. His first purchases in the early 1750s were the brilliant saltglazes of Staffordshire and the equally brilliantly decorated Chinese export, and for everyday use he bought quantities of white stoneware – good, solid, durable earthenware that lacked sophistication yet was aesthetically pleasing. It was to be replaced ten years later by a grand service of creamware, some of it by Turner but perhaps more by Josiah Wedgwood, running to some 250 pieces. Wedgwood's creamware took the fashionable world by storm in the late 1760s and early 1770s, and Washington was no exception. Washington, however, never purchased the great innovations of Wedgwood – the black basalt, the blue and white jaspers, or the great neo-classical vases. Jasper was not invented until 1774; by then Washington was a great public figure and far too preoccupied to give much attention to the purchase of china as he moved from headquarters to headquarters. Also, the acute shortage of British manufactured goods, and European goods for that matter, made it extemely hard for Washington's stewards and housekeepers to replace rusty tin plates with any china. A few pieces were bought in New York in 1776 and a large purchase at Philadelphia in 1782 at quite exorbitant prices – £12 for a soup tureen. Even in 1783 he had great difficulty in getting together a blue and white service of tableware for Mount Vernon. The Washingtons had to put up with mixed patterns and odd numbers of soup and meat plates. However, they had acquired by then a new ceramic connection – the French.

To own a porcelain factory was a distinction that many princes, let alone aristocrats, craved. Le Comte de Custine, who sailed in 1780 with Rochambeau, was an ardent supporter of Washington and of republican virtue. (In the French Revolution he threw away his title to fight for Robespierre, only shortly afterwards to lose his head.) He owned the Niderviller factory, near Strasbourg, and in his baggage he had a dinner service especially made and decorated for Washington. His initials G. W. on a cloud were crowned with laurel: simple swags of flowers were the major decoration. It was elegant but simple, neither ostentatious nor expensive, and Custine presented it to Martha Washington when he visited her at Mount Vernon in 1782.

In the years immediately after the war, Sèvres (which curiously was declining in popularity in Europe) became à la mode amongst the sophisticated New Yorkers. Robert Morris and William Bingham both aroused Washington's competitive appetite with the splendour of their Sèvres table ornaments, and he was determined that America's 'first table' would not be outdone. The Niderviller factory provided him with many pairs of figurines and Morris sent over a very splendid group, or surtout, from Paris in 1790. All of these figures were white, not extravagant in colour or gilding – indeed they had none. Equally austere was the great Sèvres service which Washington purchased from his eccentric friend the French Ambassador, the Comte de Moustier. This was the plainest Sèvres made; pure white with a little, very little, gilding. Even the most commonplace Sèvres was scattered with bouquets of flowers in colour

but this very basic Sèvres of Washington has far greater elegance –
dazzling white, just touched with gold; so right for the virtuous head of
a virtuous republic.

Indeed, Washington himself felt the elaborate decoration and vivid
colours were inappropriate and he seemed at one point about to decline
a splendid suite of highly decorated Worcester vases, offered by his great
admirer Samuel Vaughan, who was also responsible for the splendid
marble mantelpiece at Mount Vernon. Although Washington's delight
in and appetite for china never diminished, his later taste is in marked
contrast to his early purchases. All the major acquisitions – the Cincinatti
china as well as the Sèvres – possess a lofty and restrained elegance.

Susan Gray Deitweiler has made a great contribution to the study of
the decorative arts of eighteenth-century America. Her book is a mine
of scholarship, but she never gets lost, never forgets the human personalities, nor indeed the wide social context of Washington's cups and
saucers, bowls and pots. It seems a pity the book had to be printed in
Japan in a sadly greyish ink.

4. THOMAS HUTCHINSON

(i) The Ordeal of Thomas Hutchinson

Just two hundred years ago, on 1 June 1775, Thomas Hutchinson, the
Governor of Massachusetts, boarded the *Minerva* in Boston Harbour,
accompanied by a son and daughter, and sailed for England for what
was to be permanent exile, increasing unhappiness, and posthumous
execration. His only support came from the dedicated efforts of his great-
grandson, who carefully preserved and published some of Hutchinson's
papers before selling them to the British Museum. He at least lived long
enough to watch the tide of New England scholarship begin to turn in
favour of the loyalists, and to read with gratitude Hosmer's eulogistic
biography of his ancestor, the only one to be written before this remarkable, sensitive and scholarly study by Bernard Bailyn. A few weeks before
Hutchinson's departure, Benjamin Franklin, as responsible as any man
for the calumnies and criticisms which beset Hutchinson, arrived back
in Philadelphia after seventeen years' residence in England, and was soon
to establish himself as one of the heroes of the American Independence.
Scarcely a year has passed since Franklin's death without some pamphlet
or monograph extolling his virtues. And today he is being marmorealised
in the huge publication of his letters, which may take to the year 2000
to complete, and at a cost of millions of dollars. Hutchinson's papers
will doubtless remain, in Bailyn's words, 'wretchedly, disgracefully

preserved'. Yet, compared with Franklin, Hutchinson was a man of integrity, principle and honour. True, his journalistic and intellectual gifts were far less distinguished than Franklin's, but he was freer from guile and deceit. But Franklin, in the end, made the correct decision – to go all out for American Independence. Hutchinson's decisions – honourable, decent, certainly liberal – were always wrong, whereas Franklin sculled with ease in the turbulent tides of history, twisting and turning, but always mastering the buffeting of events. His timing of the moment for action was superb – intuitive, yet almost always right.

No scholar is better equipped than Bernard Bailyn for a study in depth of Thomas Hutchinson. Bailyn is far more deeply read in the pamphlet literature, both English and American, of the decades preceding the American Revolution than any living scholar. This provided the material for his best book, *The Ideological Origins of the American Revolution*, until the publication of this biography. Bailyn has also written another penetrating study, *The Origins of American Politics*. Both books are marked by a quality rare amongst historians, best described as an acute sensitivity to the springs of political morality and belief. This sensitivity is not, however, activated, as it is in so many historians, by commitment to a small range of political attitudes, but a genuine feeling for the whole spectrum. Bailyn is capable of empathy for the inner compulsions of radicals, as well as conservatives; his sympathies, his insights into the inner nature of revolutionaries and reactionaries are finely tuned, and in the main dispassionate, although perhaps his pity is more easily aroused by losers than his glee for winners.

Perhaps more important than the sensitive study of Hutchinson's personal predicament, to which I shall return, is Bailyn's insight into the whole question of loyalism which, naturally enough, has always posed a difficult problem for American historians, even today. At a recent symposium at the Library of Congress, when the impact of the American Revolution on Russia and the Netherlands was considered alongside Britain, France and Ireland, Canada, which, after all, the loyalists largely created, had no place on the programme; an omission not noticed until underscored, with a certain sardonic wit, by Professor John Pocock. The loyalists have, however, been given sympathetic study in their sad and depressing exile in Britain, particularly by Mary Beth Norton. Recently, too, there has also been a franker treatment of their strength, their location in place and class, and of their economic losses in America itself, but, as Bailyn himself stresses, there has been little study of the inwardness of their world – their hopes and aspirations; their principles, and those imperatives which compelled them to act as they did. The great stumbling block, it seems to me, has been to consider both revolutionaries and loyalists as Americans, which they were not in the 1760s, and were only becoming tentatively so in the mid-1770s. An understanding of the American Revolution will be both deeper and clearer if it is stressed that America, from Georgia to Maine, was an integral part of eighteenth-century British society, more so, in many ways, than Scotland and Ireland, and, therefore, the attitudes of both parties in the 1760s and 1770s must be understood not only in the local context of Virginia, Pennsylvania, New York or New England, but also in the wider context of British politics, both the accepted structures and critical opposition to them. The local American situation, by its very nature as well as by its acute tensions and acts of commitment, intensified divisions and sharpened the ideas which were a commonplace of London and Liverpool, and as much a part of the political debate there as in Boston or Philadelphia.

Thomas Hutchinson was what eighteenth-century politicians and placemen were expected to be – a manager. He operated as any ambitious local magnate might have done in Bristol or Exeter, quietly and persistently building his family into the system, acquiring buttresses to his power by judicious marriages with place-holding families of wealth and standing. Secure in office, backed by a dependable clan like a Pelham or a Yorke, he wanted to make the system work, but, as Bailyn makes crystal-clear, not merely through self-interest or a desire for profit and power, but because, like so many Englishmen in politics, from Sir Robert Walpole to Lord North, he believed that the British had secured through their constitution a balance between liberty and authority. Hutchinson believed that in the British colonies 'as much freedom is enjoyed as can consist with the ends of government'. Hence the tendency towards greater liberty that would precipitate anarchy had to be restrained, if necessary, by the authority of Parliament. Partly for these reasons he tried successfully to moderate the Massachusetts petition against the Stamp Act. But the Stamp Act passed, and the lack of unity amongst the colonies was given as the reason for its passage and for that lack of unity, the responsibility was saddled on Hutchinson, unleashing a ferocity, combined with malice, lies and accusations of treachery that appalled him. Finally the 'hellish fury' raised against him resulted in a mob attacking the house that he loved at Milton. And so the long journey towards exile began. For ten years, Hutchinson behaved with rectitude, moderation, never uncritical of British acts, hoping always to alleviate their effects, always underestimating the power of the opposition, seeing too clearly the personal defects of the opposition leaders – the near madness of Otis, the bitterness of Adams. Always he remained blind to their effectiveness. Bailyn conducts us through every stage of the tragedy with an acute perception of both the moral issues and the intransigence of political events. It is a marvellous study of a cautious, unimaginative, deeply committed and honourable official, working dedicatedly within a system which he thought must be preserved if his country was not to dissolve into anarchy or plunge into disaster. Time and time again his strenuous efforts for conciliation, for effective action, for the securing of firm solutions were deliberately misrepresented as acts of a traitor, of a paid lackey of George III, who clung to his office and his masters for the sake of money, honours and corrupt power. In the end, his quite moderate letters of criticism and advice on the situation in Boston were deliberately leaked by Benjamin Franklin, and so started the final tempest that blew Hutchinson out of Boston. Yet there was nothing in these letters that he had not said publicly time and time again. He denounced what he called 'the licentiousness of the Sons of Liberty', but there was no novelty, no surprising exposure in that remark or any other. Hutchinson had become, irrationally, the symbol of all that was hateful in the system of the British government, the triumph of whose policy could only mean the triumph of a *reimposed* status quo. He was to the Boston radicals what Lord North was to the friends of Wilkes – a self-seeking tool of tyranny.

And so, Hutchinson, who may be described as a typical member of the British political establishment, a firm believer in King and Parliament, with a lifetime's experience of holding office, operating always both by the methods and with the typical assumptions of his age, left America and settled in England which, in such marked contrast to Franklin, he soon loathed. He felt awkward, provincial. The King was affable, Oxford University gave him an honorary degree, later Gage entertained him to a sumptuous house-party at Firle. But he knew himself and felt himself to be a small, insignificant member of the aristocratic British political establishment which he had so unswervingly served. He longed for Milton, for New England, for the minor officialdom in which he was at home. 'I cannot help thinking that nature alone has done as much in some parts of America as nature and art together have done in England, and I should prefer even my humble cottage on Milton Hill to the lofty palaces upon Richmond Hill, so that upon the whole I am more of a New England man than ever.' He expected to get back. There was a curious obstinacy in his belief in the final triumph of constitutional rectitude, in the inane hope that a society in revolution would see the errors of its ways. Of course, one must allow that the final defeat of England seemed improbable, and that his beliefs concerning America were not so absurd as afterwards they seemed. When he advised Lord North that the American Congress would never achieve unity of purpose or action it was, indeed, a misjudgement, but it was one that could not be called either unreasonable or misinformed. It was one that any establishment politician of hard-headed judgement might have made. It required both hope and an instinct for the future to believe otherwise.

Apart from Peter Oliver, a loyalist who rollicked in London society, most loyalists in exile felt as Hutchinson did, and there is a sardonic quality in their unhappiness in the country whose establishment they had served, and in whose principles they believed.

The irony lies in the fact that men such as Benjamin Franklin, Arthur Lee, Stephen Sayre or young Josiah Quincey, were much more at ease in London than Hutchinson could ever be. Their ideas, their political attitudes, their criticisms of government were no more alien to British politics than Hutchinson's apologetics. Indeed, they felt comfortably at home in radical and opposition circles in London, or, for that matter, in the provinces. They spoke the same political language as Wilkes and his friends, and their worries about arbitrary government were little different to David Hartley's or Josiah Wedgwood's. They might be more vigorously expressed, more rigidly concerned with specific acts, but in principle their views were the same. Like was talking to like in a common language of politics. When Hutchinson spoke to Dartmouth or stayed at Firle with the Gages, it was the differences that were marked, not the correspondences. The radicals' appraisal of the American political situation was much more realistic than Hutchinson's, whose interpretation of the American conflict was always wrong, although seemingly based on common sense. He could not, or would not, see the innate power or the capacity for authority of the opposition to Britain. For him, it was composed of a clique of slanderous, ill-disciplined, anarchical troublemakers, bent at all costs on the destruction of himself and his friends; indeed, his political life was one long series of uncomprehending misjudgements. The reasons for these misjudgements often sprang from the highest motives – loyalty, respect for the law, the belief that sensible men would behave with circumspection and moderation. He was unable to grasp that in revolutionary times it may be better for sensible men to act without moderation when the final moment of decision comes. This constant failure of his judgement which led him, time and time again, to misrepresent the situation in America, and so to give wrong advice to the British government, might, perhaps, have been more strongly stressed by Bailyn. Hutchinson's position is common in revolutionary times, when cautious common sense can be wrong and political decisions, made upon the basis of how men normally behave, can be disastrous.

As might be expected, as exile ceased to be temporary, as the bitter truth emerged that his fellow countrymen would continue to execrate him and regard him as a traitor, Hutchinson settled down to write a justification of his career. Posterity, however, did not easily or quickly change its opinion of Governor Hutchinson: losers lack glamour. The world, after all, is unlikely to be flooded with biographies of President Thieu or Marshall Ky. But losers are very much a part of an historian's duty if he is to understand the forces of conflict in any age. And Hutchinson, at last, has had his stroke of luck, for Bernard Bailyn has written a biography that is a work of art; exquisitely written, delicate in insight, and imbued with a wisdom about men and affairs that is the true hallmark of a great historian.

PART TWO

THE PROBLEM OF SLAVERY

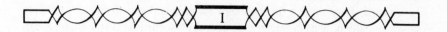

I

The Burgeoning of American History

Before I began regularly to visit America in the 1960s I had started to review occasionally for the *New York Times Book Review* and the old *Saturday Review* under Norman Cousins. As my visits grew more regular and my name became better known through my articles in *Horizon* and *American Heritage*, the frequency of my reviewing increased and so did the number of journals for which I wrote. And I was particularly delighted to be asked in 1963 by Robert Silvers to write for the *New York Review of Books*. This remarkable journal, established now, arose out of a newspaper strike to become one of the leading intellectual reviews not only in America but also in Great Britain. Silvers gave his reviewers space that critics and writers had not enjoyed since the nineteenth century and they responded eagerly. Although its bias was certainly left-wing, and Marxists figured frequently in its pages, Silvers always had room for the independent mind. He knew also how to keep in harmony with the intellectual climate and as the Civil Rights movement and the Vietnam débâcle have receded into history, so the *Review* has moved gently and steadily to the centre; now it is sturdily independent rather than committed.

The *Saturday Review*, however, was my mainstay and in 1967 I began to do a monthly column, called 'Perspective', about books of my own choosing. After that books on every conceivable subject landed on my desk – Japanese gardens, sexuality in boys, the Negro family, the Incas, the historiography of Indonesia, Nelson's letters to Emma Hamilton, tomb sculpture, the influence of Europe on Asia in several volumes, quantities of eighteenth-century history, heaps of biographies; indeed history of every kind. I never knew what new exotic fruit would land on my desk. This came at a time when I was deeply concerned with the history of human society, and at a time, too, critical in my development as an historian. By 1960 I had finished the second volume of my life of Walpole. Writing *The Renaissance* as well as brooding on the history of human society, had focused my mind on the problem of both change and inertia in society. And so, when I was asked to give the Ford Lectures at Oxford, I set myself the problem of how did the turbulent, savage, violence-ridden British society of the seventeenth century acquire the stability of the eighteenth, a political and constitutional stability which proved itself able to cope easily not only with occasional rebellion but also with profound economic and social change. It survived too the loss of America, adjusted itself to reform, and coped even with the acquisition and loss of Empire. This was a very complex problem because some of the institutions which helped to bring about that change were forged, or half-forged, in the turbulence of the seventeenth.

My reading threw up other problems but of a similar conceptual nature. I became more and more fascinated with the history and culture of China – the first great bureaucratic empire. (Someone should study it in relation to the Soviet government – a new bureaucratic empire without Confucian wisdom and grace.) I was baffled by the fact that the Chinese did not develop theoretical science or even an accepted scientific method of investigation. Why did the Chinese fail to develop science? Technologically ingenious to a high degree, science never came. Why no science? It was an article written by Joseph Needham which made me brood more on this question which he turned round – looked at the problem, as it were, backwards. Science is not a natural outcome of highly technological societies. Advanced societies do not necessarily develop a scientific attitude. Needham suggested – do not ask why China failed to develop a scientific attitude but why did Europe? This leads to the larger question – how do ideas, or a cluster of ideas and beliefs, become social attitudes? What was the compost in Europe that matured science uniquely? All that I was writing at this time, whether books, articles or lectures, tended to circulate about this fundamental question – the most difficult I think that an historian or a political theoretician like Marx has to face. Marx and his followers put forward confident answers to many of the questions which puzzled me; but they proved to be no more than helpful approximations.

I realised that one of the most remarkable of changes in social attitude related to the major problem of America's history – the question of slavery. As the Civil Rights movement grew so did the volume of historical work on slavery, and so did the involvement of American Marxist and Marxist-oriented historians. I had always been interested in slavery and the seeming double-vision it created in societies. The philosophical problems it posed for pagans as well as Christians were equally fascinating. I remember as an undergraduate studying Tudor economic history and discovering that in 1547, the English Parliament introduced slavery by statute (true it did not work but nevertheless it was a remarkable fact). I was even more amazed, just after the war, to discover in an eighteenth-century Liverpool newspaper, which I had purchased, that there was a small but active slave market in Liverpool in the 1760s: even in England there was an acceptance of slavery. By 1810 there was little – an incredible change of attitude.

Other historians were showing a growing interest in slavery. Moses Finley was devoting much of his energy and perceptive historical imagination to slavery in antiquity, and Charles Verlinden, one of the finest of Belgian scholars, produced his massive account of slavery in the Middle Ages. Other scholars were active in South America and others busy with Caribbean slavery. The more investigation took place, the more complex the problem seemed. With Needham in mind, increasingly it seemed to me, the major problem was not that slavery, in a multiplicity of forms, had flourished for millennia but the real problem was why in little more than the space of one generation – in Britain primarily – that institution became regarded not only as utterly immoral but also as an antiquated economic and social system that had no place in a modern world. Fortunately David Brion Davis, a great American scholar, had decided to take on this massive and complex problem.

From 1963 onwards I read voraciously about slavery. Indeed from 1963 onwards I read voraciously about anything historical. I seemed to have a revitalised intellectual life that could absorb itself with equal delight in the history of toys, childhood, gardening, political theory or constitutional change, or the problem of slavery. Oddly enough these interests were all to fertilise each other.

There were wonderful books published in America during this period. The older generation of Morison, Commager, Schlesinger and many others were still producing admirable work but about their history there was now an old-fashioned air. They wrote mainly narrative, political or biographical history and sometimes the major problems of the growth and development of American society seemed to elude them, or, at least, not absorb their imagination. The newer generation of historians I found more exciting, particularly the historians of slavery – Eugene Genovese, Vann Woodward, Edmund Morgan, Winthrop Jordan and, of course, Davis.

Eugene Genovese accepted an invitation to spend a year in Cambridge as Pitt Professor and I persuaded my college to offer him a fellowship. He and his wife Betsy (herself an exceptionally fine historian of France) added greatly to the intellectual and social life of the college. Gene loved food and wine and talk. Although a Marxist, he had an almost paranoic concern with the machinations of the orthodox members of the Communist Party whom he regarded with the same fascination and fear that, as an Italian boy in Brooklyn, he might have regarded the Mafia. What was so very strong in Genovese was his empathy. He could project himself into slave society and thereby grasp its complexity. Of course, he never forgot the bestiality of the institution but he also showed how generosity of the spirit could work its miracles in any society. He also realised how human cunning might be exploited with dexterity by slaves. He saw, too, that the most abject of men and women could find deep consolation in rituals, in dancing and song and in rich sexuality that no economic or social system could destroy. Neither could slavery obliterate hope, clothed in religion, that has always been an anodyne for the generality of blacks. Indeed he brought a magnificent sense of the richness of human life to his study of slavery which disguised his fundamentally Marxist approach. His Marxism, subtle as it was, brought him to dead ends, to problems of which there were no convincing answers, as, indeed, did other reductionist attempts at analysis. Winthrop Jordan, whose book *White Over Black* was another milestone in slavery studies, ran into similar trouble in finding the roots of American slavery in racism. No doubt that racism provided the whites with splendid palliatives for uneasy consciences but, as I point out in the review of his book, the concept was too simplistic.

For me the greatest contribution, the most satisfying to the slavery debate, was Edmund Morgan's *American Slavery, American Freedom*. He deals with great subtlety with the economic and social changes that led to the replacement of white indentured servants by black slaves. He is aware that both were types of servitude, that the supply and control of labour was fundamental in that change, that the language of racism could be used about the abject poor white as well as the enslaved black, although the latter's visibility may have brought a deeper sense of God's truth to the enslaving whites. With great imaginative delicacy, he shows how this brutal and exploitive society could sustain an elegant and up to a point an enlightened culture of a Jefferson. Since I reviewed this book, I have re-read it several times and my admiration grows rather than diminishes. The same is true of Genovese's book *Roll, Jordan, Roll*. And many others. The years from 1963 to 1975 were for me the great days for American history and historians – there was a new vitality, a broader vision, a deeper analysis also in Americans writing about Europe – Peter Gay, John Clive, and also less well-known figures – Eric Cochrane on Florence for example and the great popular historians, such as Barbara Tuchman and Catherine Drinker Bowen, were better than most of their British counterparts.

As always with history, this renaissance did not receive the public acclamation that it deserved.

The historical world, however, was becoming more cosmopolitan. With jet passenger aircraft coming into service in 1960, England and

Europe were only a few hours from America. It became quicker to me to get to New York by air than to Glasgow by rail. American historians began to pour into London in the summer vacation. We saw far more of each other, discussed more and, I think, became more understanding of the complexities of Anglo-American history. Perhaps it is not surprising that I forged deeper professional ties with American historians than with British. Many were more gifted, most were more generous, all were more open to new ideas, new angles of vision. And they had a deeper belief in the value of their subject. The society in which they lived was racked by problems whose historical roots were obvious, for example, the Civil Rights movement or an Imperial Presidency. There was nothing in Britain that touched the raw nerves of society like civil rights or Vietnam. Both experiences made American society, and its historians, more sophisticated, but not more cynical. They remained men of hope – for their country and for their profession. In neither was it falsely based.

(i) Slavery, Race and the Poor

Often social change is imperceptible to those living in its midst. It is like water oozing through a dam – at first a faint dampness, a trickle, a spurt, the cracks multiply and either the dam crumbles or the pushing waters are sufficiently eased to create a new, if unstable, equilibrium. To the Black Panthers and other groups of activists the change in social attitudes in America towards the Negro is derisory, and when not derisory a conscience-easing fake. To white Anglo-Saxon Protestants, conscious or unconscious, or to ethnic groups living near to black ghettos or in competition with blacks for jobs, the rushing of the waters is so deafening that they are driven towards panic and hysteria. To the uneasy liberal, the situation borders on the grotesque. He wants to be fair, to make retribution, and yet he cannot easily accept the new black contempt towards the white. He is also conscious, perhaps over-conscious, of the militant blacks' hatred of white democracy, and their growing insistence on authoritarian, almost totalitarian, attitudes within the black community.

The situation of the historian is equally acute. What has been the role of the Negro in American history? What have been the long-term results of slavery and deprivation of civil rights? Indeed what was the true nature of American slavery – was it the most evil type the world has known or no better and no worse than the rest of the New World experienced?

These problems have never been easy to answer, but in the context

of the present time they are much more difficult, for now the question
has to be posed – how far was racism itself responsible for the wretchedness of the Negro slave? Did it give a peculiarly vicious twist to slavery?
Indeed, what are the connections between racism and slavery? And of
course this raises the question of the nature of slavery – unbridled racism
combined with absolute, or near absolute, authority of the racist master
was unlikely to lead to anything but social brutality, of treating the slave
more as a chattel than as a person.

At the present time possibly the problem of racism and slavery is the
most insistent, for obvious reasons. For the professional historian there
are others equally difficult but intellectually perhaps more exciting. There
is Stanley M. Elkins's brilliant and disturbing investigation of slavery
and the Negro personality, examining the reasons for the development
of the 'Sambo' response of the Negro slave to his environment which
would help to explain the paucity of slave revolts in America. (No
amount of black protest or black re-writing of history can overcome
that fact. The American Negro slave protested less in his society than
the free peasant class of Europe, or of England for that matter, and this
needs explanation.) Less original, but more deeply and professionally
argued, is Eugene Genovese's memorable book, *The Political Economy
of Slavery* (1965), which attempts to relate all aspects of Southern life
to its peculiar means of economic exploitation. Indeed Genovese analyses
the social system, based on slavery, from its basic economic structure,
through its institutionalisation of power, to its self-justification and its
sense of pride in itself. Slave society, Genovese has shown, was far more
complex than most historians have allowed.

Apart from Elkins and Genovese many historians have recently made
contributions of great value to the story of slavery and the South. Indeed
the richness of historical writing is well brought out in the two
anthologies under review. This type of book is stupidly despised by
academicians with lunatic standards of scholarly endeavour, usually
not for themselves, but for their pupils. Yet how could the modern
undergraduate cope with the swelling bibliographies on any major theme
without such assistance? Both *American Negro Slavery: A Modern
Reader* by Allen Weinstein and Frank Otto Gatell, and *Black History:
A Reappraisal* provide an admirable selection of the best writers on the
Negro question and will give the moderately diligent student an insight
into the difficulties, arguments and material of the problem.

Here he can read in fascinating apposition the bland apologetics of
Ulrich B. Phillips, the moral incisiveness of Kenneth Stampp, the sophisticated approaches of David Brion Davis or Winthrop Jordan, and the
valuable and all too rare local studies of Edward W. Phifer, whose
account of slavery in Burke County ought to have a myriad of imitators,

since even the best analyses of slavery rely far too heavily on the great plantations of the Tidewater or the accounts of foreign travellers who kept to a well-worn track. Slaves, like the industrial proletariat, were exploited in myriad ways, and, like the proletariat too, in varying degrees of inhumanity. It is as important not to concentrate on the worst as not to forget it.

Yet in all this wonderful range of work on slavery, as exciting, as deeply original, as any going forward on any other aspect of American social history, there is one singular omission. There is no comparative study of slavery and poverty. By this I do not mean a study of the economic condition of slaves compared with free Negroes in the slums of southern cities such as New Orleans, which indeed has been examined by Richard C. Wade, but of the attitude of slave owners towards slaves compared with the attitude, not only of industrial, but of pre-industrial owners of wealth towards the poor, especially in Europe, from 1540 to 1750, for in a sense America had too few poor in the early centuries for any comparison to be meaningful.

New World slavery raises two profound problems. Why was it so easily accepted by all Western European nations at a time when slavery had ceased to be socially important for many generations in their own countries? And secondly why did abolitionists become socially and politically effective from the last third of the eighteenth century? The answers to these questions will obviously illuminate the whole nature of slavery. It is my conviction that these answers can only be found within the non-servile context of the exploitation of labour, and the ideology that goes with it. And this brings one to Winthrop D. Jordan's outstanding book, a volume to be placed alongside Stampp, Elkins, Davis and Genovese.

Jordan's thesis is straightforward. The Elizabethan Englishmen coming across primitive black men for the first time were repelled. To them black men were associated with beastliness; their inferiority made them the lowest link in the great Chain of Being. Blackness stimulated the Englishman's sense of guilt and horror. His Devil was, after all, black, and he always put a high price upon fairness of skin. The primitive societies of West Africa, with their strange and divergent customs, strengthened the Elizabethan's belief in the eternal, God-given inferiority of the Negro – a little higher, maybe, than the apes, but infinitely lower than the white Englishman. Negroes naturally were 'addicted unto Treason, Treacherie, Murther, Theft and Robberie' as well as idleness and lechery.

Hence the proper status of Negroes was slavery. Slavery fitted their natures whose outward sign was the blackness of their skin. And it was because they were black that it became easy to justify slavery and maintain it. This racism can be further illustrated by the treatment of free or freed Negroes, whose rights were subject to strict limitation; even the onus of proof that he was free rested with him, for society expected, owing to his colour, that he would necessarily be a slave. From the earliest days of slavery this element of racism – evident also in the detestation of miscegenation – was dominant and it became more and more powerful as Negroes grew in number and slavery became the dominant social system of the South. This, in essence, is Jordan's argument and it is based on a wealth of material which ranges from the sermons of sixteenth-century English bishops to obscure travellers' reports from Africa, court session records of the Slave States, newspaper files throughout the South, the lucubrations of philosophers in the eighteenth century, the voluminous correspondence of the Founding Fathers and a host of other sources. Indeed the range of Jordan's reading is prodigious.

That racism gave an added dimension to slavery cannot be doubted; but it is a most difficult question to decide on its extent. Jordan contends with a wealth of quotation from Elizabethan literature and from African travellers' tales that the sixteenth-century Englishman regarded the Negro as not only savage, heathen, biologically close to the ape, but also as theologically damned; for the Negro was descended from Ham, Noah's disinherited son, who was cursed by having black offspring. Since the Englishman's Devil was always portrayed as black, Negroes were associated with evil and linked ever more firmly to God's curse. Furthermore, they proved helpless against the 'angel-like' English, whose whiteness proclaimed them to be beloved of God: so, rightly, good was triumphing over evil.

These attitudes to the Negroes made the enslavement of them by the English both natural and ferocious. Unlike Catholic Europeans, the English had no interest in conversion and so long as the black remained a heathen savage in a Christian society the Negro slave could have no rights. Hence the slave possessed fewer human rights in English slaveholding societies than in others ancient or modern. From start to finish American slavery was racial: indeed Jordan calls it racial slavery. In one essential Jordan is correct. Negroes were considered born inferiors, born slaves if you will, to a degree that was not applied to many other groups of slaves. The Roman slave was treated just as brutally, at times far more brutally, than the Southern Negro. He certainly possessed no more rights. But, once freed, the world was open to him. He and his family could rise or fall like any other man in the Roman state, so long as he had either ability or money or both. Not so the Negro. The freed Negro entered a caste which was excluded from most of the benefits and all of the power in the society to which it belonged. And the basis of this exclusion was racial. This far one can go with Jordan.

But it could also be argued that racism went far beyond slavery, so that it cannot be viewed simply in terms of slavery. Racism was not, of course, confined to the Southern slave masters or to Southern slave society in the sixteenth and seventeenth centuries. It was just as rampant in the Portuguese empire. Franciscans in the seventeenth century in Goa attempted to prevent Portuguese born of pure white parents from entering their order on the grounds that having been suckled by Indian wet-nurses, their blood was contaminated for life. This surely is racism as extravagant as any to be found in the Southern States. Again, Jordan makes a great deal of the deliberate exclusion of the Negro from the Anglican Church, but Catholic slave owners were no more eager for their blacks to be a part of their Church. As one Portuguese slaveowner exclaimed indignantly, 'Should my Kaffirs receive Communion? God forbid that I should ever allow them.' Indeed the literature of the sixteenth and seventeenth centuries is full of savagely expressed racism directed not only to the Negro but the Hindu, the Hottentot, the Welsh, Scots, Irish, French against English, English against the Dutch.

Nor was Negro slavery the only slavery justified on racist grounds, nor was the Englishman's attitude unique, as Jordan implies. If one glances at the reaction of the Chinese mandarins of the T'ang dynasty to the primitive peoples of Nam Viet (the tropical south) the response is the same; a combination of curiosity, superiority and utter loathing. 'Both conscience and law permitted the enslavement of these subject peoples all the more readily because of two persistent views of them,' writes Edward Schafer in *The Vermilion Bird*, his remarkable study of the T'ang mandarins' involvement with the south, 'an older one, that they were not really human, and a younger one derived from the first, that they were not really civilised'. These arguments are frequently used about the Negro: yet the enslavement of the primitive people of Nam Viet never developed into the equivalent of Negro slavery, for the Chinese did not require slaves on such a scale.

Racism does not create slavery. It is an excuse for it. Racism was a rampant feature of the centuries when slavery was being established in America and it was, therefore, easy to make it one of the justifications for the institution. But racism could be intense and not lead to slavery – and racism does not explain why the European nations found so little difficulty in adopting slavery in their colonies long after the institution had become insignificant in Europe's economic structure.

Although the institution had no economic relevance in contemporary Europe, the idea of slavery was both potent and entirely acceptable on stronger grounds than those of race. The English House of Commons did not even turn a hair at the suggestion that persistent English vagabonds should be enslaved by their fellow countrymen and they passed an Act in 1547 for this purpose: along, of course, with branding the victims with a large S. It failed and was repealed, but not on humanitarian grounds. No one wanted slaves – there was enough cheap labour without them, requiring no more food and less supervision. But the idea of white slavery was in no way repellent to the Tudors, or limited by them to savages and heathens. Indeed the condition of slavery had been accepted by the Church and by society from time out of mind; a part of that great law of subordination without which the whole edifice of society might crash to the ground. Without slave status, what would happen to bonded servants, to children sold as apprentices, to the indigent poor who had no rights in society except to labour? Slavery was only the most extreme of all servile conditions. Servant and slave were more than semantically linked.

The type of abuse that was hurled at the slave was hurled at the poor, particularly in English society, from which many Southern slave masters were drawn. Take these remarks of William Perkins, the popular puritan preacher of the early seventeenth century:

> Rogues, beggars, vagabonds . . . commonly are of no civil society or corporation nor of any particular Church; and are as rotten legs and arms that drop from the body . . . To wander up and down from year to year to this end, to seek and procure bodily maintenance is no calling, but the life of a beast.

Or this from his colleague Sibbes: 'They are the refuse of mankind: as they are in condition so they are in disposition.'

These puritan divines were more charitable than many. The rogues and vagabonds were, of course, the wandering poor desperate for food. Their lot was bloody whippings, frequent branding and enforced labour. The early slave codes were very similar to the legislation designed to control the Elizabethan unemployed poor. Again, the poor, like slaves, were, it is now thought, neither expected to go to Church nor be welcomed there. And as for cruelty, treatment of apprentices could be vicious, the floggings and brandings meted out to the 'dregs of society' of Elizabethan and Stuart England almost as savage as anything the Negro knew; perhaps at times more so, for the poor were no man's property, and hence valueless if sick, weak or contumacious.

Again, miscegenation: the taboos against marrying the poor were formidable – for a woman it usually meant total ostracism – yet, of course, the young servant women, like slave Negresses, could be and were fair game for their masters. And even the Sambo mentality can be found in the deliberately stupid country yokel or the Cockney clown of later centuries. And so, too, the belief, as with Negroes, that they were abandoned sexually, given both to promiscuity and over-indulgence.

Slave, servant, worker were the objects of exploitation, the sources of labour, therefore wealth; hence we should not be surprised to find similar attitudes, similar social oppressions operating against the poor as against the slave. Slavery and poverty in these centuries are not different in kind but different in degree, and the disadvantage was not always the slave's for, as property, he might be treated with greater consideration in sickness or in old age than the wage-slave. Because America did not know poverty, rural or urban, as Europe did in those early formative years, historians tend to attribute to slavery conditions which spring from the intensive exploitation of labour, whether 'free' or servile. I do not doubt that racism gave an added intensity, a further degree of hopelessness and degradation to slavery and the slave's lot, but it is important to see the similarities in the treatment of slaves and the poor: otherwise one cannot realise how natural slavery was to the majority of men who practised it or accepted it.

To underline this, if underlining be needed, slavery was often – not always but often – at its cruellest where intensive economic exploitation was at its highest, namely on the great plantations. The comparatively mild slavery of Cuba turned into a far more vicious and disciplined form with the rise of the large sugar plantations, as Michael Banton points out in his admirable *Race Relations*, a book which really deserves a far more extensive treatment than can be given it here. Just as a discussion of slavery without a consideration of the exploitation of other labourers tends to obscure fundamental issues, so too can racism and questions of civil rights obscure the deeper issues. No amount of civil rights can alleviate the Negro's lot, for much of the hatred of the black springs from the rich's fear of the poor and dispossessed. The basis of the problem is exploitation: the gross injustice which acquisitive society always inflicts on those who have nothing to offer but their body's labour. Hence the absence of an extended consideration of other labouring poor weakens to some extent the force of Jordan's book.

Once Jordan moves into the eighteenth century there is a greater sense of mastery, and he is particularly skilful in tracing the evasions of the Founding Fathers and the reasons why they could not face the question of abolition. Jordan analyses very subtly the conflict between the insistence on natural rights and the Lockeian concept of the holiness of property. The easiest escape was to defend natural rights negatively, and after the first flush of idealism, revolutionary America had little difficulty in pushing the question of slavery onto the sidelines. But this was as far as it could be pushed: for by 1800 white America's dilemma became both clearer and more devastating to its conscience. How could they keep the purity of white America free from Negro contamination? How could they preserve all that they thought was best in American society,

even the inviolability of family life, if they allowed Negroes to be emancipated? And yet their revolutionary cultural heritage, their growing sense
that Destiny had placed the moral future of the world in their hands
'prohibited extreme, overt manifestations of aggression against them'.
Here were the roots both of a crisis of conscience and of its solution.
Slavery was destroyed, yet racism preserved. And how this was achieved
has been little understood.

The story of abolition, the reasons why the whole of Europe in the
last third of the eighteenth century began to acquire a strong distaste
firstly for the slave trade and even for slavery itself, is a vast question
which none of the great historians of slavery – Davis, Jordan, Stampp,
Genovese, Elkins – have yet attempted. It is a highly complex issue. The
important factor is not the conversion of Quakers to anti-slavery attitudes, nor the convictions of a few intellectuals; voices, some weak,
some powerful, had always been raised against slavery. The real question
is why did abolition acquire a strong social basis, why did it become a
passionate political issue? Again, I believe that this cannot be understood
in isolation from the working class and the different attitude which was
developing towards it. The most fertile ground for conversion to anti-
slavery agitation, besides the Quakers, was in England amongst the
entrepreneurs of the industrial revolution: the manufacturing districts
(as against the commercial) were inclined to produce the subscribers,
the speakers and the supporters of the anti-slavery movement; not all,
of course, but it was an area of marked sympathy.

From the middle of the eighteenth century, and indeed far earlier
amongst the Quaker industrialists, one can find a changing attitude to
the poor labouring man, the attitude that he turned into a better, more
profitable tool if he were given incentives, that is if he were encouraged
to feel that his work possessed opportunities for self-advancement and
better conditions, no matter how rudimentary. Furthermore, the new
industrial methods required more self-disciplined, skilful, better
educated, literate labourers. The more imaginative, speculative manufacturers, such as Josiah Wedgwood, Jedediah Strutt and Robert Owen,
experimented with higher wages, bonus schemes, better housing, works
canteens, children's schools and the like. Instead of labouring men,
exploiters now wanted tools, and far more tools than the old craftsman
methods of industrial organisation permitted: also their new tools needed
to be more specialised and more limited. Master craftsmen were not
wanted. Tools or 'hands' were wanted, and they could be created from
the labouring mass. Also a pool of labouring men, skilled, semi-skilled
and unskilled, selling their labour on a free market, was invaluable for
keeping down wages. In a world of violent business cycles, 'free' labour
obviously had great advantages over unfree. Manufacturers' attitudes

were rarely as crudely materialistic as this, any more than those of the slaveowners. Many were devoted to their workers, helped them in harsh times and developed a patriarchal attitude, but this does not disguise the basic situation.

And so the whole attitude to exploitation began to change, very slowly but with gathering momentum, and the poor began to turn into the working class: but this working class, of course, was sharply differentiated within itself and, in a society that needed a mass basis of free wage-slaves, was treated often with a callousness which was not less evil than slavery and often justified by the same bogus quasi-scientific arguments that were used to justify racism: that the poor were biologically inferior. And, of course, racism did not die, indeed, given the right conditions, as with the influx of East European Jews into London's East End in the late nineteenth century, it intensified. And the same is true with Negroes in America.

The flourishing state of racism throughout the world, *post abolition*, should make us chary of explaining slavery in its terms. Yet slavery was abolished, the most powerful world leaders, for the first time in recorded history, deliberately set out to get both the slave trade and slavery suppressed. It became politically and socially viable for them to pursue such a policy. Slavery began to appear as archaic and its personal brutalities and restrictions were anathematised. Slavery became the antithesis of modernity. It cannot be an accident that the leadership of the anti-slavery agitation on a world-wide scale was conducted by the most industrialised nation in the world, namely Great Britain. However, that is another and a longer story. The point that I wish to emphasise is that a study of slavery, disengaged from the general history of the exploitation of labour, has inherent dangers, leading to a false emphasis and to a too simplified causation. It is even more confusing to see slavery entirely in terms of racism.

(ii) Plantation Power

Now that the 1960s have closed, it is fitting to salute Eugene Genovese and the salutary, disturbing, critical effect that he must have on the writing of American history – performing, indeed, for his own country the service which Christopher Hill and Eric Hobsbawm did for Britain in the 1950s. The rise of very sophisticated, scholarly and sensitive Marxist history has been a feature of the cultural life of both countries, making the historians of an older generation look curiously dusty and old fashioned and bringing the English-speaking historians much closer to those of France and Italy. Not that I can accept in totality the analysis

of Genovese any more than I can that of Hill and Hobsbawm: often
there is a twist and slither in their arguments in order to achieve the
hoped for consistency with doctrine. But of that, later. Let us stress their
virtues.

They are the heirs, the inheritors, of a vital change which began to
take place in historical study at the turn of this century. For most of the
nineteenth century, historians were concerned either with annals or with
biographies. They wrote multi-volume histories of countries, reigns, wars
or people. They told stories splendidly, dramatically, and they pointed
morals and taught lessons so that all who read them might be made
wiser. History, narrative history, was, they thought, a higher calling,
none perhaps higher. About 1900, however, there was a shift. The
development of what one might call 'concept' history: the most obvious
and best-known example of this being Turner and his concept of the
moving frontier as a factor in American history. The historian's new
aim was to discern the dynamic processes controlling social change. The
proliferation of specialised fields of historical study, the growth of
learned journals, the rapid expansion of graduate schools of history
(again in some ways Turner was a pioneer) soon made 'concept' history
the dominant scholastic form of historical study. True, the old style
annals and the old style biographies went on, but with less and less
impact on the intellectual life of history and historians, particularly in
the universities. The excitement lay in economic history, in the history
of ideas, in the application of new ideas in anthropology and sociology
to historical situations. Obviously this was an ideal seedbed for Marxist
historians.

Naturally, in this new analytical game, both slavery and the Civil War
acted like powerful magnets, drawing shoals of historians into their
orbits. The cautious pursued eruditions piling up the ammunition for
the conceptualists. And new concepts flew thick and fast. Slavery was
an archaic, unprofitable method of economic organisation; slavery was
patriarchal and less hideous than rampant capitalism; slavery bred a
special mentality in the slaves which reduced social tension; slavery was
a red herring disguising the real motive, of the North. For fifty years or
more some of the best historical minds in America have been concerned
with what is, after all, its greatest social and historical problem.

True, these historians have been a minority. Often those most widely
read by the public and most earnestly listened to by the Establishment
have done their best to ignore slavery and write off the Civil War as an
'unnecessary conflict'. For, as conservative historians know, analysis
tends to lead, not to national self-approval and euphoric self-confidence,
but to criticism and doubt. Since the radical element in American life
strengthened in the later 1950s and throughout the 1960s, so too has

the quality of work on slavery strengthened. If anyone doubts this, then he should buy *Slavery in the New World*, edited by Laura Foner and Eugene D. Genovese, which brings together a collection of brilliant papers in the comparative study of slavery in the New World. The new masters are all there, Stanley M. Elkins, David Brion Davis, Winthrop D. Jordan, Elsa V. Goveia, H. Orlando Patterson and M. I. Finley: only the Grand Master, G. Vann Woodward, is absent. The challenger for his title – Genovese – is naturally well represented: I find his, Winthrop Jordan's and M. I. Finley's contributions the most suggestive in a book which is alive with intelligence and perception. Indeed, here is another admirable illustration of what I have said before – the writing of history in America is, at last, acquiring that sophistication and analytical insight which has been the hallmark of the best European scholarship for fifty years.

The burden of the book, its lesson, is that slavery cannot be studied as a separate institution, divorced from time and place. Slavery, like poverty, changes with changing society. Poverty in Pennsylvania cannot be the same as poverty in Peshawar. And poverty in Pennsylvania in 1930 was not the same as poverty in Pennsylvania in 1690. Trite. Maybe, but like many other simple approaches to historical problems, it becomes complex and revealing when applied, and the results are compared. If one studies slavery in Cuba before and after the development of the great sugar plantations, the difference is almost as startling as the difference between domestic industry and the factory. Again, such comparisons, as Genovese rightly points out, make one very wary of accepting some forms of slavery as mild and benevolent, others as harsh and explosive. In a fascinating and perceptive essay Winthrop D. Jordan shows how Jamaica, where blacks were worked more vigorously than almost anywhere else, at an almost death-haunting pace, the mulatto had far greater chance of freedom and social opportunities than in the somewhat milder slavery of the Southern States, where race and slavery were more closely related.

These comparative studies lead, as Genovese and Foner meant they should, to a realisation that slavery can only be understood in relation to the class structure of the societies that practise it. And that class structure, of course, will be intimately related to the economic activity upon which the society is enlarged. This is the theme of Genovese's new book, *The World the Slaveholders Made*. Here he attempts to explain why slavery differed so markedly in the New World, and compares not only the ruthless and intense systems in Jamaica with the milder forms in Martinique and Guadaloupe, but also the variations within Brazil and elsewhere. He makes short shrift of the old argument that Catholicism, because it encouraged the baptism of slaves and so elevated them to the rank of Christian, gave the blacks a passport to common humanity and, therefore, an easier social situation than they enjoyed in Protestant slave societies.

After all, few Catholic clergy in Brazil pressed for abolition. C. R. Boxer has produced in his recent book, *The Portuguese Seaborne Empire*, plenty of evidence of harsh treatment, reluctance to permit baptism, and as rabid a racism in parts of the Portuguese empire as would have delighted the most fervent Southerner.

Again, as Genovese shows, the Puritans were themselves no more averse to slavery when it suited their economic needs than their Southern cousins. Slavery did not root itself throughout New England (it did in patches) simply because economic necessity did not require it. The commodities in which New England traded did not demand a huge labour force in their production; tobacco, sugar, cotton did. Short of people, the South had to acquire a working population, and that could only be done forcibly. It is Genovese's view that slavery will be the more economically exploitive the closer the economy is to the world markets, and this is the reason for the most fundamental differences in various forms of slavery.

At this point it is important to remember that all slave societies of the New World were colonies, attached closely not only to the economies of their mother countries, but also to their social and constitutional structures. Absolutist, paternalist mother governments will create absolutist and paternalist colonies. Bourgeois capitalist societies, such as Britain or the Netherlands, will produce colonies in which high production and high profit will override all other considerations. Hence the difference between the Jamaican slave code and the Colbertian Code Noire of the French West Indies: one the result of bourgeois, the other of absolutist government. Again this reconciles the conflicting views of Freyre and Boxer with regard to Brazilian slavery: Freyre was mainly using evidence derived from domestic slavery, which naturally reflected the patriarchal, absolutist social pattern of Portugal. Boxer, however, derives his evidence from the profit-conscious sugar plantations that, in some ways, were exceptional in Brazilian society as a whole.

Genovese argues his thesis with a subtlety and breadth of scholarship that we have now come to expect in his work. He dismisses mechanical Marxism, and his own dialectical skill possesses the flourish and deadly intent of an expert duellist. And how well he writes – no deadly jargon, no laboured pages. So easily is one persuaded by so much of Genovese's argument that it is difficult to stop oneself from swallowing it whole.

The trouble lies, of course, in what Genovese himself recognises as his major conundrum. The society which gave birth to Jamaican slavery was also the one which fathered the Old South – namely seventeenth-century Britain, which Genovese, following dutifully in the footsteps of English Marxists, regards as a strongly bourgeois society dominated by the economy of the marketplace. This explains Jamaican slavery but does create a difficulty for the Old South, which Genovese regards as a patriarchal slave society, perhaps indeed the most highly developed patriarchal slave society the modern world has known. After all, elsewhere in the New World it was seigneurial societies – Spain, France, above all Portugal – which spawned paternalistic slave systems. So how come this startling exception?

Genovese's handling of his conundrum is very neat. Paternalism, he argues, is inherent in all slave–master relationships, and the special situations in the Old South, particularly the system of large plantations, turned a potentiality into a reality. Hence Genovese can fit all that he believes about the Old South into his general theory of slave systems. Naturally the argument is more complex than is possible to sketch here. But this bridge safely crossed, Genovese is then able to discuss the highly developed slave society of the Old South, its philosophy and its prophet, George Fitzhugh, in order to underline once more his view that its quality of life, its ideals and aspirations, as well as its social structure, differed radically from the North.

To understand the Old South is also to appreciate it. There were human values in slavery as well as inhuman ones – a theme which Genovese has consistently developed. Not, of course, that he condones slavery. Nor, and this should be made clear, does he think, as many of his critics mistakenly believe, that the society is a feudal society or even a variant of it. The Old South was a slave society, no more, no less, with its own developed pattern of class relationships and with its own *persona*: distinct from the capitalist worlds of both New and Old England whose evils the slaveholders saw with clarity and which they regarded as far more monstrous than the benign if disciplined servitude they practised. And no one else put his point of view with the urgency and conviction of Fitzhugh.

Nearly a half of *The World the Slaveholders Made* is devoted to George Fitzhugh. Fortunately Fitzhugh's blistering attack on capitalism, *Cannibals All: Or, Slaves Without Masters*, is available. And all should read it, giving particular attention to C. Vann Woodward's excellent introduction. Of course, Fitzhugh seized on a central contradiction. How could abolitionists prate about liberty and human dignity when the conditions of their factory system were more horrible than plantation slavery? Fitzhugh quoted largely from the revelations of the parliamentary inquiries into factory conditions in England, with their appalling evidence of the exploitation of women, children and men in terrible conditions for excessive hours at very low wages. Against these horrors, he opposed the picture of patriarchal plantations – stern masters certainly, discipline certainly, but there was always food, always a roof, even in old age. Slave workers could not, like factory workers, be turned out to starve in bad times, or left to die in destitution in old age. Both societies, the North and the South, were slave societies, but the South at least retained moral responsibility for its slaves.

Indeed Fitzhugh maintained that all societies, whether free or not, would be slave societies, for the nature of man demanded it. 'Some were born with saddles on their backs, and others booted and spurred to ride them.' All talk of progress, of betterment, was illusion. there would always be masters and men, and the master–slave relation was one of the best, far superior to a free labour market.

Genovese rightly sees that Fitzhugh was making a serious case. Exploitive industrial capitalism could be vile, some plantation slavery by comparison was almost benign. However, I believe that Genovese puts too high a value on Fitzhugh and does not allow enough both for the contradictions in Fitzhugh's own thinking, often more apparent in private than in public, and for Fitzhugh's desire to shock.

The World the Slaveholders Made enriches our understanding of the slave system of the New World; it sparkles with originality and it is a most important contribution to the swelling historiography of slavery. But there are weaknesses. The major one for me is the rigidity with which Genovese distinguishes between seigneurial society, or patriarchal society, and the competitive bourgeois, market-dominated societies – principally New and Old England and the Netherlands. Moreover, Genovese has relied too heavily on Christopher Hill and Maurice Dobb for his analysis of English society. England did not secure a full bourgeois revolution in the seventeenth century. Patriarchalism remained a powerful feature in English social attitudes; aristocracy recovered much of the ground which it had lost before 1640 after the Restoration in 1660. A profound respect for rank, hierarchy and status infused the very marrow of seventeenth-century England, as indeed one may see from the original constitution of South Carolina devised by no less a 'bourgeois' apologist than John Locke. True, some feudal trappings had been abolished, and a world in which the bourgeois could develop and expand had come into being, but the structure, worm-eaten though it might be, was still monarchical, aristocratic and patriarchal; and in some ways the divisions between the social structures of New England and the Old South only reflect in a more extreme way the divisions which existed in the mother country itself. A fact which Fitzhugh seized upon. He realised that these two aspects, symbolised by Filmer and Locke, existed together very uneasily in sevententh-century English society. After all, he resuscitated Filmer to refute Locke.

The same sort of insistence on the two opposed societies – patriarchal and bourgeois – also inhibits Genovese's appreciation of the exceptionally strong patriarchal streak in early industrial capitalism. Indeed, words that he applies to the best resident planters, the care for the housing, food, health and old age of the slaves, could be written with equal justice about Wedgwood and his workers, or Jedediah Strutt and his. I do not know enough about early industrial capitalism in New England but, I suspect, one could find easily enough similar examples of benevolent patriarchalism. And it does make one wonder if Genovese has not somewhat overdone the differences between North and South and whether they had not more in common than he allows. Others have pointed out that many Southerners had feelings of guilt about slavery, indeed even some planters and that Fitzhugh himself could write in praise of Northern industry and hope for closer relationship between it and the South. I find it difficult to accept Fitzhugh as presented by Genovese.

Fitzhugh's claims are, I think, somewhat inflated although his importance needs to be stressed. In the end what worries me most is the distinction between patriarchal and bourgeois societies that is made too hard and fast for my liking. As in England during the seventeenth century, so in America during the nineteenth, they were inextricably mingled. However, if the lines of Genovese's argument are drawn more vehemently than, perhaps, the evidence allows, they surely are drawn in the right places. Our understanding of the slaveholders' world has been greatly enhanced by Genovese's work, and he has established himself without question as one of the leading historians of the South. In Genovese, America has a Marxist historian in every way as gifted and as subtle as Hill, Hobsbawm or Soboul, and at times just as opaque.

(iii) The Problem of Slavery in the Age of Revolution

Perhaps the greatest problem which any historian has to tackle is neither the cataclysm of revolution nor the decay of empire, but the process by which ideas become social attitudes. Voices, often powerful, of men of intellect as well as men of religion, had been raised against slavery since the days of the Sophists, but their influence on society's attitude to slavery was entirely negligible. Even though villeinage, let alone slavery, had almost died out in England by the sixteenth century, the English Parliament had no compunction in introducing slavery as a punishment for incorrigible vagrancy in 1547.

Two hundred years later, blacks were still being advertised and sold in London, Liverpool, Bristol and elsewhere without unduly disturbing the public conscience of those cities, although by that time the debate about the moral validity of slavery was growing, indeed very strongly among Quakers. It must be stressed, however, that Quakers in England, if moderately influential in commerce and industry, were a small and highly inbred sect; their social impact in 1740 or even 1750 was slight. Yet by 1788 the House of Commons was inundated by over one hundred petitions against the slave trade, containing tens of thousands of signatures: the defenders of slaves and of slavery were acutely aware of their growing isolation and of the increasing difficulty of defending their positions politically. The swiftly running tide of anti-slavery feeling was steadily gathering the momentum that was to lead to the abolition of the British slave trade in 1807 and eventually of slavery itself – an economic and social institution that had existed since the beginnings of recorded time.

By the 1770s the debate on slavery was intense not only in England, but also in America, as well as in France or even in Denmark. It must be remembered however, that at this time too, owing to economic and social pressure serfs were being bound much closer to the soil in Eastern Europe and, above all, in Russia, where the rights of serf-owners had intensified – so much so that the difference between serf and slave was now marginal. Even so, the Czar of Russia grew uneasy about slavery and the slave trade, and listened with sympathetic attention to one of the leading abolitionists, William Allen. By 1820 the question of slavery had become a social question of great intensity in Europe; and in Great Britain, especially, bitter opposition to the foreign slave trade had gained unquestioned acceptance in large segments of society and was leading to intensive international political and social action.

Here is one of the great reversals of social attitude. How could it be that in the space of a generation or less in England over 100,000 men could be so certain of the iniquity of the slave trade and so disturbed by its practice that they took political action by petitioning Parliament? On the other hand, Revolutionary America – pledged from inception to suppress the slave trade – failed to respond despite strong abolitionist movements in the South as well as in the North, and indeed several generations elapsed before slavery became a desperate critical issue.

Equally divergent was the experience of Revolutionary France, where slaves were emancipated in the full flush of revolution, only to be re-enslaved by Napoleon. Another half-century passed before they regained their freedom. In spite, therefore, of a growing social antipathy to slavery as an institution throughout Europe and America, outside the South, the results of the abolitionists' campaign were complex, ambiguous and by no means so inevitable as they now appear. Here are problems worthy of a great historian.

Nine years ago, in one of the most scholarly and penetrating studies of slavery, *The Problem of Slavery in Western Culture*, David Brion Davis displayed his mastery not only of a vast source of material, but also of the highly complex, frequently contradictory factors that influenced opinion on slavery. He has now followed this up with a study of equal quality, and, like his first book, this will endure, one of the peaks in the vast mountainous range of the bibliography of slavery. Some of the same ground is covered again, but in greater detail, and from a more complex viewpoint.

This new book deals with three types of structure which influenced slavery and the rise of the abolition movement in the age of revolution. The first section is a masterly study of the influence on slave societies of the change in the international power structure that was a consequence of the American Revolution. The importance of the West Indies declined both economically and strategically for Great Britain, thereby weakening the influence of the planters and their bankers at Westminster and so throwing the apologists for slavery on the defensive. On the other hand, the Founding Fathers were caught in a moral political dilemma in which whatever idealism they might have about slavery and its abolition had to be sacrificed to preserve Federal unity. A drive for immediate abolition even of the slave trade (if not of slavery itself) would have resulted in either civil war or the Balkanisation of America. Thus the highly traditional and conservative political structure of Britain was paradoxically more open to the abolition cause than that of the idealistic, revolutionary democracy of America. All of this is beautifully presented and argued.

After a quick look at France, Davis then comes to the heart of his book – the growth of the abolitionist movements, their successes and failures between 1770 and 1823 – and again, although France is never forgotten, the emphasis rightly is on America and Britain. Here the interplay of religion, politics and economics, the influence of great historic figures – Jefferson, Granville Sharp, Wilberforce, Benezet – are analysed with brilliant skill.

Davis gives great weight to the role of the Quakers, emphasising that many of these abolitionists were also in the vanguard of the industrial and commercial expansion, and alive, therefore, to the need for both the discipline and productivity of labour. Any solution of this problem, however, had to meet their ethical commitments, which now included an abhorrence of slavery. Quaker influence in England spread to many of the progenitors of the Industrial Revolution – Josiah Wedgwood, Richard Arkwright and the rest – whose paternalistic and disciplined factories mirrored so many features of the Southern plantations, but without the slavery. Again the success and failures of the Quakers in the Southern states, in Pennsylvania and in the North is traced with great lucidity. The pro-slavery elements in both countries, particularly Britain, are never underestimated and the social complexities are never simplified. In his last section Davis discusses the intricate equivocations of English law and its judges toward slavery in Britain.

Undoubtedly the finest chapters of this book are those which deal with the evolution of the abolition of the slave trade in England. The surge of abolition became possible not so much because of the dedication and moral fervour of Quakers and Evangelicals, important though that was, but because abolition no longer posed a massive threat to British wealth. Indifference towards the slave trade among men of power (which may be seen from the relatively moderate attendance in the House of Commons on abolition debates – a point missed by Davis) was probably as important as commitment. And there were other subtle forces, too, at work in the power structure of English society – a sense of imperial destiny, of world mastery: a desire to police the world with British navies on a moral crusade; a need to make lesser powers execute her will. All these motives possessed their attractions for men who had little use for blacks but took a stand against the trade.

Yet Davis never lets us forget that, be this as it may – admit and accept the selfish motivation, stress the contradiction in a Wilberforce blind to child labour but heart-felt about slavery – there was indeed a commitment to a moral crusade and to the destruction on moral grounds of a very real source of national wealth. Those who pressed for the Act to abolish the slave trade were overwhelmed, not surprisingly, by the magnitude of their own selfless morality. That they do not seem absurd and hypocritical is a measure of Davis's empathy and skill in leading us to a profound understanding of their world.

Davis is mainly concerned to describe the course of the movement for abolition in America, France and Britain, and to make us fully aware of those factors which promoted, inhibited or changed its direction; but in so doing he does, at times, lose sight of the larger social context in which the abolition movements was embedded. This is particularly true of Britain, where there were important social factors which have eluded him.

Sensitivity to the plight of slaves, particularly towards the horrors of the ocean passage as well as to the rape of people from Africa, was but a part of a far wider growth of human sensitivity in England and to a lesser but marked extent also in France. Attitudes were changing rapidly in the late eighteenth century in respect to cruelty towards animals, towards children, towards women, towards the plight of madmen and of the sick. And it is not surprising that many abolitionists were preoccupied with other aspects of human suffering beside slavery and committed to their relief.

This profound change in social attitude – of course by no means universal, indeed the attitude of only an influential minority – is not a result of the Enlightenment, indeed the Enlightenment is a reflection of it, or perhaps more accurately the Enlightenment confirms this attitude with conscious reasoning. However, this growth of sensitivity is a most important factor in the history of abolition. A chapter on the social background of abolition would have given added depth to Davis's discussion and would also have led him, I think, to the new and important mechanism that permitted the wider dissemination of abolitionist ideas.

In England there was a literate, politically intelligent public of far greater extent than in any country of Western Europe, indeed far larger than was to be found in America; furthermore it was strongly concentrated in London and the large towns, yet served by a complex network of newspapers, pamphlets, prints, handbills, advertisements, media in which entrepreneurial expertise had long been exercised both to extend propaganda and to make profit. As Dr John Brewer has shown, politics in the 1760s had been commercialised by Wilkes in medallions, buttons, prints, circular letters, pamphlets. Every trick of modern promotion had been used to extend his influence and to convince the literate public of his stand for liberty against the tyranny of George III. Such methods had been used before, but never exploited with such skill.

Hence the abolitionists had at their disposal a system for the distribution of propaganda, for the creation of public opinion, and one which had already been tuned to the politics of protest. America was not so equipped until the 1820s or 1830s, and France only briefly, at the height of the Revolution. The point to stress is that abolition was exploitable. When Josiah Wedgwood produced his famous medallion of the slave in chains with its caption 'Am I not a man and a brother?' he was fusing moral force with a keen sense of profit. It paid him as well as pleased him to push the sales as hard as he could.

A market in politics and a market in protest existed for the abolitionists to exploit; and like all markets it was not averse to sensationalism, to horrifying pictures of slave-ships and atrocities. Without that market, it is unthinkable that the abolitionists could ever have obtained the thousands of signatures to their parliamentary petitions. And again it must be emphasised that the political public in England had been sensitised to protest – through Wilkes, through the American Revolution, through the abolition movement and, above all, by its own growing sense of exclusion from power. West Indian slave-traders and owners were a narrow group in the constellation of that oligarchy which was thwarting this public's own political aspirations.

This public base, of course, was not enough to secure abolition – that was secured by the processes so brilliantly described by Professor Davis – but it was an essential element, and one which he might have examined more fully and to advantage. However, the complexities of change in social attitude are exceptionally diverse, and how properly to weigh them presents even greater difficulties. Yet no one has written a work about the abolition of slavery that carries the conviction of Professor Davis's book. And this rich and powerful book will, I am sure, stand the test of time – scholarly, brilliant in analysis, beautifully written.

(iv) Slavery and Human Progress

Since World War II professional history in America has become infinitely more sophisticated and analytical, more European, than ever before. The great historians of the 1930s, Morison, Commager, Nevins, Mattingley and the young Schlesinger, were largely cast in the traditional nineteenth-century mould of narrative historians and biographers. Their works were powerful, enriching, often original, and reached out far beyond the confines of the profession to a wide national audience. Perhaps because America had no mediaeval history, indeed the United States has little sixteenth-century history, the influence of European scholars such as Pirenne, Bloch, Febvre and other luminaries of the new history of the 1920s was slow to take root. The slogan of this school, phrased by Febvre, was 'No problems, no history'. Historical problems naturally occur more frequently in complex, well-defined, long-continuing societies; simple colonising societies in a largely empty continent have fewer. At least one huge problem however has confronted all historians of the United States of America – the question of slavery continuing in a society founded to protect liberty and secure freedom. Historians of distinction had recognised the problem before World War II, but immediately afterwards a torrent of articles and monographs, many of exceptional distinction, poured from the American presses. Young American historians had been stimulated by Eric Williams's *Capitalism and Slavery*, a wrong headed but stimulating Marxist interpretation by an outstanding Caribbean scholar, and by European studies, particularly Charles Verlinden's *L'Esclavage dans l'Europe médiévale* (Vol. 1, Bruges, 1955), an outstanding and original work which created vast interest in what was virtually a new field of European history, but one which had close links with the first century of American slavery in the Spanish colonies. Non-American contributors to the history of slavery have continued to enrich the subject but for the last twenty-five years it has been dominated by American scholars of quite exceptional brilliance – Woodward, Morgan, Genovese, Jordan, Patterson, and so one might go on listing names as numerous as those on the Tree of Jesse.

The intellectual content of these studies, particularly in Genovese, has been enriched by Marxist influences. No doubt the fading of Macarthyism in the 1960s also helped to produce a freer and livelier intellectual climate. Other historians have turned for enlightenment to other disciplines such as anthropology, sociology and psychology; others to music as well as myth; the econometric historians of slavery, dominated by Fogel and Engerman have attempted to turn the economics of slavery, upon which so much historical interpretation depends, upside down. Their *Time on the Cross*, a deeply fissured book, dubious in statistics and unacceptable in argument, nevertheless created new insights as well as new problems for the historians of slavery. The work goes on and will go on for perhaps another decade before it begins to subside, as subside it will. It can hardly be a coincidence that American historians' preoccupation with slavery has been contemporaneous with the growth of the civil rights movement. As that movement achieves its goals, so, I expect, will interest in slavery diminish. But that prospect lies well in the future and this year has seen two more major works on the subject; Orlando Patterson's *Slavery and Social Death*, a book of magnificent scholarship, brilliant originality and penetrating analysis, and David Brion Davis's *Slavery and Human Progress* (Oxford University Press, 1985).

At the beginning of his career Davis set himself one of the most difficult of historical problems. How do the ideas of an élite become a widespread social attitude? How did the views on slavery of a few Quakers and Evangelicals become the automatic belief of hundreds and thousands of men and women within two generations? This dramatic change to slavery can be illustrated by the following advertisement published in the Cowburn's *Liverpool Chronicle* on 15 December 1768 (the only copy known is in my possession):

TO BE SOLD
A FINE NEGRO BOY
of about 4 feet 5 inches tall
of a sober, tractable, human Disposition, Eleven
or Twelve Years of Age, talks English well, and
can Dress Hair in a tollerable Way

Ironically the newpaper at the time was giving its support to 'Wilkes and Liberty'. Twenty years later even a Liverpool newspaper would scarcely have dared to publish such an advertisement and had it done so, it would have led to public outrage, vigorously expressed. This advertisement provoked no comment of any traceable kind. In twenty years the social attitude to slavery in England had changed dramatically. To many – particularly nineteenth-century liberals – revulsion to slavery seemed both natural as well as sanctioned by the Christian religion. This revulsion is now so generally felt that it is hard to remember that until the late eighteenth century, slavery, except for a few intellectuals, had been acceptable to all societies and practised by most of them since the dawn of history. After all slavery has its roots in the most fundamental human group – the family – whether white, black or yellow.

What is remarkable is not that slavery existed but that it was ever abolished. How did it happen? To this problem Davis has devoted his professional life – his views are enshrined in two books – both peaks in the great Himalayan range of slavery studies – *The Problem of Slavery in Western Culture* and *The Problem of Slavery in the Age of Revolution*. No simple answers emerge from either book which delineate the complexity of the problem rather than suggest easy solutions to it. Where he is quite exceptionally perceptive, both in his earlier books and this new one, is the stress which he places not only on religious belief but on how the commitment to the anti-slavery cause created in many a sense of religious rebirth, a strong emotional belief that through opposition to slavery they were becoming agents of their own moral regeneration. Hence the strength of the anti-slavery movement in both Britain and America amongst Quakers and Methodists and Evangelicals, who believed deeply in personal salvation. Almost all the leading protagonists of the first drive against the slave trade and slavery were deeply religious men and women, converted more by their hearts than their heads. Often such conversions resulted in dramatic action – slave owners, like Garretson, freed their slaves; slave-traders such as John Newton gave up their trade and preached the horrors of their sinful earlier lives with the fervour of a St Francis.

Certainly the development of a deeply moral and emotional commitment to anti-slavery was a new dimension. What voices had been raised before had been largely intellectual and only occasionally religious. But even so, the quick, almost overwhelming response and momentum which the anti-slavery movement achieved required other and more complex social and economic factors to explain it. Ideas rarely convince by themselves; there is usually a pressure to believe. As Davis shows, along with this moral vision was the conviction, that grew steadily in the early decades of the nineteenth century, that free labour was likely to be more productive because it was free, that a man was more likely to work harder when he had wages to dispose of as he wished. Indeed the belief that slavery was an outmoded and incompetent means of production was believed so totally across the political spectrum that it could take contradiction in its stride. The abolitionists, for example, opposed Cuban sugar on two grounds: one, that it was blood-stained; and secondly that its low price, which undercut the market, was due to cheap but highly productive slave-labour. The fact that the second reason contradicted one of their major convictions did not perturb them. Because the belief that slavery was not as profitable as free labour was so deep-rooted, a sense of outrage greeted Fogel and Engerman's *Time on the Cross* which led to more careful assessment of the economics of slavery. Although no one would agree whole-heartedly with their statistics or their conclusions, subsequent research has shown that slavery could be very profitable, even as late as the 1860s.

Although it is true that slavery was often very profitable, the majority of thinking men, whether radical or conservative, by 1860 had, however, come to regard it as an antiquated institution, a phase in the history of human society which should be abolished as soon as possible. Even the slave-holders of the Southern States, of Cuba, or of South America were, almost to a man, defensive about their peculiar institution. Indeed by 1860 such societies were beginning to collapse from within, feeling helplessly that they belonged to an antique world. Profitability is not the only factor in social buoyancy.

At this point, I believe, Davis fails to notice another great change in social attitude which took place between 1760 and 1830, every bit as profound and as momentous as the change in attitude to slavery: indeed, I regard it as a trigger to that change. Davis does consider the influence of science and rightly points out that the attitude of many scientists, particularly social scientists in the eighteenth and early nineteenth centuries, strengthened the intellectual case for slavery by arguing that blacks were an inferior sub-species of humankind: less intelligent, more emotional, without innate moral sense and at the mercy of their sexual drives, a stage further back than whites in the evolution of mankind. However, Davis does not consider the other social attitudes which science had been breeding for a century and which were now taking hold of society. Technological development and the rapid growth of man's power over nature had bred an astonishing acceptance of the idea of modernity which had little to do with the specific ideas of scientists. It pervaded most of the education of the British middle and lower middle classes, and the belief that the betterment of mankind would come by acceptance of man's rationality and control over nature was widespread, even in religious circles. There is not space to explain the interrelationship between those two social attitudes, but there is no doubt that the steadily growing belief that slavery was an outmoded as well as immoral institution, left over from antiquity, was fortified by the remarkable acceptance of the idea of modernity. Of course, Davis is well aware that many regarded slavery as an old-fashioned institution and that this was a powerful factor in the anti-slavery campaign. What he does not consider is the mechanisms in society which were giving power and conviction to these ideas. For example, in one of the earliest, most successful and most popular pieces of scientific propaganda for children, *The Newtonian System of the Universe Digested for Young Minds* by Tom Telescope, published in 1761 there is a sharp denunciation of the slave trade. Nor is this an isolated view; between 1760 and 1800, an increasing number of children's books, scientific as well as religious, used in middle-class homes, echoed the same theme. After all, Tom Telescope's book sold over 30,000 copies in England and it was as popular in the north-eastern states of America as it was in Britain. The way children were taught to hate slavery, and this partly precedes the emergence of the abolitionist movement, is an area which badly needs investigation by those historians of slavery concerned with its abolition.

Indeed, I wish that Davis had ranged more widely than he does over the changing world of the late eighteenth and early nineteenth centuries when quite fundamental shifts occurred in the attitude of the ruling classes towards human and social relationships. Slavery cannot, I think, be abstracted from other social constraints made to make men work, if one is to understand why slavery had been for so long an acceptable human institution and why it has in historic terms, only recently been abolished.

Males have always been reluctant workers. In many ways the Rape of the Sabine Women symbolises man's first slave raids, raids for women for work as well as enjoyment and the breeding of more men. The deadly toil of food-gathering, back-breaking garden cultures, were women's tasks, and the more the better, for the use or abuse. The acceptance of slavery is easy to understand if one grasps the fact that slavery is inherent in the family.

In India, as in Papua, the age expectation of women is lower than males, although biologically this should not be so – their work kills them early. Only forms of bondage and the need to survive kept men steadily at work, at tasks he would never choose for himself and as soon as there is need for mass labour – in silver mines or salt mines – there has to be organised plantation-type slavery to get the work done as in antiquity in Greece or Spain, or in southern Iraq in early Islamic times. Once established, of course, other aspects of human nature exploit the potentiality of slavery – it is often easier to buy sexual pleasures than earn them; that has always been a powerful factor in chattel slavery or concubinage: again sometimes the conditions of slavery and the conditions of the so-called free labour are uncomfortably close – domestic servants, like household apprentices, were more comparable to those of chattel slaves than we care to admit. Women and children at all times tend to be in the condition of slavery.

Except for nomadic societies mankind has usually been short of labour or short of people willing to undertake life-destroying, repetitive toil. And although the direct influence of rapid population growth on the decline of slavery is almost impossible to demonstrate, surely it can be no coincidence that they occurred at the same time. The Tudor government in England was quite willing to reintroduce slavery into England and passed an Act of Parliament making enforced slavery legal but it failed, because there was an inexhaustible well of paupers to draw upon, cheaper far than slaves, and much easier to control. Perhaps it is not coincidence that the fastest growing society in Europe in the late eighteenth century was to launch the anti-slavery movement.

Surely related to this also was the rapidly changing attitude to labour first in Great Britain, then elsewhere. Almost everyone prior to the second half of the eighteenth century believed that the poor had to be compelled to work, like slaves. But throughout the second half of the eighteenth century there was a growing belief amongst industrialists that men and women could be entitled to work and work hard by rewards as well as penalties; an attitude that chimed with the concepts of modernity and which helped to make slavery seem outmoded as well as immoral. And if it is remembered that middle-class education at that time was based from earliest childhood on a similar attitude of rewards and punishments, how much easier for such an attitude towards poverty to become acceptable. Indeed, is it too far-fetched to link the new attitude to children (after all for most of human history the slaves of parents; in most societies children could be sold, discarded or even murdered in times of famine with impunity), and the less marked but discernible new attitude to women, with the changing attitude to slavery? Industrialisation provided a much more subtle and basically more humane way of getting the world's work done. The sense of moral regeneration in those who took up the cause of anti-slavery was undoubtedly a powerful, very powerful, factor in the achievement of abolition, and Davis is right to make it a central factor in his book. He is absolutely right to stress the contradiction of beliefs in many a liberal mind or attitude. Although his space was limited, I for one would have liked to have seen him cutting brilliant figures on the thin ice of more general speculation about the change in the social attitudes which led to the abolition movement. New ideas certainly require definition and dedicated leadership if they are to triumph but they also need to be nurtured by a social compost of considerable complexity.

(v) American Slavery, American Freedom

One of the great conundrums of American history is how could Jefferson write the Declaration of Independence, with its insistence on the inalienable right of all men to liberty, to equality, and to the pursuit of happiness, whilst he was depriving two hundred slaves on his own estates of precisely those rights? Nor was Jefferson alone. George Washington – at least in his rhetoric – was equally opaque. He said that he was prepared to see America drenched with blood, rather than be inhabited by slaves. By that, of course, he meant that the somewhat mild yoke of George III and his officials was worth a civil war, not, of course, that he should die in the last ditch to free the blacks. These, like the rest of the Southern supporters of the Revolution, he kept firmly in bondage. Slavery was worse than death for a white man, even when most loosely interpreted, yet it was to be a permanent condition for the blacks. How could those men be so hypocritical? Naturally there were men of the time who saw the contradiction, who hated it, and who were tempted to break away from the South because of it.

Yet, in spite of this glaring contradiction, it would be absurd to accuse Washington, Jefferson, Madison, and the rest of the Virginians who fought for independence and subscribed to the Declaration, of self-conscious hypocrisy. They believed passionately and sincerely in the rights of men, but equally they could not conceive of a Virginia without slavery. Why was this so? Why did freedom and slavery go hand in hand?

This is the problem which Edmund Morgan has set himself to solve. As he rightly points out, it lies at the very heart of America's experience, from the first tentative settlements to the present day. He believes, rightly, that Virginia is the crux of the problem, and, good historian that he is, he also knows that social attitudes have long roots in time. Hence he starts his investigation at Roanoke, and then moves steadily forward to the Founding Fathers. It is a wonderful book, learned, perceptive, convincing; the chapters on the seventeenth century are stronger than those on the eighteenth, and the weakest of all is the last - not so much in its argument as in the detailed working out of it. It requires, as we shall see, greater substantiation. Nevertheless, it is the greatest contribution to the history of slavery of the 1970s. One sincerely hopes that it will receive greater attention than *Time on the Cross*; historians ought to be sufficiently well trained to beware of books which fly in the face of human reality, no matter how festooned with arithmetic. Every page of Morgan's book speaks of a sensitive understanding of human nature, as well as a scrupulous attention to scholarly exactitude.

Six years ago (in the review, entitled 'Slavery, Race and the Poor', see pp. 133–41), I stressed that attitudes to slavery could only be understood in the context of poverty and of the exploitation of labour, pointing out that the Elizabethan poor, flogged, branded, forced to work, were the source from which the American attitudes to slaves were derived, not racism; that racism was an added degradation and a continuing excuse for slavery; it was an ingredient, not a cause. And I regretted that no American historian of slavery had studied the institution in the context of labour exploitation and poverty. That is no longer true, for one of the themes of Morgan's book is the way the exploitation of labour changed in Virginia, the causes of that change, and the social effects of it. The white-bonded servant gave way to the black slave with remarkable consequences for Virginia and America. Let us look at Morgan's argument more closely.

Firstly, he argues that the founders of Virginia, and particularly the promoters of the Company in London and their propagandists, such as Hakluyt, were ambivalent towards natives. He makes much of Francis Drake's relations with the Cimarrons, and Hariot's sympathetic account of the Indians at Roanoke. The intention of these early chapters, which seem somewhat remote from his major theme, is to portray the first English in America to be freer from the racism that Winthrop Jordan argued infected the Elizabethans. And, perhaps, Morgan errs a little too much the other way. Drake was using the Cimarrons in exactly the same way that Cortez had used exploited Indian tribes to topple the Aztecs; to his allies Cortez was all kindness and courtesy; after all, he took an Indian mistress, too; not that that prevented him from torturing, killing or enslaving the Indians, once they were subject to him. Although one can argue for the most part with Morgan, that there was a strong religious motive that masqueraded as racism, it should also be remembered that to all Europeans heathens were coloured. However, the role of racism is not an essential part of the argument, and I feel that Morgan could have compressed the early history of Virginia with great advantage into one chapter. The colony only became viable when John Rolfe planted West Indian tobacco seeds, and the first cargo went off to England in 1617; only then did the colony need a large supply of labour. Up to that time incentives had been few.

Tobacco created a gold rush society in Virginia, rather than a settled community looking towards a future of steady growth. Men wanted to get rich as fast as possible, and often their dreams were of becoming a country-gentleman back in England. They did not build substantial houses, for they did not believe in permanence. They went bull-headed for tobacco and profit – food supplies came a very poor second – the Indians, if need be, could always be plundered for corn. And they imported servants – bonded servants; their property for a term of years. These were overwhelmingly male, young, often very young, and their servitude was far more arduous than a servant's life in England, bad as that might be. They lived in hovels; they had a poor diet; and they were subject to ferocious discipline. They often died before they completed their years of servitude; if they ran away or transgressed, not only could they be mercilessly flogged, but also they could have their servitude increased. Nevertheless, if they lived, they finally got their own land, their own small chance to grow tobacco, and may be to struggle up the ladder of profit. Amongst them, probably from the earliest times, there were some slaves, a number of Indians, a few blacks. And Morgan makes the telling point that there was some comradeship between the slaves and the bonded servants; they escaped together; lived together in the woods killing their master's hogs; there is evidence of mixed marriages, of blacks and whites fornicating, evidence, indeed, that poverty bound them together and racism did not yet divide them. Also their masters had not yet defined their own attitudes to race – slaves were too few to make it necessary for them to do so. Their main problem was the bonded servants, and how to control them. As the century progressed, they did all they could to extend the years of servitude which became the usual punishment for crimes great and trivial; by buying up land they forced many freed men to a life-time's dependence as hired hands. But as the great mortality of the early decades passed, more and more bonded servants lived to their freedom, a disgruntled proletariat began to develop in Virginia, one desperate enough to threaten the oligarchy in Bacon's rebellion of 1676. And so the institutional change in the exploitation of labour took place – not deliberately – social changes rarely result from deliberation. More and more slaves were imported; they were more expensive than bonded servants, but they never secured freedom, and, better still, they bred slaves. As the slave population grew, racism naturally followed; so too, did the spectre of slave rebellion. Racism and fear tied the small men to the greater. The class divisions between whites closed; as they did the prospect of an unruly, dangerous, radically-minded white mob which haunted Europe and strengthened its need for hierarchy vanished in Virginia. Tension eased, the animosity of the whites could be directed against royal officials and the grievous burden of royal taxation. Oppression no longer existed within the white Virginian community, only without by a Britain that revelled in aristocratic social inequality. Hence the fight for equality and freedom became *external* to Virginia; such words had no relevance within the white community of Virginia, where freedom and equality always reigned. Slavery had placed the workforce firmly and totally under control; unlike the workforce of England or Europe, it could not mob, it could not riot, it could not hold London to ransom, as it had London at the time of the Gordon Riots. Also, the poor were deprived of their natural leaders – the skilled artisans – by racism, by the colour of the poor. Again, once plantation slavery was established, the investment in labour became larger and immovable, so the big planters ceased to be Englishmen in Virginia, but Virginians, and the flimsy wood houses gave way to the brick mansions of an established gentry. Free from social and political tension, rooted now in their own land, free as few societies have been from unrest and class hatred, the patriarchs of Virginia could, thanks to slavery, become the American freedom-fighters. This, in essence, is Morgan's very subtle thesis; naturally it is argued in greater detail with a wealth of factual support.

The most brilliant part of the book, I think, is the description of how slavery grew and servitude decayed in Virginia, not through any political decision, but because of the pressure of social and economic necessities on the ruling class.

Only minor criticisms can, I think, be levelled at the chapters on the seventeenth century. The beginning is too long, but that is a matter of structure, not content. In his desire to demonstrate that racism is not the major cause of slavery, Morgan sometimes gives a religious interpretation to evidence which, to others would seem to be howling with racist overtones. But, in essence, he is right. There is no social need for racism until there is a vast army of black slaves. One point, I think, he misses in these chapters. Except for Bacon's rebellion, brief and fatuous as that was, the bonded servant behaved with a docility which his English counterpart never displayed. Morgan thinks the English poor were passive (p. 326). Quite wrong; they were continuously rebellious, very violent in food riots, enclosure riots, turnpike riots; they often threatened arson and mayhem, and committed them. Surely the reason for the passivity of Virginian bonded servants in the seventeenth century was their youth; the median age in Norfolk County between 1662 and 1680, according to Morgan, was between fifteen and sixteen; with slower maturity of the seventeenth century, these were scarcely more than children, and seventeenth-century children were used to harsh discipline and frequent punishment. And in the earlier decades, when male mortality was so high, many, if not most, would have perished as young adolescents. Probably the freed men became more rebellious not only because they felt frustrated by lack of land, but also because they were an increasingly large group of mature men. One would like to know far more about the age-structure of immigrants, both male and female.

Morgan does what he can with the scant evidence. One can only hope that lists of registers will still turn up. If the average age of servant and landless worker steadily increased, and the workforce depended less on children and adolescents, who were so easy to discipline, this, too, would be an added incentive to slavery.

However, the major difficulty arises at the point where slavery established, freedom begins to wave her flag. As if uneasy himself, Morgan almost rushes his book to a close. He has spent long and fascinating chapters on Roanoke, and on early Jamestown, but the central core of his thesis is covered in three chapters – one has to deal with the role of racism in creating a gulf between the slaves and white poor; another covers the intricate argument of the oligarchy's shift towards populism, and the last explains its addiction to freedom. All these chapters are fascinating, but the last the weakest. There is not enough here on the difference of ideas; one would wish to know more and in exact detail about the education of the Virginian élite; how they acquired their attitudes to slavery as well as freedom; not merely Jefferson, but the average planter. And there is a far more haunting doubt in my mind about this chapter. The Virginian planters were not the only society to solve the problem of the unruly poor by adopting wholesale slavery. Yet did other societies become, in similar circumstances, addicted to freedom – Jamaica, Barbados, and the rest? And the planters of Martinique were not notable for their support of the declaration of the Rights of Man. If Virginia is unique, then why? To me Morgan's final argument is remarkable, suggestive and may be true, yet with the evidence which he presents it is far from completely proven.

I would suggest that some of the attitudes to freedom, to liberty and to equality derive from aspects of British society in the seventeenth century. This had never been so deferential as some British historians would maintain. Also, its democratic experience was wider; its belief in the small freeholder as the purest form of political man was deeper than is commonly realised. These strands of belief or social attitudes, call them what you will, were woven into the fabric of colonial society before Virginia was committed wholeheartedly to slavery. Morgan has some admirable and perceptive pages on Trenchard and Gordon, on Burgh, and on Fletcher of Saltoun, but one would wish to know more of what sermons were preached or read, what pamphlets from England or New England or Philadelphia were circulating in the early decades of the eighteenth century. Only then will we be able to tell how far attitudes to freedom, which were a commonplace part of the general structure of opposition to English oligarchy and corruption, had acquired special strength in Virginia because of the factors so brilliantly analysed by Morgan. Or we may find that attitudes to freedom were as easy to inherit as attitudes to poverty. The further from London, the more powerful do we find these attitudes to freedom in England itself. And Virginia was very far, like Philadelphia or New England, where the same attitudes are to be found.

But the great merit of this profoundly important book is to put back slavery in the context of poverty and the exploitation of labour; here Morgan insists, rightly, on seeing this as a part, too, of Englishmen's experience and attitudes. The second half of the thesis, 'American Freedom', also needs to be seen in the context of British, particularly English, society.

(vi) A Nightmare World of Fantasy and Murder

This is a remarkable book, *The Loss of El Dorado* by V. S. Naipaul. It is history by a sensitive and highly intelligent novelist and as remote from professional history as one can imagine. And yet it often presents truths about society that are both more profound and more moving. Recently professional historians with a radical bent have directed their analytical gaze on the Caribbean and the nature of its slave societies. Here and there, as in Orlando Patterson's study of Jamaica, *The Sociology of Slavery*, bitter facts emerge to startle the heart and fill one with fury at the thought of the bestiality and brutality with which black slaves were treated. But in most studies of Caribbean slavery, it is the intellect that is engaged, alert to the comparative situations, aware of the sociological analysis: these preoccupations blot out the empathy needed to realise the searing pain that racked and tortured slaves caught in the evils of vindictive punishment inflicted by frightened whites. Pain and torture, however, are not the only aspects of this complex Caribbean world that tend to lose their force in professional studies; so does the fantasy and the illusion, the boredom, the hopelessness which influenced black as well as white in these colonial backwaters.

V. S. Naipaul is concerned with the island in which he grew up, Trinidad, 'the fag end of the world', which had bemused Spanish conquistador and Sir Walter Raleigh alike. To them it was the gateway to El Dorado, the mythical kingdom that lay inviolate in the mountains beyond the jungles of Guyana, a land where gold was more common than cloth. This dream of satiated greed drew Berrio, the conquistador, at the age of sixty into fantastic journeys through rivers, swamps and jungles of the Orinoco; his was a personal heroism that matched a Cortez or a Diaz. Sir Walter Raleigh dreamed a dream of a mixed Anglo-Inca empire in a paradisiacal world of exotic beauty – the two races mingling blood as well as culture and wealth. It ended like Berrio's in frustration and death. These grandiose illusions produced only a sordid reality – an unprofitable and unwieldy backward fragment of the Spanish empire where the Indians were steadily exterminated and replaced by African blacks. Trinidad drifted on, with little profit to colonists; the blacks, free and slave, living not intolerably with the whites and mulattos – a mild slavery, a mouldering colonisation, a forgotten island. Reform in Spain, revolution in France, war in the Caribbean changed all that.

And the bulk of Naipaul's book deals with Trinidad after 1797, when the British occupied it in order to use it as a springboard for the revolution in South America which was to open up to them vast opportunities for trade – another fantasy of greed that was dispelled by the wilder fantasies of the Venezuelan conspirators. For the British and the South Americans were as much a prey to illusion as any Raleigh or Berrio. But the British brought complexity to Trinidad, complexity and continued suffering for the blacks. French émigrés from Martinique and Guadeloupe brought in their negroes and their horrifying punishments for poisoning, suspected or real – negroes quartered, the living tied to the dead and burned. Flogging and torture became a daily round. The British governor, who believed in severe punishment, signed a warrant for the torture of a mulatto girl, Luisa Calderon.

This terrible cruelty and its complex consequences for slaveholder and slave, for reactionary and radical, for revolutionary and renegade, is the heart of Naipaul's book. For the British were neither simple nor coherent; they were complex and divided. The governor, Picton, a savage, brutal, direct man, hanged German mercenaries as well as blacks for the sake of authority and discipline. He loved money. He was infatuated with his mulatto mistress, who treated her blacks with a ferocity that he would have admired. He was hard-hearted, ruthless, greedy for money, yet, as Naipaul realises, even hungrier for fame, for warlike action. As the prospect of revolution in South America ebbed and flowed, Picton was caught in a strangling web of personal frustration that erupted in violence. He, too, possessed a dream that was only realised when he led his troops through the breach against the murderous fire at Badajoz and got himself killed at Waterloo.

Picton in Trinidad was but one face of Britain. His First Commissioner, Fullarton, wanted regularity, order, imperial rule; he was sympathetic to the abolition of slavery and preferred a Trinidad of smallholders, white, mulatto, if need be black, firmly ruled, but protected in basic human rights. The jail at Port of Spain horrified him, the barbarities inflicted on negro and mulatto enraged him. These things gave purpose and direction to the almost paranoic hatred of Picton which he conceived on first meeting him. Personal warfare between them flared up; the case of Luisa Calderon became their battleground.

In these troubled waters, the South American idealists, the handful of resident English radicals, and the few coloured revolutionaries were tossed like leaves in a gale. And, as Naipaul well realises, beneath this storm fresh and powerful economic currents were changing the nature of Trinidad society. And with intenser exploitation and harsher discipline came the slaves' revenge and the slave fantasies – the sudden poisonings, the play-acting at night, slaves transformed into kings and queens, with courts and generals and militia that could suddenly dissolve into the reality of the hangman's noose, the whip and the shackle when, on discovery, the whites' terror took over.

But what a story and what a writer! Not only are the personalities vivid, but also they are realised in all their complexity – their dreams made as moving as their brutalities are horrifying. Nothing is simple, nothing is easy in this world which Naipaul recreates, except his exposition. Narrative, description, sudden stabs of analysis are handled with enviable dexterity. From the point of view of professional history, this book could be faulted here and there, largely through what it omits, not so much for what it contains. At times, the documentary evidence almost submerges the novelist and occasionally there is a sense of anachronism. Nevertheless, professional historians should read it, ponder on its skills and techniques and ask themselves as candidly as they can whether or not the truth about men and societies in time is not more forcibly, more convincingly conveyed that in the limited and rigid techniques which now dominate the writing of history. One can only hope that *The Loss of El Dorado* will be widely read. It is a remarkable achievement – intelligent, humane, brilliantly written.

(vii) The Royal Navy and the Slave Trade

The most enlightened of the British people throughout the nineteenth century regarded their government's attempt to suppress the slave trade as one of the great moral crusades of their country. They were proud of their ships which kept a ceaseless patrol along the fever-ridden coasts of West Africa, coasts on which the sails might hang listless for days beneath the tropical sun: featureless coasts, full of creeks and sandbanks and mangrove swamps that the knowledgeable slavers exploited to the full. Boredom and sickness were interspersed with danger as the small, lightly-armed cutters crossed the bars and challenged a well-armed Spanish or Portuguese slaver or stormed the stockades where the slaves were held.

Parsons in their pulpits lauded the navy's efforts, missionary societies printed pamphlets that told of the horrors of the slave trade – the manacled necks, the brandings with hot irons, the whippings and the lashings, the fearful conditions on the slave ships, overcrowding, disease, bestial punishments. They harrowed their readers with tales of women and children thrown overboard in order that the slaver might evade capture, and left to drown or be eaten by the sharks which followed the slaving ships like gulls a fishing smack, ready for the titbits. They gloried in the retribution that the navy inflicted – the boats seized, the slaves freed, the vile traders left to their fate on the hostile African shore. They were puzzled by the reluctance of other nations to join them in their work, and hurt by the constant accusations of self-interest and hypocrisy.

As Americans, Spaniards and Frenchmen were quick to point out, most of the goods with which the slaves were bought were of British manufacture: a sizeable slice of Birmingham's and Manchester's trade. And Britain only wished to suppress the slave trade in order to exploit and colonise Africa for herself and to bring ruin on the slave-using countries. And what hypocrisy to weep over slaves, when English children, scarcely more than babies, were devoured by the horrible factory system about which very few, if any, anti-slavery societies raised their voices. Also the naval action was a farce, a cheap way for Britain to license its navy to commit piracy. The naval officers won prize money for capturing slave-ships and freeing slaves; and their effect on the trade, in the 1820s, little over 5 per cent, was ludicrously small for the effort. Indeed, the attempt to suppress this trade was an example of perfidious Albion at its worst.

And so the arguments have gone on ever since – a high-minded noble cause or hypocritical self-interest? Mr Ward sets out all the arguments carefully and critically in The Royal Navy and Slavery, but his heart is with the British sailors in the mire and misery and heat of the African coast. He is happier with yarns about the ships, with warpings, haulings on the wind, broadsides and heave-tos than the mysteries of social and political behaviour and its morality. He gives his approval to the British, he needles the French for their evasions, and bluntly condemns the American government's supine behaviour under the pressure from the Southern States that permitted slave trading to exist because it regarded the American flag as so sacrosanct that it would not permit any American ship to be searched except by American naval patrols, of which for most of the time between 1808 and 1860 there were only two. If Britain was hypocritical, at least, she was not alone.

Of course, just as no personal situations are free from self-interest, so no national ones ever are. The high-toned morality of the British certainly covered a considerable and wolfish appetite for commercial and economic expansion. They were out for profits, just as the slavers were. Maybe; but the difference is profound. The British intention, whatever the motive, was to stop the slave trade, to end the iniquitous and inhuman trade in men, women and children. In that there was nobility. In the constant effort to persuade other countries to join them, to put their naval patrols alongside their own was a germ of international cooperation in a humane cause – an event all too rare in human history. And this policy whose results, although small, were wholly good, was not sponsored by the most powerful economic interests of Britain – indeed, they detested it. To them it was grossly expensive, fatuously ineffective and sanctimoniously hypocritical. For the most sensitive part of the middle class it remained a crusade. They lacked full political power, but here at least they could make their voice heard and frighten the government into pursuing their policy.

Such situations are rare, but a similar one could develop in America, where there is a great, an almost unbearable longing, in the most intelligent and sensitive segments of the middle class for idealistic actions in government rather than devilish acts in the name of an ideal. The motives become pointless – better a slave freed out of moral arrogance and economic self-interest than babies and women shrivelled alive in the name of a Christian crusade. In the long history of Africa's torment, the anti-slavery patrols of the British navy were not its worst moment.

PART THREE

HOPE AND ANXIETY

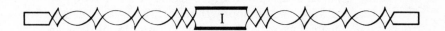

Introduction: At Large in America

I first met Senator Daniel P. Moynihan when he was a very young man working on his PhD at the London School of Economics. He had answered an advertisement put out by two young friends of mine for a third man to share their flat. The result was an astonishing ménage of vast ambition, intellectual stimulus and endless energy – a volcanic experience that was to enhance their abilities as well as their lives and give Moynihan admiration as well as affection for Britain – rare in a New York, Irish Catholic. His two flat-mates were quite extraordinary young men.

Frank Fenton had taken a brilliant first in Greats at Oxford, but could not be persuaded to stay there. He wanted the wider world and got it. He became an American citizen, and is now a lobbyist for the US Steel Confederation in Washington, having previously worked for US Steel in Pittsburgh, a post which sent him endlessly flying up and down and round about the globe. He possesses a superb memory, excellent dialectical skill and total fascination with himself. In conversation he could suppress his natural and ferocious egocentricity and give his life a kind of universality, embedded in descriptive anecdote and wit. A man of violent prejudice but one whose prejudices changed with chameleon rapidity so that he became a liberal by experience if not by intellectual commitment. Above all, he was a great enhancer of other people's lives as was his friend Dante Campailla, a young lawyer, his father Sicilian, his mother descended from a long line of rigidly Calvinist Dutch preachers – Dante was one of the most vivid personalities whom I have ever met. A brilliant cook, easily the most brilliant amateur cook I know, an excellent jazz pianist, a man with an irrepressible lust for life, and an incomparable writer of letters; at times a raconteur of genius who does not so much enhance life as inflate it, but behind the gusto lies a thick slice of Dutch character, remorseless industry, endless stamina, and capacity for extreme discretion that at times borders on the secretive – valuable qualities for a successful solicitor. Pat fitted into the Campailla–Fenton ménage like a nut into its shell. Indeed, I believe that it had a profound effect on his education and his approach to the world, strengthening his creativity and giving him extra dimensions in his political thinking. As a Roman Catholic he had a profound conviction in the importance of tradition and traditional institutions. Both Fenton and Campailla, whilst critical and, indeed, often satirical of Britain, were profoundly conservative, and an admirable antidote to the socialist predilections of the London School of Economics. Moynihan was wonderfully open in his approach to English life. He sailed in the tiniest and fastest boat on the Broads whose berth accommodated only half of him so he gave it up and slept on the cabin floor. He took the gales, blizzards and torrential rain in his stride. The quality of his personality was easy to appreciate, but the depth of his political skills, his capacity to sense emerging issues long before others, the range of his social and political interests, the shrewdness with which he developed his career, of course, I could not fully grasp until I saw him in his American context. That opportunity came in 1960, by which time Fenton was working with US Steel in Pittsburgh but, fortunately, he came frequently to New York and I renewed my acquaintance with Pat. He was, then, partly working for Averill Harriman and partly pursuing his academic career. Within a week or two of my arriving in America we had re-established our relationship. We went together to Gaige and Tollner and on to the Brooklyn Heights, ate in the Village and drank at the four ale Irish bars that Pat knew so well. He took me to places like the meat market in Lower West Side at which I consumed the most remarkable steak of my life, the size and shape of an American football. He taught me more and more about New York and we had some violent political arguments – one of which was of profound importance and taught me a very great deal. It was an argument that lasted the best part of a weekend and some of my attitudes to politics and society crumbled.

I was much taken by the high-rise apartments that were going up around Columbia University, over towards the East River at about the high nineties. I praised them. Pat's eyebrows elevated sharply. His eyebrows could ask a question more politely than any one's on earth. His language became ornate and fanciful – he praised the Lower East Side, the humanity of its slums, their warm neighbourliness, their sense of community, their capacities for small personal charity and larger self-help. He castigated the high-rises as isolation towers, barrack ghettos, breeding places of aggression, violence, crime and hopelessness – especially hopelessness – often in the old slums, blocks of modest prosperity, and even a little block of respectable success, might be intermingled giving hope to the young who longed for a better life and were willing to work for it. Whereas for a young man or woman clambering up airless, graffiti-stained stairs, or trapped in a urine-stinking elevator, there was no sense of hope, and hope was what America was all about. It began in hope, grew in hope and could only sustain itself by hope.

Pat put forward these views in long, seemingly rambling but always ornate, sentences. Often like the Niger in its delta, the argument appeared to be about to be lost. It never was. Pat's was a curious technique – more a politician's than an academic's, for he was conveying a sense of life, painting a picture, as well as conducting an argument. I wriggled and twisted the best I could, talking a little stupidly about hygiene and the economy of space as well as common recreational facilities to which he listened with polite and disbelieving attention. I grew slightly angry which wisely Pat viewed with satisfaction. Anger in argument rarely spells victory.

Pat bridged two worlds of feeling – one academic and intellectual, the other the intuitive grasp that the politician has of the hopes and fears of classes and groups of men. Later, he broadened my world politically in many ways – through his books, particularly *The Melting Pot* written with Nathan Glazer and his dramatic studies of the black family – that caused fury amongst the politicians of the left but was extraordinarily prescient. I also learned a great deal about American politics from his wife Elizabeth, one of the astutest political tacticians I have ever met on either side of the Atlantic.

The Moynihans ran a remarkable household: lunch might arrive at five o'clock; breakfast was adventurous and best coped with alone although Pat could boil a good egg. When the meals came they were delicious for Liz cooked not only with skill but with *élan*. Sleeping off a bit of the jet lag one might come downstairs to a party of extraordinary distinction – Mr Justice Goldberg, the Kristols, the Bells and Glazers, the Schlesingers, the Trillings, Sandy Van Ocker, Abe Ribicoff and dozens more, a kaleidoscope of intellectual life of America whether the Moynihans were in Washington, New York or Boston. I got to know the American political world in all its intricacy in a way which would have been impossible without Pat and Liz. My debt to them is profound, and I am sure in a way, too, that Pat has not fully realised. He converted me to hope; hope as a touchstone for the judgement of a society – not power, not grandeur, nor welfare, but the provision of hope for ordinary men and women and their children. So this section begins with the last important speech I was to make in America – the Commencement Address at Washington University, at St Louis. The morning was blue and hot, even at 8.30 am when we assembled. I was in a wheelchair as I had been badly smitten with pneumonia when giving the Churchill lecture at Westminster College, Fulton two weeks previously. It was the kindness of my host, and the excellence of the medical care at St Louis, that enabled me to get out of my chair and address the 7000 gathered on that handsome campus. It was the message I had got from Pat; the lesson I had learned from over twenty years of visiting America: it had become my credo. I spoke from the heart as well as the head.

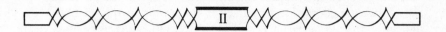
The Commencement Address at Washington University, St Louis, 1983: A Time for Hope?

Mr Chancellor, Fellow Graduands, Ladies and Gentlemen. My first duty, Sir, is to thank you, your Trustees, and the Faculties of this great University for the singular honour that you are to bestow on me and my fellow honorary graduands today. One always, I think, feels a little abashed when receiving an honorary degree for one hears the complimentary phrases about one's work spoken aloud; phrases which one would hesitate to speak in the privacy of one's own mind even in a moment of egoistical delirium. Abashed we may be, but we shall certainly leave this ceremony fully determined to strive to be more creative than we have been and to produce further work that is worthy of Washington University's highest honours. By so doing we can truly express our gratitude.

'A Time of Hope?' There are, I believe, two aspects of hope which greatly enrich human life – hope about ourselves; and social hope, hope about the world that we live in. During the last hundred years both in Europe and in the United States, hope in both these contexts has had a severe battering.

The hope for oneself and the hope for one's world, of course, are very much involved with each other but, today, I want to treat them separately because when one is young, hope, thank God, comes easily to most of us. The years at a university are pregnant with hope – about one's own happiness, about one's career, about one's future in life. Of course, I know there are clouds, disappointments of every kind, even tragedies, but there is infinite resilience in young people, a wonderful and moving sense of the possibilities of life and happiness. And it is my belief that one of the most important aspects of education and university life is to cherish that sense of hope.

One of the great destroyers of personal hope over the last century has been the spread of half-baked Freudianism on the one hand and on the other of genetic determinism, equally misunderstood. The belief that, in a sense, we are doomed to be ourselves has been known to mankind for millennia. I could never have walked six feet tall, short of being cloned before birth. I was doomed in the womb to be short, fat, pink, brown-eyed and possibly above average intelligence. We will grant all of that. We were bequeathed our bodies and basic intelligence. And the same half-truth of determinism can be said of our characters – depressive, manic, sensual, frigid, aggressive, pacific, all the strange varieties of men and women; we are, of course, genetically related, yes, to parents, and their parents and so back into the great pot of genetic soup. And I would grant that our characters are interlocked too with our bodies and its complex chemistry. However, that basic determinism still leaves a huge area for will, for choice, for decision as well as the most important force of all upon our lives – our future to which I shall turn in a moment.

It is all too easy for our educators and our gurus to try to force on us the belief that we have one identity which we must discover in youth and live with to old age. I believe most young men and women are closer to Walter Mitty or Woody Allen; that within each of us lives an assortment of strange and not very peaceful characters. True, there are some men and women with very tight egos who know, it seems from childhood, who they want to be and how to maximise every drop of talent to get there. I used to envy them. I no longer do. I prefer the richness of conflict; the battle of choice which our differing selves bring to us. Indeed, I think it is because most men and women have a variety of selves that for them nurture – in the family, in the school and above all in the university – is so important. A primary duty is to teach crafts and skills, and these should never be narrowly conceived. The ever-increasing specialisation of our academic disciplines presents great problems for general education but they should be surmounted. The best universities, I believe, are those which present opportunities for students to taste other disciplines, to get excited about other forms of knowledge than they are majoring in, and there should always be moderately easy means to change disciplines – to desert history and take up medicine, to cease to be an engineer and become a classic. One of the most fascinating of my colleagues began as a scholar in classics, took part of his degree in English, the rest in philosophy: he then turned away from graduate studies to begin again as a junior medical student, and finished up as Professor of Anatomy. In old age he has begun the serious study of Egyptology. The best-read historian I have ever known, and he read history in eight languages, was a professor of Pure Mathematics. Intellectual appetite, like all our appetites, is most wolfish in the late teens and early twenties; those are the years of ebullience, of delight, of experiment, of creativity and of hope. A university must feed that hope so that it avoids frustration. And we should always remember that formal education is only a fraction of our university experience. We make friendships here which last for life; we can quarrel, grow affectionate, argue in agreement or bitterness without thought of consequence which we can so very rarely do, once we graduate. Variety in thought and experience helps to keep hope alive – so long as there are choices, new worlds to explore, one stays a hopeful person.

Hope is closely allied with enjoyment – intellectual, social, physical. Of course that hope will be diminished by age, by experience, by the necessity to choose but it need never quite disappear; but it must be nurtured. And, I think, it is particularly necessary for the well-being of our societies on both sides of the Atlantic that students should leave their universities with hope for themselves and their countries; they should be encouraged to learn how to bounce back after setbacks, after tragedies, minor or major. It is essential for the world's well-being that the intellectual élite remains hopeful, joyful about life and man's prospects.

Of course, unless one is a very competitive personality like my Professor of Anatomy, it is difficult to preserve one's hope in a society which is without it. And that is the reason for my question mark in the title of this address. Is it possible for the most hopeful young men and women to go on hoping in this our world? The horrors are there – the prospect of a nuclear holocaust, the growing famine in Africa, the murderous governments that litter the world like a rash; the monstrous citadels of repression; the sheer burden of people: the sheer limits of resources. It looks dark. But less dark, I suspect, to the historian who recalls that the Black Death killed a third to a half of the world's population and then went on decimating it from time to time for over two hundred years; or knows that the average age of man when this great country was first colonised by the Pilgrims and the Virginians was 29; that most children born never survived beyond the age of five. For thousands of years, the life of mankind was short, disease-ridden, illiterate and this was true of the West as well as the East, for those who lived in cities, or those who did not. We accept so easily what we have achieved; indeed accept it so easily and think that it is so pitifully materialistic that we are taught to scorn it.

One of the great dangers of our present time I think has been the rejection of so much of man's achievement, an achievement which perceptive men longed for in the eighteenth and nineteenth centuries. Of course they longed for more. They thought torture would cease; that justice would prevail, that men would grow in moral strength. Perhaps in the light of what has happened in my lifetime they seem a little naïve

– two World Wars – my first memories are of men in khaki – puzzling men to me as a child because they lacked arms and legs and some could not see when they came from hospital to my home for tea. And between these wars Fascism, Depression, the Nazis, a Second World War that gave hopes again of a new world but only to find ourselves deluded with a harsh, hostile world; with two great monster powers who can eradicate the human race at any moment. Elsewhere civil wars or worse, famine, discord and corruption.

Such facts may make the hopes of the men of the Enlightenment look hollow and self-deceiving so that it becomes all too easy to mock them. And yet I would maintain that the world is a far better place now than it was even fifty or forty years ago and with so much potential that the world should be surging into hope, hope for a future, for yourselves and your children greater than my generation ever knew.

The achievements of the West, and particularly of America, are too readily taken for granted or ignored. And, alas, they are taught less and less frequently in our schools and universities. I am aware that New York is not America, any more than Venice is Italy, but sometimes in its love for the new and the futuristic it underlines a trend which may be weak elsewhere but one which may strengthen. At present, American history in New York is under great threat, many years ago it was subsumed into social studies, now it looks as if the teaching time devoted to it is going to be radically reduced from an hour a week per teaching year to an hour for one semester only but, worse, the history to be taught will be themes – three only, politics, the role of immigrant groups and foreign policy. World history and the history of Western civilisation are to be limited and again reduced to themes. No attempt is to be made to keep to chronology. Human rights in the Soviet Union is likely to replace study of the Renaissance or Reformation or even of Marxism itself for the innovators want the themes to be contemporary.

The most important feature of historical study in its elementary stages is to bond the student to his society, to make him aware of its tradition, its constitution, its achievements in science, technology and the arts. Not to be unaware of failures but also to savour its achievements and to discern its goals. To give the student pride as well as to engender wisdom.

And there is so much for America to be proud about – never have so many people lived so long, so well or – and this is just as important as long life and comfort – in freedom. Freedom to express themselves in every way. It is all too easy to take our lifestyles for granted – for Western Europe and America have a basic common culture, a common desire to make democracy and the freedom of human thought work. Both the democracy and the freedom of thought have immeasurably enriched mankind. It is easy to despise the motor car, the refrigerator, the air conditioner, the processed foods and the supermarket when you have them. Most of the world still long for these simple comforts invented by us – the Western world. And the industrial revolution, begun in my country in the eighteenth century, and brought to increasing fruition here, has not finished: indeed we stand on the threshold of a new and exciting revolution. The command of knowledge during the next century is going to be of revolutionary proportions and will change all our lives. This should be the basis for your social hope. Knowledge, the capacity to acquire it, to order it and to transmit it in freedom is the basis of man's achievement.

And a time for hope does not mean unawareness of dangers (knowledge helps to spell that out too), or the possibility of tragedy or even failure. Hope does not mean blinkered optimism. Mankind is, as it were, struggling up the north face of Everest; it may meet disaster, it may have to turn back to search for another route, but it will never succeed without hope fortified by determination. And the leadership which is at present America's must have faith in its capacities: in its abilities to respond to challenge. It is time to get your recent failures and tragedies in proportion; every country has suffered rebuffs as you did in Vietnam, has committed horrors, has denied some of its citizens rights which should belong to all, but most societies have refused to recognise their shortcomings or take action. You do. You began as a revolutionary society, and in many ways – in most ways – have remained one.

And so for those graduating today it is not a dark time; you have every right to be hopeful and confident.

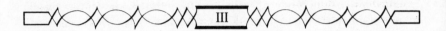

III

President Kennedy and After

Indeed, my early days in America were full of hope for John Kennedy had been elected to the White House, true by the narrowest of margins and with the help of Mayor Daley of Chicago, an old-style political boss who always delivered a healthy Democratic majority from Cook County. Kennedy's success was a curious mixture of machine politics combined with charismatic leadership. Hoping for victory this young Irish-Catholic American had already surrounded himself with a bevy of academically trained intellectuals, largely from Harvard, who complacently assumed that politics were no more difficult than the economics, sociology and history which they taught. Their fate proved somewhat short of grandeur and their delusions of power quickly evaporated – Galbraith, the intellectual guru of the party's left, was shunted off to India as Ambassador; Arthur Schlesinger to the West Wing to write speeches, on occasions, for the President. Others of stronger political experience did better. Walt Rostow, in particular, becoming a shaper of policy rather than a commentator on it.

Pat Moynihan, far more political than academic, and quickly recognised as such, slipped into an important advisory job. He concerned himself with transport, and then used his imaginative flair to remodel Pennsylvania Avenue – at that time a run-down and seedy link between Capitol Hill and the White House. This helped to secure him a post in the Department of Health and Education. Although few academics exercised real power, they certainly were wonderfully useful in public relations, creating a sense of a new era. In the same way, Jackie Kennedy's redecoration of the White House helped to publicise the sense of a new, sophisticated presidency in which style, intellect and moral purpose would combine to lift America towards yet greater goals.

In spite of the bitter taste of the Bay of Pigs, the disturbing buffoonery and bombast of Khrushchev, and the more alarming success of Sputnik, the Cuban crisis and the unleashing of America's technological skills for the conquest of space kept the spirits high and hopes alive. But they were to be sternly tested. I was dining at Christ's with Staughton Steen, a mathematics don, when the college butler whispered in his ear and Steen looked startled. He hesitated for a time and then blurted out that the American President had been assassinated! The inane wife of the Professor of Geometry turned to me and said, 'Does it mean that nice Mr Nixon will take over?' That inanity increased my sense of utter desolation, a desolation over a public event that I had not known since the days of the war, as great as I felt on that bleak, blue morning in June 1940 on the top of Snowdon where I heard a crackling wireless announce the fall of Paris.

The desolation was quickly obliterated by action. Almost immediately I was called from the dinner by an urgent telephone call from New York. Parton and Thorndike had decided to produce with UPI an instant memorial to Kennedy that told the story in pictures and appropriate text of his last days, from the assassination to his burial. I was to liaise with UPI in London and if need be secure tributes for Kennedy from Britain and Europe. In exactly ten days, *Four Days* was on the market – a hardcover pamphlet restrained and moving both in pictures and in prose, covering the assassination and the public and private grief it aroused. The team at American Heritage had worked non-stop day and night not only going over UPI material but a plethora of other sources too. It still reads astonishingly well and the pictures still stir my emotions. Easily the first tribute in the field, it sold quickly over a million copies and went on selling for many months. It was a journalistic *tour de force* in the highest standards of first-class journalism. It was beautifully written and possessed the gravity which the occasion demanded.

Camelot was lost and as the years passed, particularly after the assassination of Robert Kennedy, it seemed little more than a dream without much substance. Kennedy had already created, perhaps, more problems than he realised – certainly in Vietnam – and probably raised too many expectations that could never have been gratified. At first Lyndon Johnson seemed ham-fisted, crude, almost oafish, but he was to prove the best President in domestic affairs that America had had since Roosevelt. In Johnson's administration Pat played an important and growing role. He was as unhappy as anyone about the appalling diffi-culties of Vietnam, for Pat was one of those rare American politicians who knew a great deal about Europe and Asia as well as Africa; he had a deep sense of the major historic forces at work in the world. Any perceptive Democratic President ought to try to entice him into the State Department. He never underestimated the nature of the military conflict in which America was involved in Vietnam. As it was, however, domestic affairs – civil rights, welfare, family structure, education – became the

fields that absorbed his attention. And he was willing to look at unfash-
ionable and disturbing facts, accept their truth and try both to create
feasible policies and to raise political awareness about them, even though
it led, alas, from time to time to criticism that bordered on personal
abuse which he took with a kind of *insouciance* that was, alas, only
skin-deep. Nevertheless it was Vietnam that in the end brought about
his resignation from the Administration which he did without fuss.

Every time I visited America in the 1960s and early 1970s when Pat
was in all the Administrations I made certain of spending a day or two
with him and Liz wheresoever they might be. I always learnt. Pat could
at times be too loquacious (his Irish ancestry?) but he was never dull
and his paradoxes, always provocative, made me think afresh about
numerous social problems. Long before most of us, he realised that rich
as America was and is, the expectations raised by social welfare were
beyond its capacity to meet them. It was not merely the sick, the old,
the homeless, the single parents and the unemployable who created the
burden: but the ever-growing number of people on welfare for whom
low wages were not a sufficient incentive to leave it for work. This
stimulated a black economy which doubled the government's losses –
welfare paid out, no taxes paid in. He was acutely aware too of its social
dangers – the poorest segments of the community were black which
made it dangerous for politicians to meddle with: any attack on social
welfare could be denounced as racist, as Pat was to discover very disas-
trously when he served in Nixon's Administration as his domestic
adviser.

My contacts with Pat and his circle of friends and advisers also
brought opportunities to express my own ideas, and the essays which
follow owe a great deal to my talks with him. He, of course, is in no
way responsible for the ideas I express. No doubt he would take sharp
exception to many of them.

Perhaps something, however, should be said about the essay which
follows, 'History and President Kennedy'. This was never published as
Kennedy's assassination occurred almost as soon as I had written it.
Although I have changed the tenses, the piece was written about a very
alive and active President, but it went into my drawer. I think that it is
worth printing now because it gives a sense of why people like myself
were so hopeful about Kennedy. The project began because Kennedy
had read my life of Sir Robert Walpole and let it be known to Arthur
Schlesinger and others that he had greatly enjoyed it. I came into contact
with Frederick Holborn, the son of the great German historian, who
acted as a kind of cultural secretary to Kennedy and he and Arthur
Schlesinger made my visit to the White House both easy and stimulating.

After the President's death I became acquainted with Mrs Kennedy.

Her beauty was almost a shock: and she possessed a capacity to seem utterly captivated by what one was saying – a splendid, life-enhancing experience. As her redecoration of the White House had shown, she possessed as excellent sense of style. But what did surprise me was the sharpness of her intelligence, and her range and knowledge and absorption in all forms of artistic expresssion including literature. Had she had eight years in the White House I have no doubt that she would have been regarded as one of the greatest First Ladies of all time and that artists would have been more common, for the first time, than racketeers in the White House. Her departure from the White House was as sad, almost as tragic, as her husband's.

(i) History and President Kennedy

President Kennedy was an historian. He was trained at Harvard in historical method; he studied research problems at the London School of Economics; with help he wrote two history books – *Whilst England Slept* and *Profiles in Courage*; even as President he found time to review a volume of the Adams papers for the *American Historical Review*. The moment he became President, he assembled a number of very able historians to take part in his Administration – Arthur Schlesinger Jr, John Galbraith, Walt Rostow, George McBundy and a score of less well-known men of high academic talent; indeed the Kennedy Administration was alive with historians. Did this weight of historical advice and his own insight into history enable the President to control the present? Was he more effective in directing America's course towards the future because he was aware of the dynamic rhythms of the recent past? It was to answer questions such as these that I visited Washington and the White House in 1963.

History possesses two faces – tradition and change; although it embodies the past, it always points to the future. Social, economic and political forces are restlessly at work, changing, modifying, at times even destroying the inheritance from former generations. And like an army of industrious ants, men will heap up the sandbags of tradition to stem the tidal flow; at a cost they may succeed; at times the flood sweeps them away: on rare occasions a great statesman, realising the force and necessity of change, curbs and directs the tide along channels of his own devising. In this conflict between change and tradition, there is usually a moral problem, often of great complexity, yet requiring to be dealt with in terms of such transcendental simplicity that a whole nation can respond, in spite of self-interest, to its deeper needs. In 1963, the great moral problem both within and without America was the liberty of men, their civil and human rights, their urgent desire for freedom. How far were the President and his historical advisers conscious that this grave moral problem was becoming each day a more irresistible historical force, that would secure, either peacefully or brutally, its own solution. In this history-soaked Administration what was uppermost? What seemed imperative? The preservation of tradition or the acceleration of change? Or was there, even, an unawareness of the problem?

The sheer beauty of the White House drove away preoccupation with graver historical problems and reminded me sharply that history is also nostalgic, evocation as well as analysis. The White House gleaming in the sunshine was a part of the poetry of Time, the symbol of America's heritage. And the nature of its traditions was underlined both by the restrained elegance of the House itself, provincial rather than metropolitan, and by its air of informality. As Arthur Schlesinger Jr took me towards the President's office, there were knots of people standing about chatting; we drifted into the state dining room, already laid with gold plate for the dinner for the King of Morocco; and so to the cabinet room brightened by Secretary Dillon's charming grandchildren, wandering through it: the little boy looked hard and long at the President's chair: there, at least, the future confronted the past! Pictures, furniture, decoration combined to form an emphatic visual statement of America's idea of itself. All the more sophisticated elements of America's decorative arts have been used to create a style, a sense of tradition, an emphasis on the continuing greatness of America and her people. Indeed the Kennedys have used the White House brilliantly and imaginatively to make it more than ever before the living symbol of America's past. This, of course, is very much in tune with one of the major trends of American life. The frontier has disappeared; and preservation is becoming a national mania, and so is the pursuit of culture. Everywhere Americans are turning more actively towards their own past; folk museums sprout like weeds across the prairies and even Omaha has its Historical Society. The crisis of the great assimilation of European immigrants is over; and now Lithuanian and Sicilian can speak of 'our past' and mean America's. And so the Kennedys' style, urban and sophisticated, responds to one aspect of America's historical development, and must add both to their popularity and power. Kennedy has used the White House as no other American President has done, and made his way of life there a real political asset. And for this he has exploited both tradition and nostalgia. Only an historical-minded man could have sensed intuitively that a political opportunity existed in the House itself. History as the common man understands it has been captured by the Democrats: Eisenhower and the Republicans never realised the existence of this golden asset – Eisenhower's only mark on the White House is the holes of his golf studs made in the parquet of the President's Office.

The President is, indeed, very historically-minded. He needs books like some men need drink. Even by his bath-tub he has a book rack. Apart from a passion for James Bond, the President's reading is history. He enjoys biography, and the history of action. Churchill's *Marlborough* (the one book he has read twice recently), Duff Cooper's *Talleyrand*, Philip Magnus's *Gladstone* and *Kitchener*, Moorhead's *White and Blue Nile*, Hugh Thomas's *Spanish Civil War*, Barbara Tuchman's *Guns of August*, along with Harold Nicolson's *Congress of Vienna*, Trevor-Roper's *Historical Essays* and George Dangerfields's *Decline of European Liberalism* are some of the books on un-American historical themes that he has recently read or re-read.

The President's reading tends to run along two historical themes only – the way men acquired, maintained and used political power, and secondly, the nature of political decision and action: and the absence should be noticed – little or nothing on the history of ideas or philosophy, no straight economic history, no historical analysis in depth: the preoccupation is largely with the narrative of history rather than with its structure.

Perhaps, however, more fascinating than his own reading, and far more interesting than his concern for his own history, are the seminars which he encourages and attends whenever he can. To realise the full implication of this innovation of the Kennedys (for Bobby is equally concerned in this), imagine R. A. Butler, Edward Heath, Christopher Soames and Ernest Marples, after a hard day's work in the office or in the Commons, rushing down to Admiralty House, after a quick snack, to listen to Professor Ayer on *Logic* or Sir Isaiah Berlin on *The Russian Novel*. But that is exactly what happens at Washington; both Ayer and Berlin recently addressed the Washington Seminar; more often than not, however, the subject is historical – recent topics have been the American Civil War: The Era of Reconstruction: Woodrow Wilson: The History of the Supreme Court. The President attends whenever he can, the Attorney-General is always there, so usually is Robert Macnamara, the Minister of Defence, who probably is currently the hardest-worked administrator in the world: Judge White of the Supreme Court rarely misses; and others are more sporadic: some, like Dean Rusk, never attend.

The White House, intellectually as well as physically, presents to the American people a conscious tradition and style. History, as tradition, seductive, urbane, secure and perhaps a little self-satisfied, is stamping its image on the intellectual and fashionable life of America. That, too, brings certain advantages. It breeds confidence, a sense of stability, and an awareness of the dignity of life that can bring great moral strength at moments of crisis. But these virtues are bought at great cost, as they were bought at great cost by England in the eighteenth century, a period which could fruitfully be the subject of several White House seminars.

Although the Kennedy Administration is deeply conscious of its own historical traditions, its attitude towards other nations is more cavalier, or at least more concerned with history as change rather than history as tradition. And it is no accident that S. W. Rostow, one of the most brilliant economic historians America has produced, should be at the heart of the operational planning of America's foreign affairs. As an historian, he sees the major problem of the modern world to be the destruction of traditional patterns of society by rapid modernisation and industrialisation. Such change creates turbulence, or as he himself said,

> We must expect over the foreseeable future an environment of turbulence as these nations – committed to modernise, but not yet sufficiently modernised to make growth their regular condition – undergo radical economic, social and political change. Such change inevitably meets with resistance and involves conflict both among men and within the minds of men, torn between the heritage of the past, the confusion of the present and hopes or fears for the future.

The historical present, for the world beyond America is, for the Administration, one of inescapable change, of ancient patterns destroyed, and an irresistible impulse towards a scientific and industrial society. This sense of revolution, combined with the profound conviction that such a revolution is best achieved by a free society, has shaped some of Kennedy's most moving rhetoric. Hence his willingness to accept the fact of social revolution in Africa, in the Middle East, anywhere so long as the forms of freedom have been maintained; probably even the loss of a country here and there (particularly if not strategically important) to communism would not trouble either him or his advisers over-much; simply because their reading of history has bred in them a rugged confidence that time is on their side; that man's innate desire for plural rather than monolithic societies is in the nature of the historic process; even deeper, perhaps, goes the belief that the pattern of living of advanced technological and scientific societies will be the American way of life. Even in Russia, they already discern movements in society that will lead to greater demands for individual freedom, personal judgement, and a relaxation of prejudice that can only strengthen the attitude that America supports. It is not my present purpose to argue the strength or weakness of this attitude to the historical process, but to report it. Certainly it has given added flexibility to American policy, endowed its foreign aid programme with real tactical insight, strengthened its position with

Africa, with Latin America and the Middle East. Blunders there have been, but the crass idiocy of Dulles has gone. Kennedy believes, and everyone I spoke to stressed this again and again, that he can ride the tide of history. And certainly as never before, an American Administration has made it absolutely clear as to what it understands the process of world history to be; and of the efforts that it is willing to make to direct the tide into less turbulent channels.

Yet once one turns from the influence of history and historians on the Kennedy Administration's vision of the world beyond America to its attitude to America and its people, the change is striking and profound. Obviously during the campaign, and in President Kennedy's early speeches the same consciousness of the need to foster the process of historical change was as great within America as without. The very phrase 'The New Frontier' implied a struggle to create, if not a new society, at least a better one, more conformable to the ideas to which, through its constitution, America is pledged. The current bitter quip in liberal circles in Boston, New York and Washington is that the New Frontier is lost in fog. American politics, many think, have become as boring as politics in the age of Pelham; the great themes – civil rights, education, health – have become engulfed in a great swamp of patronage and management, so that the only thing that finally matters is political arithmetic – the number of votes and the power they confer. One of the most startling experiences for an eighteenth-century English historian was to talk to Richard Donahue, one of the President's Praetorian Guard, who fought every inch of the campaign, and is now a special assistant at the White House. It was like talking to John Robinson who managed the elections of George III. Only the hard facts of political power counted and the hard facts of political power are votes and those that can deliver them. Naturally Donahue's respect for Mayor Daley, the Democratic boss of Chicago, was immense; his impatience with Stevensonian liberals was scarcely concealed. ('Who the hell else can they vote for, anyway?' he asked.) From long conversations with him and others it was clear that every political act had to be measured in terms both of political personalities (patronage) and of local government (the right to patronage). So, over the whole of America, come Republican, come Democrat, has been woven a web of political patronage and management. It is accepted; it is traditional. But in such a system great legislative acts can rarely take place; they disturb the delicacy of the machinery, upset the arithmetic. Here history as tradition, not history as change, dominates all thinking.

Murder, riot and arson are subjecting this pattern of political life to violent strain. But even the grave troubles in Birmingham, Alabama did not alter in any radical way Kennedy's political method. There, personal pressures were applied, intimate persuasion, backstairs bargaining were all regarded as preferable to a direct confrontation of the moral issue. Bankers, departmental store bosses, influential manufacturers were telephoned or visited by Bobby Kennedy, by Dillon and others, pressuring them to let in a token Negro and so ease the situation for the Administration. The President avoided, and still avoids, presenting the issues fully to the nation. Great statesmen must risk their parties, must gamble their political futures for the highest human good. Kennedy could risk the world for Cuba; over Birmingham he was scarcely willing to stake a Southern Democrat. The political bosses may be suspicious of Kennedy's concern for foreign affairs, but they are terrified of the civil rights issue which could play ducks and drakes with their political structures. And Kennedy listens more attentively to his bosses than to his historians. The needs of the next election obscure America's future.

The bosses do not mix history with real politics. For them history is merely record. How Dade County voted in 1956: who kept North Dakota firm at the Convention: the way Humphrey was smashed in West Virginia. And, of course, it is the historically sanctified pattern of the American constitution that gives strength and stability to these politics of management.

Indeed so inflexible has the American system become that, ironically, historical change is more likely to be accomplished now through the Supreme Court than by massive legislative action, for so many of the civil rights acts remained socially impotent and negligible until given judicial teeth by the Court. With the appointment of Justice Goldberg, a liberal of acute intelligence, great charm and strong principles, the balance in the Court is once again with the forces of progress. No President, no Congress, no Senate, could have strengthened the black radicals so quickly or so powerfully. And here again the analogy with eighteenth-century Britain can be drawn, such small advances that were made in civil rights in England were made, not through Parliament, but through the Courts. When the judicature has to do the work of the legislature, it is always a sign of political paralysis, for rapid social change is the last thing that a judicature wants.

History as tradition, indeed, has the internal policy of the Kennedy Administration in its grip. The American constitution was designed for a nation of planters, farmers and merchants in a few small seaboard communities. Pushed and pulled a little by events, nevertheless it remains in essence what it was, and the march to the New Frontier has got lost in the thickets of political traditions and barred by the spiny, rock barriers of a rigid and written constitution. Opportunities for radical reform, for rhetoric that could rally the nation lie thick about Kennedy:

yet he views them with caution and side-steps them, until trapped by events.

And here, the significance of the President's own historical reading and inclinations develops added point. His interest is caught by the story of men seeking, holding, losing, political power, by the narrative of political history or by tales of war which, again, are the tactics and strategy of success. He is not interested in the history of ideas, of structural analysis, or the history of political institutions. Politics is a game to win, a machine to maintain, a loyalty of men, not a movement of ideas, the pursuit of justice, or even a bold bid for the future. In those problems that do not directly touch on maintenance of his party's power, he will listen to the dynamic rhythms of history, seek their meaning and attempt to master them.

Within the American frontiers the tides are blocked; there is no confrontation with the past, no willingness to fight the battle for the future, if it means immediate political oblivion or a break in the democratic machine. In world affairs Kennedy looks every inch a statesman, in domestic matters a mere politician. Abroad, he looks clear-eyed to the future; at home he moves with the sure foot and lack of vision of the somnambulist.

(ii) The Private Grief of Public Figures

How much privacy have great men ever enjoyed? How far has it been possible to separate their public and private lives? Throughout recorded history and discernibly beyond there have been persons and families of distinction who have been known by name and fame and special status to all members of their communities. High priests, kings, Caesars, popes, emperors – all have belonged to the world in a very special sense. The kings of France dressed and undressed in public, were ceremonially fed before their court; they had an audience for their wedding night, and their wives laboured in childbirth in rooms crowded with nobility. Although it is true that the royal bed was railed off, the rest of the chamber would be thronged with courtiers, listening to the queen's groans, peering and peeping, joking and talking bawdily.

For royalty death was no easier than birth. The courtiers of Carlos II of Spain stood about as the doctors tried the warm entrails of a pigeon on his belly. His priests, putting more faith in San Isidro, brought his mummified remains to the bedside. Their prayers and the hushed gossip of the grandees were drowned by the chants of rival priests, who carried round the room the corpse of San Diego of Alcalá, sitting in its urn. It was not much better for Queen Caroline of England rolling in agony in her own putrefaction, whilst her husband, distracted with grief, upbraided her for looking like a dying cow. The grossly fat Prime Minister knelt by her side and could not get up. The Archbishop of Canterbury mumbled his prayers. The Queen, still in possession of her wits, sent for the Lord Chancellor to make absolutely certain that Frederick, Prince of Wales, would not inherit one iota of her possessions. As she said on this deathbed, she wished him in the bottommost pit of hell. And there in the corner was little Lord Hervey, rouged, powdered, flamboyantly epicene, taking it all down and doubtless inventing what he could not quite hear. He knew he was present at a moment of history, that posterity would be wide-eyed and open-mouthed for every gory detail of the Queen's death. To be royal was to live even the most intimate moments of one's life before the hostile, loving, or indifferent eyes of one's court.

And yet there was, in a sense, privacy. The court was an enclosed, narrow world. For the nation as a whole, the Queen died, the prince was born; not for them the detail, the sniggering, the gossip. Lord Hervey naturally did not dare to publish his memoirs. They stayed secret generation after generation, and when at last they were sent to Windsor – to Windsor, mark you, and not to the publisher – a prudent descendant tore out and destroyed a large section which dealt probably with the sexual antics of the Prince of Wales. And until very recently there have always been circles of privacy, zones of silence, that protected the famous and the great. Even as late as 1936, England's millions lived in ignorance of Edward VIII's relationship with Mrs Simpson, and the abdication crisis came like a thunderbolt from the blue.

Of course, privacy for princes became more difficult as mass means of communication developed. Although the Roman nobility and the cardinals might gossip about Pope Alexander VI, hinting at strange orgies and darker dabblings in incestuous sin, thousands of peasants, completely oblivious, thronged to kiss his foot in Holy Year. A few decades later the gulf between private life and public fame was more difficult to bridge, for the printing press and vitriolic pen of Peiro Aretino had popularised the lampoon. The private lives of the great were really threatened.

The absolutist kings of Europe, of course, kept a firm hand on the press and clapped courtiers too imprudent with their verses into jail or exiled them to their provincial estates. But England had a free press and the second half of the eighteenth century witnessed a remarkable and ribald outburst of satirical verse and coloured cartoons that left no aspect of royal life alone. George III's madness was a matter for newspaper gossip, so were his domestic habits; and his sons' riotous sexual lives were pilloried in the press. Moreover, when George IV attempted to divorce his wife, intimate details which would now be considered, in England at least, unfit for publication, were boldly printed.

Privacy for the royal family and many public figures, oddly enough, became better protected in the late nineteenth century. To some extent this also holds for the twentieth century. No British politician has been ruined as Parnell was, although English politicians have been no less adulterous than their Victorian counterparts. And the same is true of American Presidents. It is doubtful if Woodrow Wilson's physical incapacities and utter dependence on his wife could have been so well concealed in the early nineteenth century. One odd aspect of the growth of illustrated newspapers was to check curiosity. Seeing someone almost every week opening bazaars, signing documents, greeting potentates may satiate rather than quicken curiosity. And possibly a royal image was created that no one wished to see sullied. More important, perhaps, was the sharp realisation by the Bristish monarchy that those who lived by the press could be ruined by it. They knew its dangers. Certainly, in spite of a mass press and ubiquitous photographs, the British Royal Family have been extraordinarily skilful in concealing anything they wished to if not from all, at least from millions of their people. And the physical state of Churchill after his first stroke in Washington during World War II was carefully hidden from many of his colleagues, let alone the public.

There are strong arguments for maintaining a degree of privacy no matter how public a person may be. An open debate on Churchill's health could have done no good, only harm. His fitness for the conduct of affairs had to be judged by his doctors and colleagues – a desperately difficult decision, as Lord Moran has shown. And again it is reasonable that, within limits, the sexual predilections of men of power should be surrounded by zones of silence. Lloyd George was a warmly lecherous man, with the keen eye, quick response and tactical skill of a master politician. But his escapades with housemaids were irrelevant to his position and quality as a statesman. On the other hand, they could have developed into situations in which this aspect of Lloyd George's character could have been a matter for public concern and one in which exposure was essential. He lived on thin ice, trusted his friends, exploited his wife, and got away with it. Neither he nor the public were harmed.

The privacy of public persons must always be a hazardous frontier. Curiosity is not enough. We all feel it. We are all delighted to get 'in' stories and repeat them with glee. And, of course, every eminent person must expect to live with public curiosity as in a constant guerrilla war: kings and princes and their families did in the past; Presidents and their wives must expect it in the present. Death, however, makes a vast difference.

Once dead, a public man must become public property, to be assessed by biographers and historians. A great deal of indignation greeted Lord Moran's revelations of Churchill's physical condition. Could he not have waited? Could he not have spared Churchill's family the pain? This seems to me absurd. Sir Winston's health was an important factor in the history of the decade after the war. And for such a family to react oversensitively reflects a failure to realise that public families are more than private families.

They become, whether they wish it or not, a part of history. Of course, there might have been situations in Churchill's life that were best kept secret until his immediate family were dead – situations, say, of no relevance to his public role, but of interest in a purely biographical sense. Nevertheless, the decision to maintain silence must always be difficult, for curiosity about those rare creatures dwelling on the Himalayas of power can only be regarded as legitimate. And probably a catch-as-catch-can attitude is the one that ought to prevail.

Thus when Jacqueline Kennedy asked William Manchester to write *The Death of a President*, the risk was hers – in choice of author, in the exactitude and stringency of conditions; indeed, in what she told the author. Are there, however, stronger arguments for the invasion of the public, or failure of those in the public eye to protect themselves? One that I have heard put forward is that the Kennedys exploited the press to achieve their eminence: hence they can scarcely complain if they become the used instead of the user. Not very convincing.

A better argument is that President Kennedy was a figure of history; therefore every fact about him is worthy of record. In a sense this is true, but its application is fraught with danger, for facts too can lie, and even history can mislead unless it is very carefully and sensitively handled. How his children, for example, reacted to his death is utterly irrelevant to any historical question that is ever likely to be asked. Childish utterances could be true, yet in the hands of an accomplished writer be easily made to mislead. Actions or words, the result of sudden intolerable grief, torn out of context, might also be valid, but, high pointed by dexterous use of literary techniques, carry far more meaning than they should and so lead to a distortion of history rather than to its illumination. About anything so dramatically tragic as the assassination of the President there is always the danger that the concept that every fact about him belongs to history may be used to cloak sensationalism for its own sake. Historians certainly do not require minor incidents at the airfield to demonstrate the arrogance and insensitivity of LBJ or the combative spirit of some of the Kennedys. Of course, one would like to have such incidents recorded, to be able to use them sooner or later to decorate a paragraph or point a sentence, but if their revelation is going to cause pain and bitterness, or add to a sorrow that has been deep enough for anyone to bear, then to wait ten, twenty, thirty years would be a matter of indifference to any historian. And the demands of history cannot be used as an excuse for such exposure. For journalists, of course, it is another matter – their trade is all-in wrestling.

Seen in perspective, the privacy of public figures is still greater than one might expect even if, at times, it is less than they might desire. It has always been a battle from the days when kings, visiting their mistresses, put on disguise to elude their courtiers, and it always will be. But let us have no hypocrisy about it. More often than not such battles have had nothing whatsoever to do with the needs of history.

(iii) Where Do We Go From Vietnam?

Politics are like a great mountain chain: the abundant foothills, the numerous alps, the rarer peaks and, rarest of all, the great Himalayan giants that make the peaks and alps seem but foothills. Opportunity to climb a Himalayan giant comes to few statesmen: one must be born in a great country; even then the struggle for power will be so sharp and harsh that luck will be needed to become a President or a Prime Minister, as much luck, perhaps, as skill in climbing. True, the political ability for such a local success need not be of the highest order: think of Coolidge or Bonar Law, or of the other forgotten Presidents and Prime Ministers of America and England. Also, even if the statesman's quality is of the highest, the opportunity to move into world statesmanship of enduring significance may never come. Events are needed. What would have been Franklin D. Roosevelt's role in history without the Depression or Winston Churchill's without World War II? Or, for that matter, Kennedy's without Cuba? Significant, of course, and perhaps more than significant, but events are needed to give a statesman the moral authority to speak to the multifarious millions who inhabit this world.

The event, however, is for the statesman but the opportunity to project a vision, to bring mankind to a sense of its ultimate necessities. The politicians who become statesmen of the highest class are men who in the last resort combine conviction, courage, with a will of steel be they Stalin or Gandhi. The best of them know instinctively how to pluck the future from their enemy's grasp.

Vietnam gave Johnson his chance to impress himself on the world as a statesman of the highest class. Has he failed, and is it possible even to judge his performance in the turmoil and horror of this Vietnamese war? It is difficult, but I believe Philip Geyelin has done it in the best book about the President yet written, the most carefully analytic, the wisest and the coolest. And Geyelin's indictment makes grievous reading, grievous because Johnson obviously had many of the qualities of a Himalayan climber: he is tough, resourceful, deeply moved by a sense of human needs – by poverty, sickness, the tragic plight of mankind's millions. He is huge in personality, a man built, one might think, on the scale of eternity. But there he is, well below the summit, frost-bitten, snow-blind, lost; clawing feverishly along a route that ends in a precipice. And now even the mountain is crumbling beneath him.

No one, of course, pretends that the Vietnamese situation was easy: it was getting much worse before Kennedy died. But such situations require not mere response to events as they occur, with an eye cocked on the consensus, but bleak, realistic, intellectual analysis of how the future can be won even though it may mean losing the present. A plebiscite in England would probably have kept the British in India, and certainly the bulk of the Establishment, too, were against withdrawal. But there was no other course, if political complications of a monstrous order were to be avoided, complications which would have created more agonising horrors than the religious massacres that followed Indian Independence. And for that withdrawal the public had been prepared if not consulted. But, even now, there seems no preparation by Johnson for what must inevitably come: sooner or later America must get out of Vietnam, win or lose, and what then will be the meaning of this bloody drain of men and treasure? China will still be there, still Communist, and much stronger. And China will have to be lived with.

But it's not only the discussion of Vietnam that makes this book worth reading, for it also lays bare the complexity of the President, and his essential weakness. What becomes apparent is Johnson's distrust of intellectual capacity. What a loss America has had in the great exodus from Washington of those outstanding intellectuals whom Kennedy grouped around him. Fortunately, they seem to be re-forming in New York and Boston, ready doubtless for 1968, when, maybe, conviction and courage in a President will once more be combined with high intelligence. This book spells out the need and, after reading it, one could wish it could be sooner.

Geyelin's book also raises larger issues. How long can the West go on putting supreme power in the hands of self-taught, amateur politicians? Kennedy had had some training in political and economic theory, and so has Harold Wilson; but this is unusual. The dominant figures of the West since the war – Truman, Eisenhower, Churchill, Macmillan, de Gaulle, Adenauer – were totally devoid of strict intellectual training in politics and economics, as is Johnson. But look to the other side – Stalin, Khrushchev, Kosygin, Mao, Chou En-lai, Ho Chi Minh. In the practical arts of day-to-day politics they may not be so adept, and their blunders many, but who is winning and who is losing? All these were, or are, men rigorously trained in political theory as well as in political tactics. Such men are professionals in the strictest sense. They have scarcely ever missed a major strategic opportunity, whereas the West's golden chance to exploit the rift betwen Russia and China seems to have been lost for the sake of General Ky.

In a short review, it is hard to be fair; time and time again Geyelin stresses the great qualities which Johnson possesses and which, at times, even operate in the world of foreign affairs. Maybe the President will cut his losses, change his route, and find his way to the summit. If not, America will suffer deeply, both within and without. Reading this book would be salutary not only for the President, but for the nation. It points the way with inexorable logic.

(iv) Another Year of Defeat

Another year of defeat, another summer of bitterness and estrangement: once more the liberal feels impotent and caught. A year ago hopes were high that the mounting wave of detestation of the war in Vietnam might become an irresistible surge that would place in the White House a man of humanity and style. Alas, bullets killed that hope. But at least there was a mild achievement: Johnson did modify his policy slightly and, more dramatically, throw in his hand as President. It will be no liberal gain if Nixon sits in the White House instead of him. None at all. The Vietnam War will go on and on and on. But the blows to the liberal cause go deeper, far deeper than Johnson, far deeper than the festering sore of Vietnam. The assassinations of Martin Luther King and Robert Kennedy brought the cold feel of death close to all of us. Implacable hatred of liberality, humanity, idealism was rampant and closing in.

After these tragedies, did America remove the gun, attempt to cleanse its public life of the violence that scars its image like suppurating eczema? Not a bit of it. The old claptrap was poured out about inalienable rights to self-protection. Protection for whom and from what? For the Right and from the Left, of course! A lesson given at Chicago. A lesson that may be repeated frequently enough if Nixon and Agnew get firmly into the saddle. There can be few who doubt that liberals, not Communists but honest liberal Democrats and Republicans who hate war and love justice to their fellowmen, may be in for a hard, grey four years; possibly longer.

Nor will they get much hope from anywhere else. Liberalism has been defeated in France, decisively and bloodily – and there its future is desperate. It is hard to believe that Prime Minister Wilson's government, which a mere two years ago filled many with optimism and hope, will survive much longer. Even in England the dark cloud of racism and prejudice is steadily growing. And as for Russia – the brutality of its action fills one with despair. After the death of Stalin there seemed to be a tiny flicker of hope in the Russian situation that the buffoon Khrushchev could not quite blow out. The writers' trials and the jackboot on Prague have made it quite clear that Brezhnev and Kosygin's views on liberalism are akin to Stalin's.

To me last summer brought back the taste of the 1930s, when hope was steadily extinguished, when the whole of human progress with its broadening social justice seemed about to vanish forever. Indeed, for men and women of my generation hope has been rare. For us Russia has proved a long betrayal – harsh, intolerant, conservative in the worst possible sense, far more conservative in its attitudes to art, morals, and social and economic structure than any Western capitalist power. Of course, one may argue that much of this has been due to a need to survive in a hostile world, but it is a dangerous argument to suggest that because a nation survives and becomes a great power the route that it took was the only one possible. We tend to forget not only the optimism but the liberalism and flexibility of the early years of revolutionary Russia – the evidence of which, of course, is now suppressed.

Revolutionary Profiles, by A. V. Lunacharsky, is a case in point. Mild as they are, these essays are not fully available in the USSR, for they praise the qualities of Trotsky, display quite honestly some of Lenin's weaknesses, and laud the experimental aspects of the Revolution. They give a sense of intellectual adventure and of great tactical flexibility in the revolutionaries, ruthless as they had to be in the appalling situation in which they found themselves between 1917 and 1921. Their world was basically a hopeful one and not without its liberal qualities. These old revolutionaries, of course, were liquidated by Stalin in the days when Russian Communism grew so monstrous that not even the naïve young liberal Socialists of England could believe in it any more. Since then we have witnessed Russia's near defeat in war, its remarkable resurrection, and its final transformation into a military and industrial state of formidable power.

And if anyone doubts Russia's technical capacities, they should read *Soviet Space Exploration: The First Decade*, by William Shelton, a cool appreciation of the USSR's remarkable triumphs in the last ten years when, for the first time, they outdistanced America in one major technological field. But, alas, Russian strength has not led either to confidence or to liberality. There are no hopes for liberals in the Soviet Union for the foreseeable future. The economic and social basis for conservatism is as strong as in any capitalist nation, perhaps stronger, since the whole vast structure of Russian bureaucracy will survive only if it remains conservative: otherwise tens of thousands of bureaucrats will lose their jobs and their status. What hope there is in the Communist world must rest in the satellites – just as a great deal of hope for change in Imperial Britain rested in the colonies, in their capacity not only to resist, passively or otherwise, but to sap the will to rule.

Prospects for liberalism amidst the great powers look dim, very dim, but we can console ourselves that this has normally been the fate of liberalism. If one glances at the history of Britain in this century, one realises with astonishment how rarely has it been governed by a liberal or Socialist government – for less than a third of the time, and much of that was government so feeble that it scarcely deserves the name. The same is true of America. All too frequently the solid conservative forces have triumphed. Yet both countries are infinitely more liberal, more concerned with social justice, with the poor, the sick and the deprived than they were half a century ago.

The areas of superstition, of intellectual intolerance, of outrageous social prejudices are less than they were, great though Wallace's vote may be. Similarly with Britain: the Conservative of the 1960s, willing to accept socialised medicine and socialised industries and the total dismemberment of the British Empire, would seem an outrage to his grandfather. In spite of Conservative power, liberal attitudes spread and dominate.

The answer is to be found in the nature of industrial society itself; industry cannot grow and function without widespread higher education and, as the George Wallaces realise, that means the chance of more and better-informed liberals. The educational process that industrial society demands also brings the highly educated to positions of executive power. They, at least, appreciate the economic dangers of blind conservatism: the sheer cost of poverty and sickness, the obstacles to growth created by ghettoes and illiteracy. Whatever the political situation, they accept the liberal demand for their abolition. Even Nixon talks like a liberal on urban problems. However, the process of liberalisation in industrial society is a heartbreakingly slow one for the sensitive and impotent intellectual. What he would wish to do in a year takes a generation, even in a free society.

It is likely, therefore, to be even slower in countries in the iron clutch of an indoctrinated bureaucracy that never has to put its authority to the test of a vote. Even so, some flexibility will have to come if the Soviet Union and her satellites industrialise their countries fully. Although it will need generations and the absence of war, even localised war, the liberal should take comfort. Industrialisation has liberalised the world to an astonishing degree in spite of the frequent tyrannies and despotisms of this century.

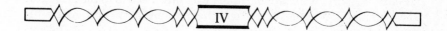

Coping

Throughout the 1960s, it had been a constant fascination to be close to Pat Moynihan, a fascination that contained spikes as well as sparkle. I was appalled by the abuse he suffered (particularly for his work critical of the black family that was totally, totally justified not only for America but also for Britain). I watched keenly the struggle, after his resignation from the Johnson Administration, between the two powerful drives of his ambition – one towards Harvard, the other to Washington. During this time, too, his politics were being honed by the battering not only of his own hope but also of America's with its grievous crisis in Vietnam, the riots in the inner cities, and the violence on the campus – the radicalism of the deed had reached and seduced a great segment of middle-class American youth; the private bomb, manufactured at home which exploded almost anywhere, echoed the public bombs that rained down on the nearly empty jungles of Vietnam. This was also the time of the mindless murder as a social or political act. This created a crisis for liberals and liberalism deeper than experienced before in America. Were they to blame for the social and political disintegration of young America? During the mid-1960s Pat and many of his friends, the Kristols, the Hofstadters, the Glazers and many more were trying to replace liberal idealism with realism and the art of coping in place of grandiose plans for society. These were the years of great ideological shift, almost seismic, which was, nearly a decade later, to affect Britain and Europe and lead to the emergence of radical conservatism. It was the beginning of the end of the ideological commitments made by many intellectuals in the 1930s and 1950s. After all campus riots and race riots were not peculiar phenomena, restricted to America. The rage of middle-class French, German and British adolescents spread with the ease of cholera – and equally fatefully.

Nevertheless it came as a shock to read that Pat was visiting the new President, Nixon, and that he was being offered a post. An even greater shock when it was announced that he had accepted and would be the President's Assistant for Urban Affairs with direct access to the President. The burnings and bombs were to be his responsibility. Fortunately for Pat – as he records in his excellent book, *Coping* – the rage of violence had begun to blow out, like a season of hurricanes petering away in dangerous yet diminishing winds. By 1968, the major crisis was drawing to a close. Now in the 1980s, it seems that it will never return, although of this I am far from sure. I cannot imagine how Americans would now take an economic crisis of the depth of 1929 and the 1930s that followed. And, I think, that America has been living more dangerously than it realises both at home and abroad, and perhaps most dangerously of all in Washington.

When Pat was fully ensconced in his post, I was taken by him to the Oval Office and taken aback by the astonishing interior decoration chosen by Richard Nixon; never had my eyes been assaulted by such acid yellows and electric blues; explosive even for a Californian beach house; weird in Washington. And quite out of the character I imagined Nixon to be. But it did help me to understand why Nixon had read Robert Blake's life of Disraeli with such absorption. By the time I came to write my piece on Disraeli/Nixon I had, through Pat, and, of course, through his policy, learnt much more about the President. Nixon was drawn to risk-taking yet remained deeply suspicious. His foreign policy was both brave and realistic. Only he could have started an approach to China, it would have been too politically dangerous for a Democrat; only Nixon could have begun the long journey to the acceptance of defeat in Vietnam. In domestic affairs he was again hesitatingly drawn to the bold and innovative. I remember being woken up in the middle of the night by Presidential aides at San Clements who, unmindful of time-change, reached me at 4 am to brief the President about Speenhamland (England's one disastrous attempt at a guaranteed minimum wage back in the early nineteenth century). But for the crashing absurdity of Watergate, Nixon's presidency could not have failed to be regarded as distinguished. But the man was flawed. And his judgement of people was patchy. This is not the place to discuss the vicious and distorted leak of a private memorandum of Moynihan's to the President* that might have destroyed a lesser man than Pat – a Churchill, a de Gaulle, a Mitterrand even would have purged his private office at that point. Nixon did nothing.

When Watergate broke, I was in Texas, teaching in Fort Worth at

---

* Pat had written a private memorandum to the President recommending that the Black Panthers should be treated for a time with 'benign neglect'. The leak was distorted to imply that Pat was recommending 'blacks to be treated with benign neglect'.

Texas Christian and I spent hours glued to the television set. I admired a great deal of America's response but not the final outcome. Watergate showed that presidential powers might still, if abused, be very dangerous for the American people. An example had to be made. It was not. Reagan prudently did not keep tapes so Irangate lacks the high drama of Watergate, but it reveals the same terrifying lesson. Congress is not properly in control of the Executive. Presidents and their men can exercise far more unchecked power than any Hanoverian king or his courtiers. And the exposures of Irangate are not going to change that either. Sooner or later the Constitution will have to be redefined.

Fortunately Pat was not involved in Watergate at all for he was far away in New Delhi as America's Ambassador. It seemed an odd choice at the time but once again Pat was enlarging his political experience, and also finding time to write, for the amazing thing about Pat is that no full-time job has yet prevented him from writing books of great importance for American politics. From Delhi he went on to the United Nations, and it was about this time I introduced him to Benjamin Sonnenberg, one of the wisest New Yorkers of all times, whom he had never met. Ben took to Moynihan at once, this was obvious because if Ben liked anyone he could never resist using a touch of the needle, just to show that he was in no way besotted with admiration. We were sitting comfortably in the library at 19 Gramercy Park sipping brandy and suddenly Ben cut the club-like warmth with what seemed a brutal question. 'Do you know Mr Ambassador,' he said, 'why you will never get to the White House?' For once Pat stammered and was lost for words, finally shrugging his shoulders, rolling his eyes and saying, 'No, no, no!' 'It is,' Ben said, 'because you are far too clever, far too ingenious.' We smiled, we chuckled, but somehow the club-like atmosphere did not come flowing back. By then, the trauma of the cities, the nightmare of Watergate, the foolish pardon of Nixon had all taken place and America had sailed into smoother waters.

(i) Nixon as Disraeli?

Asked which British Prime Minister they most admired, both Harold Macmillan and Harold Wilson had no hesitation – Sir Robert Walpole, who stayed in office for twenty-one years and left his party in office for nearly a century: a man who mixed consummate wheeling and dealing with such sound policy that he created a monolithic political stability. The same English statesman fascinated President Kennedy. Other British and American politicians have opted for Chatham and Pitt, a few for

Peel and Gladstone as their heroes. But Disraeli? Not, one would have thought, a politician's politician, even less a statesman's statesman. But first Henry Kissinger referred to himself as being a Disraelian Conservative in domestic matters and then Daniel P. Moynihan, having read Robert Blake's *Disraeli*, passed it on to President Nixon, who, it seems, was fascinated by this curious, exotic politician who flitted like a tropical butterfly down the corridors of power, dazzling in colour, light in substance, unpredictable in movement.

And here is the President himself making no bones about it in a recent interview: 'I would say that my view, my approach, is probably that of a Disraeli Conservative – a strong foreign policy, strong adherence to basic values that the nation believes in and the people believe in, and to conserving those values, and not being destructive of them, but combined with reform, reform that will work, not reform that destroys.'

One could readily understand Senator McGovern's seeing Nixon as Disraeli and so identifying himself with William Ewart Gladstone, that stern political moralist, who dominated English political life for three generations. Gladstone detested Disraeli as he detested no other man, seeing him as an evil political immoralist – opportunist, unprincipled and, worst of all to Gladstone, a wanton, gunboat imperialist. But for President Nixon to be attracted to Disraeli and for his close and intimate advisers to hear a resonance between Disraelian Conservatism and Nixonian Republicanism is strange, if not weird. It may be, of course, that they are wiser than they know, or perhaps more cynical than we allow. And men, of course, are often attracted by their opposites – by people who release what they suppress in their own natures. Is there a tiny Bohemian aristocrat screaming to get out of President Nixon?

Let us look at Benjamin Disraeli: he was, perhaps, the most extraordinary politician ever to be British Prime Minister. He was a Sephardic Jew of the third English generation, baptised, however, in the Church of England and brought up as a Christian by his father, Isaac, a well-to-do man of letters. Disraeli followed at first the same profession and wrote novels: indeed, he went on writing them throughout his life.

As well as being a man of letters, he thought of himself as an aristocratic Jew and identified himself, therefore, with the great English aristocracy, pursuing titled hostesses, haunting noble salons and slipping into bed with Lady Sykes, whose husband took a compliant Regency attitude to his wife's infidelities, so long as she endured his. When Disraeli's career demanded it, he married another mistress, as much for money as for love, and then became protectively devoted to her and would tolerate no laughter at her absurdities. After she died, he pursued elderly aristocratic women with the extreme ardour of an adolescent, indeed, almost to absurdity. His manners, like his dress, were exceedingly ornate, and he handled flattery, as he himself said, 'with a trowel' and so reduced the formidable Queen Victoria to adoration. Amorous, amoral, flamboyant – no Nixon here.

Disraeli also possessed immense political courage and a capacity for rhetoric and sarcasm, using both with deadly effect in the House of Commons. He enjoyed power, more, perhaps, like Dr Kissinger than President Nixon, for he realised that it was the base for that never-ending, passionately enjoyed social life that he clung to even when dying. Within weeks of his death, heavily rouged yet looking like a living corpse, he still went to and gave enormous dinner parties. In religion, as in politics and society, he was sceptical and sardonic. No Victorian Billy Graham haunted his years at 10 Downing Street. Indeed, in every way his attitude to life was both aristocratic and Bohemian. He loathed the masses as much as he hated their self-appointed spokesman, Gladstone. Indeed, it is difficult to imagine a political personality more remote from Nixon's.

Were Disraeli's political principles closer? Were his tactics, his manipulations of power, his achievements in government such that they compel not only admiration but discipleship in men so far distant in time and place as President Nixon and Dr Kissinger?

The apologists for Disraeli like to see him as the first Tory democrat, combining a reverence for traditional institutions with a desire to ameliorate the conditions of poverty that, left untouched, would be likely to fester and so threaten the traditional fabric of society. They saw him as the protagonist of Tory democracy, a man who used liberal principles in a conservative context. In two of his most popular and powerful novels, *Coningsby* and *Sybil*, Disraeli, it is true, dealt with what was known as 'the condition-of-England question', and adumbrated his famous conception of England as comprising two nations, the rich and the poor. He wrote:

> Two nations between which there is no intercourse and no sympathy: who are as ignorant of each other's habits, thoughts and feelings as if they were dwellers in different zones or inhabitants of different planets; who are formed by a different breeding, are fed by a different food, are ordered by different manners and are not governed by the same laws.

This was written in 1845 when, although 41 years of age, Disraeli had neither tasted nor exercised political power, although he had displayed his capacity for invective on the back-benches. Disraeli was in fact writing as a political novelist, not as a politician, with an eye towards a public deeply disturbed on the one hand by the threat of Chartism, with its implications of social revolution, and on the other by the threat of the new galloping industrial world that was shaking the old world of landed authority. His observation was exact; his rhetoric passionate. What was his Conservative solution to these social evils? Disraeli wanted a return to the 'high spirit of a free aristocracy'. The population must be inoculated with 'loyalty and religious reverence'. A strong monarchy, a powerful church and an absolute but benevolent aristocracy, Disraeli thought, could be the only enduring solution of the social ills he had described. Certainly Tory but scarcely democratic. Neither did experience change his views. In the preface to his collected novels in 1870 he summarised his political philosophy. It is as cloudily worded as anything he wrote, but even so, its tenor is clear. He was against self-government, even against the parliamentary system, against progress, against the application of reason to social and political problems. The aristocracy, and *he* says it, was a race apart and ought to rule. Could there be a resonance here between President and Prime Minister? Doubtless there may be many times when Nixon would prefer no Congress to the one that he has, and the fickleness of democracy must have been borne in upon him by an election result that placed him flatteringly in power but bound his hands in Congressional impotence. But even Nixon's worst enemies would scarcely accuse him of either regarding himself as an aristocrat or believing that aristocracy is a race apart. Or is this, too, a secret dream – Kissinger–Metternich–Nixon–Disraeli? And to hell with democracy.

Disraeli had little opportunity to translate whatever concern he may have had with social questions into political action until the age of 70 when, at last, he secured the premiership with a sufficient majority and sufficient ministerial ability to remain in power for six years. True, he had in the past supported most Bills that tried to reform working conditions and hours in factories, whether sponsored by Radicals, Liberals or Tories, largely because he felt that the new rich manufacturing classes were a threat to landed aristocracy and ought, therefore, to be taught that same responsibility to their workers as the aristocracy naturally felt for its serfs. He was more concerned to make the industrialists suffer than to alleviate the conditions of the workers.

During Disraeli's great premiership, from 1874 to 1880, there was, however, considerable social legislation, and perhaps Nixon and Kissinger have seen in this the benevolent conservatism of Disraeli. This legislation, alas, had little to do with Disraeli himself. Indeed, as Blake points out in his biography, Disraeli was so empty of legislative ideas that his Cabinet was hard put to compose the Queen's speech, which was to outline the programme of the Government to the waiting Parliament. Fortunately for him, the dedicated Civil Service had been hard at work digesting into legislative form the labours of Royal commissions and inquiries set up by the Liberal Government. Much of Disraeli's social legislation sprang from this source and, as Blake wisely writes, would probably have been carried out by any Government. Disraeli's role was to back his hard-working Home Secretary, Richard Cross, who initiated most of the reforms and was often in a minority of the Cabinet. Frequently, Disraeli seems to have been blithely ignorant of the contents of Cross's Bills, but as they did ease one or two thorns in working-class flesh, Disraeli quickly grasped their political value. In 1875 he thought that these reforms would be excellent vote-catchers among the working class, but when it came to the general election of 1880, he completely forgot to mention them in his manifesto. Scarcely an act of a dedicated social reformer. Again it was opportunism: measures evaluated in terms of power and not principle. In such an attitude one can always find the motives of Disraeli.

Should this create a fellow feeling in President Nixon? One can only hope not. Nor could it be called a brilliant tactical manoeuvre – stealing Whig measures of social reform in order to dish the Liberals. Many Liberals hated these reforms, since they believed passionately in *laissez-faire*. No question here of Conservative men exploiting Liberal ideas. Everyone must hope that President Nixon's concern with poverty, welfare, guaranteed incomes and social justice runs deeper than his British hero's; otherwise America has a bleak prospect.

I expect, of course, that the President's admiration for Disraeli springs from an earlier, more dramatic episode in his career. The occasion was the passage of the famous Second Reform Bill of 1867, when Disraeli, having dished the Whigs, seemed to run off with their clothes. Here, some might say, is a brilliant example of Conservative opportunism – surely the most brilliant theft of Whig measures by Conservative men ever – a perfect example of taking the best of reform and moulding it to one's own purpose in order to strengthen the Conservative forces of society. Presumably this apparent Disraelian achievement aroused the admiration of Nixon–Kissinger. If so, they should have read more closely and pondered more deeply.

The story can be briefly told. By 1867, the working classes in England were beginning to know their strength, and they wanted to vote in parliamentary elections, from which the 1832 Reform Bill had still excluded them. The pressure was great, and Russell and Gladstone decided that reform must be considered. Their Bill put the Tories in an uproar, as it seemed to strengthen the boroughs (Whig) at the expense of the counties (Tory). The Radicals thought the measure too limited. Some men, only loosely tied to party, thought democracy so evil that it ought to be fought to the death. With brilliant tactical skill, Disraeli welded this hotchpotch opposition together and the Government was defeated. The Tories took over with Lord Derby as Prime Minister and

Disraeli as leader of the House of Commons. They did not, however, take office to stop reform for good and all; everyone knew some reform had to be undertaken. They took office to bring in their own kind of reform to defend the landed interests. Disraeli was in no hurry to do this – 1868 or even 1869 would do. But before even he could get breath, Derby felt the urgency of the situation and pushed the Cabinet, including Disraeli, into action. What followed was a shambles – the Reform Bill changed from day to day, at one point from hour to hour – principles and safeguards came and went, and when finally the Bill was going through the Commons, Disraeli accepted Radical amendment after amendment that made his Reform Bill infinitely more democratic than the Whigs'. This was not done by design, but to survive in power. To retain power, the Tories accepted amendment after amendment and discarded the safeguards that most of them regarded as sacrosanct. After a generation in the wilderness, power, and the maintenance of power for the Tories became more important than principle. And like all political opportunists, Disraeli's judgement was clouded with hope. The grateful new electorate that he had conjured up would return the Tories to power with a vast majority.

In fact, the new working-class electorate created by the Reform Bill remained Liberal, and when the Tory Government got into trouble over another issue, the voters returned the Whigs to power and kept the Tories out for another six years. This was not success but disaster. And yet, the opportunist as ever, Disraeli insisted on regarding these events as victory, as a necessary step in 'educating the party' and laying the groundwork for his later, more solid rise to power. The idea came to him after the event: as with many Conservative political opportunists, explanations were easier after events than the examination of principles before them. I can imagine that the long, exciting story of the Second Reform Bill might have fascinated President Nixon. He would naturally have admired Disraeli's resilience, agility, capacity to turn threatened disaster into personal success: the absence of any other motive but survival in power might not have struck him as odd. Some might regard ability to discard principle as a sign of greatness.

But much as Dr Kissinger may deny it, I myself feel that his and the President's real resonance with Disraeli and Disraelian Conservatism has next to nothing to do with Disraeli's domestic policy, or with liberal measures being carried through by conservative men, for where Nixon's career links really closely with Disraeli's is in foreign affairs. No one loved to flaunt Britain's imperial power in the face of the world more than Disraeli; no one detested more heartily Gladstone's claim that the affairs of nations should be conducted on moral principles.

In his early years as a politician, Disraeli was, like his fellow Tories, not much interested in the empire; indeed, preoccupation among politicians with Britain's imperial destiny up to the 1870s tended to cut across parties rather than unite them, but Disraeli changed that. For two reasons: he sensed that working-class voters might be caught by slogans of imperialistic power – the xenophobic hard-hat is not an American invention – and, perhaps more important, empire stirred Disraeli's fever-hot imagination and provided him with a new field in which he could exercise immense power. And Disraeli loved power as deeply, as passionately as President Nixon. And so, during Disraeli's period of supreme power from 1874 to 1880, Britain's imperial destiny engrossed his attention to the exclusion of almost all else except political patronage. And the results were startling. Britain took Cyprus and a large stake in the Suez Canal Company; India acquired an Empress; the Afghans and Zulus found themselves the object of savage, punitive wars. British power was vaunted, displayed and, at times, brutally used. Disraeli rushed in to save Turkey from the Russians, ignoring the public outcry over the horrible atrocities committed by his ally in Bulgaria; with even greater relish he sat down at the Congress of Berlin with Bismarck to some tough *Realpolitik*. He enjoyed the carving up of territory even though England's interests were scarcely involved. Like Nixon, he worked hard to secure peace among the great powers, because he feared the outcome of an international war, though he had no compunction about plundering the weak or blasting the primitive. So the Congress of Berlin resulted in European peace, yet sowed the seeds of devastating war. Disraeli called it 'peace with honour'.

The purchase of the Suez Canal shares showed Disraeli at his most cavalier. He borrowed the money from his friends the Rothschilds. He boasted to the Queen that he had achieved a bargain at a fabulously low rate of interest and had safeguarded the routes to India. But truth and Disraeli rarely worked hand in hand: he had done neither. The Rothschilds charged him the same rate of interest (13 per cent) as they charged the bankrupt Government of Egypt, and the Suez Canal Company had no power whatsoever to protect or to police the canal: it merely collected dues. And as for making the Queen Empress of India, it was disastrous, for it strengthened the role of the autocratic princes of India at a time when they should have been disappearing into the attics of history. Furthermore, his flamboyance, his provocative punitive wars against the Afghans and the Zulus, his paranoid fears of the power of Russia created the image of an aggressive, arrogant and ruthless British imperialism. Certainly it captivated some of the jingoistic British working class, but it also exacerbated international rivalry, bred not only fear, but jealousy, suspicion and even hatred of the British. The only discernible principle in Disraeli's foreign policy was aggrandisement, power exercised without principle. At the time, however, Disraeli's foreign policy seemed as successful as it was flamboyant and novel. Peace, temporary only, among the great was secured at the expense of the weak. In the long run, Disraeli's exercise of British power resulted in a mare's nest.

Foreign or domestic, Disraelian Conservatism adds up to little more than the pursuit and use of power. Some might call this pragmatism. They would be wrong; immediate decision without a thought of long-term consequence is the reverse of pragmatism, as Gladstone well knew. And one can only hope that if Nixon and Kissinger turn back to their hero, Disraeli, they will understand him better – his shortcomings, his irresponsibility, his almost total lack of principle or philosophy. And they might do well to remember that Disraeli was spurned by the entire intellectual establishment of Victorian England; honours offered by him to Carlyle and to Tennyson were brusquely rejected. They judged him, rightly, as a man without public – or, for that matter, private – morality; a man who was vulgarising all that was honourable in British life. When it came to the suffering of others, the beastly killings and maimings of simple and bewildered peasants in foreign lands, even his own party longed for him to show a flicker of human sentiment. He did not.

(ii) Inflation, Frustration and Tea

LONDON. Watergate, Watergate, Watergate: endlessly the flood of news and rumours pours from television, radio and newspaper, but it washes over the mass of the population leaving hardly a name or an event behind.

And now they have a scandal of their own, involving two peers of the realm, both Ministers in the Government. Lord Lambton was photographed in bed with two call girls. Earl Jellicoe, a senior minister, figured prominently as a customer of one of them. But the outcry has come and gone like a sudden thunderclap, leaving only a rumble behind. Ten years ago, a similar sexual scandal involving a Minister, John Profumo, lasted for weeks and rocked the Government so badly that Prime Minister Macmillan was nearly brought to resignation.

Indeed, the difference between the two cases is remarkable. Then public distaste was overwhelming. Today journalists, public figures, letter-to-the-editor writers are scoffing at the sanctimonious leaders in the prestige newspapers and pointing out that every Government since the eighteenth century has had its share of adulterers, whoremongers and, frequently, homosexuals, many of them excellent politicians. So would it not be sensible, they argued, to return to early nineteenth-century standards, when private morals were as irrelevant in politics as in business? Lord Palmerston, a Prime Minister and nearly eighty, fathered a bastard just before a general election. Lord Chancellor Brougham regularly sent his footman out for a whore when nature got in the way of his work, and no one cared.

The Establishment itself has also taken this latest scandal without much fuss. Its members recognise a great deal of difference between this and the Profumo case and, indeed, the Watergate case. Profumo lied to the House of Commons. Both Lambton and Jellicoe admitted guilt at once, made a straightforward apology and resigned their offices with alacrity. Their sexual habits may be blameworthy, but their political behaviour has been exemplary. By the side of Watergate this is a commonplace little scandal, and it raises only one fundamental issue: should the sexual standards of politicians be higher than those of other classes of men? Watergate is totally different in kind and degree.

Men of affairs, intellectuals, those near to the source of power are, of course, hypnotically fascinated by Watergate. Those who supported McGovern – perhaps one-third of the British Establishment – feel a certain glee. Those who supported Nixon were temporarily stunned and silenced, though they have begun to recover and fight back, led by Bernard Levin in *The Times* of London. He argues that Nixon could never have known about Watergate since it is the first duty of subordinates to hide their illegal acts from their superiors – and that, even if Nixon knew, Watergate is no worse than what others have done.

Men like Levin – Dr Samuel Johnson had many of his qualities – have always been close to the heart of the Establishment, for their occasional liberalities cloak their deep and committed conservatism. By and large, however, the Establishment is getting bored, and gradually Watergate is dropping down the columns of the front pages, or is now tucked away inside the newspaper. Of serious discussion, which the case demands, there has been next to none. Not even a quip that one might have expected about the name. The Water Gate, in British history, was the gate of the Tower of London through which traitors passed. It was safer to take them by water, for the crowded streets of Tudor London created conditions that favoured riot and rescue. So the Water Gate of the Tower became known as Traitor's Gate. Men and women who passed through it usually ended on the block; few, indeed, who passed through the Water Gate came out alive.

However, among constitutional historians, there has been much private discussion of the deeper issues. For years now, some of them have been worried by the American Constitution. It was designed to avoid the seeming corruption of the British Constitution in the eighteenth century, in which the Executive – headed by the King – appeared to dominate the legislature to its own corrupt advantage. For the Fathers of the American Revolution, the British system gave too much power to monarchy. Such a view was simplistic, but it prevailed, and the Founding Fathers went bullheaded for the separation of powers.

So long as America was largely a loose federation of states, mainly concerned with agriculture and commerce, the Constitution did not greatly matter. But expansion of American wealth in this century, coupled with the growth of armies and communications, the development of the FBI and the CIA and the inevitable multiplication of office-holders, has placed inconceivable power not only in the hands of the President, but also in the hands of his personal aides – and power that does not, on a day-to-day basis, have to be accounted for to either Legislature or Cabinet.

A written constitution evolves slowly and with difficulty. For many decades now, there has been an embryonic dictatorship in the womb of the Presidency. The abuse of Presidential power did not start with Watergate. Such vast executive power will sooner or later always lead to abuse, great or small, until there is fundamental constitutional reform, and the President and his staff made more directly accountable for the daily actions of government.

What puzzles a number of English intellectuals is the lack of any powerful voice for drastic reform. English administrators are no different from American and, given the opportunities of the White House, would doubtless abuse their power. They do not do so, not because of higher moral virtue, but because they are subject to tight rules and, if need be, to constant interrogation in the House of Commons. The best check on any Executive is for it to be answerable day by day to a party and to a legislature.

Barren as yet of intellectual content, Watergate has, however, altered American relations with England and Europe. Indeed, it is hard to see how 1973 can any longer be the Year of Europe, as Kissinger planned. Would America enter with the same confidence into long and complex negotiations with either Prime Minister Heath or President Pompidou if there were even a remote possibility of their being impeached? Surely a shadow must fall across the conference table, at least for some months, until the heads of Europe see what the future holds for Nixon. And how sad this is, for the one great triumph of Nixon's Administration has been the dogged, subtle and successful diplomacy of Henry Kissinger.

The stinking, whalelike corpse of Watergate is, of course, a tragedy in other ways, for it has distracted attention from problems of far greater moment. Nevertheless, they keep reasserting themselves. The dollar's weakness is creeping back into the headlines, behaving fearsomely like the pound of a decade ago. Surely anxiety and fear must spread to the hordes of American tourists who have started to swarm into England even earlier than usual this season. They get less and less for their dollars, and meet more and more reluctance in shopkeepers and innkeepers to take them except at a sharp discount. Like confidence in government, once gone, confidence in currency is hard to repair. To see the most robust currency of the English-speaking family develop symptoms of the disease that has plagued England for nearly three decades produces despondency. The dollar, not the Presidency, ought to be America's major short-term preoccupation: action there is urgent whereas action on the reform of Presidential powers will require years.

There is less gloom, less despondency about ourselves. At the turn of the year, the prospects looked disastrous. A head-on conflict between the Government and trade unions leading to endless and crippling strikes seemed inevitable. Unemployment was high, the currency sluggish, people wearily resigned to social and commercial chaos. None came. The unions overplayed their hand; the Government evaded them by taking outrageous risks, by releasing a boom of unprecedented proportions. Whether the Government can control it, or whether there will be spectacular inflation of South American proportions is anybody's guess. During the twelve months ending on 31 March, for which we have figures, the cost of living rose by 8.7 per cent against America's 4.7 per cent. For the moment, Prime Minister Heath's price freeze is holding everything but food and so there is a relaxation of tension. Everybody is busy laying his hands on all he can buy or borrow to buy.

In the seventeenth century the Dutch were gripped with a tulip mania: astronomic prices were being paid for rare bulbs, men were beggaring themselves to possess them. England is now gripped in a junk mania. Every tiny market town – indeed, thousands of villages – now sport the sign 'Antiques' where, for ludicrously high prices, one can buy what our parents consigned to the trash can. Even Christie's and Sotheby's are caught up in the fever. Old wine bottles, even old corkscrews, are soaring to $250 and, for rare ones, nearly $500. Further down the line, postcards of World War II, photographs of grandparents scarcely dead, dreadful mementoes of seaside holidays of the 1920s, and the broken toys of yesterday's children are all traded, and actively traded, as antiquities. Indeed, no nation in human history can have had so much junk for sale as Britain today!

German, Italian, Belgian, Dutch and Japanese salesmen no longer merely haunt the London auction rooms: they burrow deep into the countryside. Recently, a dealer in Bungay, a remote, sleepy, charming town tucked away on the borders of Norfolk and Suffolk, sold a small Queen Anne bureau to a German for well over $2500, a bureau which, five years ago, might have cost $250. Twenty miles away in Debenham, the Italians had swooped on a dining table going at over $4500. Such prices have not been known in East Anglia until this year, and yet most shops are half-empty. Indeed, at Framlingham, six miles on, the Belgians had emptied a shop of all that it had for sale.

As with antiques, so with wine. British merchants now will not publish the prices of their fine wine: they are available only on application. The reason is the weekly, almost daily, rise in prices as speculators increasingly buy fine wines as a hedge against inflation. Last year it was Bordeaux wines that doubled and trebled and sometimes quadrupled in price; now the hunt is on for port, which has in consequence become extremely scarce. The first rumours are now circulating that sherry is poised for a great leap.

Once a month, a wine expert, his voice doom-laden, predicts the bursting of the bubble. The chances of a burst in the immediate future are, I think, small. Fine wines are now a commodity like cocoa or soyabeans, but they are as rare as diamonds or platinum. What is more likely than the price falling is that they will cease to be drunk, merely traded. A dozen Château Lafite are as tradeable as a gold ingot: hall-marked, impeccable, a saleable asset from Berlin to Tokyo. Quaintly enough, however, the heart and pulse of the wine market are not in any wine-producing country, but in London. The trend was set by the fine-art dealers, Christie's and Sotheby's – and they fix the prices, not wine merchants in Bordeaux or Beaume or Bonn.

Nothing at this moment in May is more soothing to the spirit than London's squares and parks, full of new leaf and blossom: the grass unbelievably tender and smooth, as only English grass can be – a setting made for a confident and anxiety-free world. The rows of nineteenth-century houses that still give London its style were built for a stable society that saw itself stretching on towards eternity. But, as in any great city, there are violations and horrors, banal high-rise office and apartment blocks that are as incongruous in London as thatch would be on a skyscraper. As ever, more violations and more horrors are threatened. The irony bites deeper: splendid neo-classical buildings are destroyed, but the replacements, like the Centre Point office building that soars over Charing Cross Road, remain empty year after year – thanks in large measure to England's complex tax laws.

Nevertheless, the extent to which Victorian London survives borders on the miraculous. It remains one of the most enfolding, most welcoming of cities, if not the most exciting or the most seductive. And yet the colour is deceptive. It is becoming a feverish city, and at times violent and ugly.

London is one of the greatest university cities in the world, a fact which we forget because of London's size, yet it houses in its colleges and polytechnics well over 100,000 students – some, perhaps many, capable of outrage. Only the other week, Londoners were shocked to read that Professor Hans Eysenck had been dragged from the platform at the London School of Economics and brutally assaulted before he could speak a word. (His controversial views included the notion that heredity, rather than environment, is largely responsible for low IQ scores among blacks.) The London School of Economics suffered more grievously than any other college in the student upheavals of two years ago, but this latest outbreak of loutish hooliganism, in which some outsiders were involved, has created intense indignation and a renewed bitterness towards students, alas, at an unhappily crucial time for students, who are seething with indignation. Their protests could bring a difficult summer for London.

Mrs Margaret Thatcher, the Minister for Education, is pouring what little money she has for education into nursery and primary schools. Universities are kept short, but shorter still are the students' grants, which, in the wake of inflation, have become so pitiful that even the cautious Vice Chancellors, rarely given to criticism of the Government hand that feeds them, have publicly protested to the Minister. They realise well enough that they are sitting on a boiling volcano. As impossibly low grants are combined with contracting job potential for graduates, the situation could get out of hand at any moment. And, of course, the irresponsible behaviour of a band of thugs towards Professor Eysenck would be used to defame students taking direct action.

A growing sense of frustration does not belong to students alone. Only a few weeks ago, civil servants, well-groomed, bowler-hatted, mostly very conventional golf and bridge-playing suburbanites, were out on strike, picketing the pavements of Whitehall. At the same time, the great hospitals of England were on the verge of closure because those most selfless of workers – the nurses, porters and auxiliary staff – were at breaking-point and struck. Schoolmasters, once the most docile and conservative of professionals, are now dominated by radicals – an avowed member of the Communist Party was elected by a large majority as General Secretary of the National Union of Teachers. As meat vanishes from the tables of the lower middle class, housewives grumble, threaten and combine.

All the ills, all the flash points, all the threats to social order and stability spring from the same source – chronic inflation, which breeds social injustice with the speed of a fever virus. The television screen is alive with conferences, discussions, documentaries about inflation – economists, sociologists, psychologists and politicians by the score suggest one nostrum after another.

Curiously enough, no historian is ever asked for an opinion, as if inflation were a novel disaster that has just struck twentieth-century man. A pity, because historians could throw considerable light on the problem, although, alas, they could bring little hope for the success of expedients that are being tried. Perhaps that is why neither the Government nor television companies in my country will employ them.

Europe in the sixteenth century was plagued with an inflationary spiral that lasted almost a hundred years: it was gentler by our standards, but grievous for the primitive societies it ravaged. It knew the boundaries of no country – as acute in Sweden as in Spain, in England as in France. Its causes were similar to our own – a sharp rise in demand for food, clothing, housing because of increased population without a matching rise in productivity. As with us, the price of food rose first and highest, clothing materials followed and then the rest took fire. Every government tried the measures that modern governments still hopefully try – wage control, price control, currency control, embargoes on imported goods, frantic scrambles to discover at home essential materials imported from other nations. Nothing worked, and Europe plunged into a half-century of chronic political instability and economic stagnation.

The gloomy lesson which historians would have to tell, if they were ever asked, is that inflation in any country is not controllable by that country alone; measures by single governments are ropes of sand in a roaring tide. However, united action by the governments of the Western world on the deep roots of inflation is unthinkable; only a crazed optimist could consider it. So it is likely that the fever of inflation will persist.

Whether the diagnosis is right or not, no one can deny the fever, or that London is suffering from a severe attack. Go to Sotheby's, or Bonham's, or a country sale, walk in Bond Street, eat at any restaurant, drink in any pub or visit any supermarket or travel agency, and see the thousands of pounds being spent. Yet outside the frantic spending lie the dark pools of poverty: as the history of inflation teaches us, the poor and the aged are the fever's first victims, but not the last. Bitter social tension is the one certain result of inflation, and one of which America should be aware.

Yet, although life may be hectic, the temperature high, social confrontation waiting in the wings, the pleasures of London are real enough. The opera is superb, the ballet exquisite, the theatre good and still cheap. The guard is still changing at Buckingham Palace; the ducks still waiting to be fed in St James's Park, which sparkles with cherry, and smells of lilac; little girls in their hacking caps trot their ponies in Hyde Park, and lines form patiently for a glimpse of the Crown Jewels. The Royal Academy Summer Exhibition is drearier than usual, but as usual the pictures sell. And England's daintiest tea-taster has decided that Claridge's is better than the Ritz – the cucumber sandwiches just that degree softer to the discerning tooth. Good tea, bad pictures and the endless round of tradition: in spite of its hectic temperature, London *appears* at least very much itself.

(iii) The Fatal Flaw

The *Midi Libre* squeezed in a small headline to report that President Ford had pardoned ex-President Nixon. It did not comment. *Le Figaro* found a little more space, and reported the fears of some commentators in Washington that this might be the 'cover-up of the cover-up'; the same brief treatment was all that the *Daily Telegraph* readers found in their paper in Britain. It proved difficult to find careful assessment of the impact of this incredible decision in the European papers, only Alistair Cooke on the BBC gave it the time and the consideration that it deserved. He did convey some of the incredulity and sense of enormity which the decision had created in America. Nor was it easy to find many Americans in provincial France with whom one could discuss President Ford's action, because few Americans were to be found. There were a few college adolescents frisking about the *Théâtre Antique* at Arles, very subdued, quiet-voiced, only betrayed as Americans by their T-shirts, and a morose elderly couple, who strayed into the hotel in the Gorges du Tarn, who obviously wanted to fade into the furniture and forget Washington and its horrors. Nor were the French themselves very interested; *La France*, strike-bound, blocking Le Havre, and the prospect of petrol rationing, obliterated both Ford and Nixon; Giscard d'Estaing and his *dîner intime* for the leaders of the Nine held Paris's attention, not Washington.

Back in England, only those friends who, like myself, love America with an almost obsessional love, wanted to talk and talk and talk about Ford's pardon, its motives, its possible consequences, and we sucked like leeches on the memories and impressions of two who were just back, and only then did one sense the profundity of the shock, almost seismic, with which this decision had been received. Certainly I had felt that myself, but the reception in Europe, in England, had been so off-hand that I began to doubt my own reactions. Picking up contacts again in England with those who are deeply concerned with America, one senses both bewilderment and despair — particularly despair. We are like a convalescent who, after an operation feeling secure once again, believing that health will soon be his, is told that he must go back to the operating table, that the disease is still rampant. What informed comment in Europe has not yet fully grasped is that President Ford's action is as significant, as fraught with dangerous consequences, as any in the whole Watergate drama.

For months and months that drama absorbed Europe, as one incredible disclosure followed another, but the curtain seemed to ring down after the ghoulish performance of Nixon to his White House staff. And the long, agonising drama has not left America's image untouched, far from it. Whilst many Americans have been congratulating themselves on the successful working of the Constitution, seeing Watergate as a vindication of the freedom of the press, of the Judicial Committee of the House of Representatives, and of the impeachment process, many Europeans are aghast and incredulous about the working of that system; its injustice, yes, injustice; its paralysing slowness, in many ways as destructive of America's authority as Watergate itself. More worrying still was the naïveté of political behaviour, from Nixon to Goldwater, or indeed from Mansfield or Albert, or anyone else of Capitol Hill, a naïveté repeated also by President Ford.

One can partly excuse the endless prevarications, delays, political inertia of the Republican leadership to America's lack of historical experience, but not entirely; the Constitution itself can be faulted; and so can, and most importantly, the political judgement of almost everyone involved directly and indirectly in Watergate.

All societies in Europe, indeed in most of those in the rest of the world, have experienced frequent political traumas. One has only to recall the history of France since the Revolution of 1789 to realise how widely different, how idiosyncratic is the American experience. France has experienced four major revolutions, three overwhelming defeats, loss of territory, invasion, occupation, the repeated destruction of war, and all the cataclysmic political repercussions of which they were the catalyst; heads of state, kings and emperors have had to run for their lives, or been publicly executed; politicians have been assassinated, imprisoned, exiled, hunted down like animals. Even Britain's history, far less traumatic than France's in the nineteenth and twentieth centuries, is still intensely dramatic in comparison with America's experience. Apart from the Revolution itself, only the Civil War, the Depression, Pearl Harbor and Vietnam sent such seismic shudders through the whole of American society. And who could compare Pearl Harbor with Verdun, or Vietnam with Vichy? Since 1789 generations of Americans have been untouched by political or social upheaval in a way unlike most Europeans or Asiatics. In consequence, the removal of a head of state by whatever means – public trial, enforced resignation, brutal expulsion, create few qualms in most political communities in the world. Malenkov, Nkrumah, Willy Brandt, Haile Selassie, Sukarno: how quickly they have vanished into limbo along with a host of others. Europeans, Africans, Asiatics know all too well from the turmoil of their experience that the highest officers of state, even those chosen overwhelmingly by the people can be disastrous, through personal corruption or political ineptitude, and so must be quickly removable – a lesson so painfully, so slowly, so half-heartedly learnt by America. Indeed, is it learnt yet? What so many European friends of America fear is that the Nixon débâcle will be regarded as a wild aberration of American politics, the consequence of a strange fissured personality who surrounded himself with unprincipled, power-hungry subordinates. Few are prepared to accept that Nixon and Watergate also spring from the system itself. But for the idiocy of having tapes made, and the greater idiocy of not destroying them on grounds of national security as soon as their existence was known, Dean would now be a discredited witness, Ford would be still protesting the greatness and innocence of Nixon, and so would most of the Republican senators, no matter how many of the President's subordinates were under indict-ment or in gaol. What appalled so many friends of America was the political ineptitude of the Republican leadership in Congress to allow a President to remain in office in circumstances so detrimental to the public image of America's political system, both at home and abroad. In no other country in the world would a President have survived whose hand-picked assistants were either in gaol or under indictment. To insist as so many Republicans did, on 'a smoking gun' shows almost grotesque political misjudgement. The opportunities for the corruption of power are as great now as they were before Nixon's White House exploited them. Tyranny was never stopped by the exposure of a tyrant. The usual result is merely to make those who follow more careful. What is needed is greater political, i.e Congressional control of the staffing of the White House; a far closer link between these officers with party and with party discipline. What so many friends of America fear is that the fact that Watergate was exposed, that a guilty President was removed, will be used to justify the system as it is. It is hard to grasp that but for the luck of the tapes, there could have been no justification, the system would not have worked at all. It will be a grave pity if the Watergate experience re-sanctifies a constitutional system which is so manifestly open to abuse. It is unlikely that Nixon will be the last venomous, power-hungry man, touched with paranoia, in the White House.

The near paralysis of Republican politicians in the face of over-whelming evidence of Presidential guilt, hoping that it could be dismissed as misjudgement; this and their dumb insistence on waiting for 'the smoking gun' did America irreparable harm. For whilst waiting for that gun to emerge the vital problems facing America, inflation at home, authority abroad, grew more complex through inattention and inertia.

More damaging, more desolating to the friends of America, was the disposal of the President. *Alice in Wonderland* begins to look like plain, down-to-earth common sense. No Mad Hatter's tea-party could quite equal a situation in which a man who has betrayed one of the highest offices in the world, who was likely to be charged with felonies as well as misdemeanours, should be allowed to retire on a huge pension, with the support of a large government-paid staff. And then, if this were not enough, to be pardoned for all and every crime committed although, of course, admitting to none. Nor does it end there. With effrontery bordering on enormity, there is now a plea to Congress for transitional expenses which, with secret service protection costs, runs to nearly a million dollars a year – true, they have been somewhat pruned, but in itself is farcical. They should have been rejected with contumely. No matter how discredited or guilty, it seems an ex-President must live like a Roman Emperor. In Europe for many centuries there has always been a law for the rich and a law for the poor, but the miscreant of power has usually had a short shift – frequently the gallows, often exile and always obloquy – but now, in America, sad to say, there is a law for the powerful and a law for the weak. Many were disturbed by the soft sentences in the plea bargains; they led inevitably to the greatest folly of Watergate – the Presidential pardon.

No one underestimated the magnitude of the problem that faced President Ford or Congress. All European countries from time to time have had to dispose of emperors, kings, presidents, even Popes, and anti-popes, and the problems of getting rid of the person whilst retaining the majesty of the office always has proved a grievous problem, and led at times to strange barbarisms. The barons of Edward II of England decided that he must be dispensed with, but the majesty of kingship had to remain unsullied; it could not be seen to be stained with violence and murder. With what can only be described as black humour, they exploited the pleasures that had partly caused Edward's downfall. They inserted a funnel in his anus, passed up it a red hot poker, which killed him, recomposed his features, and passed off the death as natural, for there was not an outward blemish on the body. Edward II vanished, but the corpse remained a symbol of unsullied majesty. Sometimes the enormity of disposal has been so great that the office, as well as the man, needed to be abolished – as with Charles I and Louis XVI. To do so required not only the nation to act as a tribunal and a judge, but also new concepts of law and justice had to be developed. The trials of Charles I and Louis XVI were designed, unavailingly, for such ends – to demonstrate justice at the very highest level, to show both the people and the world that not even kings were above the law.

Neither trial stopped a monarchical backlash, and such theatrical trials have their dangers, as doubtless impeachment running its full course might have had. The English quickly discovered that exile was the best method of treating delinquent kings, for all attempts at return could be denounced as treasonable. And when Edward VIII had to be removed – for no crime, merely misjudgement of a nation's mood – exile, honourable and cosy, was again used. Exile, with obloquy, is what the Russians now use, for presumably Malenkov is still running a power station somewhere in the wastes of Siberia; or acting as a minor official in a provincial town. But presumably no one group of American politicians, either President Ford and his advisers, or the leaders of Congress, ever sat round a table and asked what policy towards Nixon would disturb the nation the least, heal its wound the soonest, and, at the same time, pay more than lip-service to the much vaunted premise that all men are equal under the law. Would the removal of citizenship, the confiscation of property, the withdrawal of all benefits, perhaps even a single ticket to Costa Rica with passport withdrawn, have been too harsh a sentence? One or all would – in the eyes of the world as well as those of America – have created an image of justice preserved which the pardon has obliterated, combined, as it is, with an unseemly wrangle for yet more money, and the even more unsavoury spectacle, as Nixon's phlebitis comes and goes like a yo-yo, the circumvention of the witness box. Costa Rica would have been a far better solution; obloquy for Nixon, relief for the nation. But nations, like people, learn only slowly even through trauma, and so perhaps the next time Presidents' powers are abused, as they will be, politicians will act more promptly, the public more harshly, and the culpable President with a greater sense of shame.

Watergate, like the Dreyfus affair in France, earlier in the century, will lie like a great stain on the image of America, fading only slowly with time. And yet it is only one aspect of a deeper trend of many facets; a trend which can be described as the Europeanisation of America. The grand pioneer stage of the rape of a continent which gave such limitless opportunity, in which, if need be, America could turn its back on the world, is over; gone, too, are the days when its size, its emptiness, the very youth of its experience enabled it to evade the problems and issues which have plagued European societies for centuries. Now world-involved through a Sargasso sea of dollars and overseas investments, urbanised, class-structured, burdened with sacrosanct political institutions grown arthritic with age, it is a prey to all the problems that have wracked Britain and France and Germany these last two centuries – including the danger of tyranny and the suppression of freedom. No longer can any European view America with eyes liquid with hope, as did the immigrants of the 1890s. For them it was a land, compared with Europe, of freedom, justice, of equality and of opportunity, in which it was so easy for men and women to find their own destinies, unshackled from their pasts of ghettoes and suppression. Now the vision of America is sharper, more realistic, probably more critical and yet, I believe, more compassionate, at least more comprehending.

The diminution of America to human size, after the extraordinary inflation of her image through World War II, the atomic bombs and the Marshall Plan, started with Korea, accelerated with Vietnam, and became a blind rush with Cambodia, followed by Watergate and its ineptitudes. After Korea, Vietnam, Cambodia, how can Americans denounce imperialism or neo-colonialism? Held at ransom by oil sheiks, no American can speak loudly or confidently about self-sufficiency. Nor can he rattle the dollars in his pocket when innkeepers in Rome, let alone Paris, regard them with a certain suspicion and discount them heavily, rather than eagerly pay a premium as they were wont to do twenty years ago. And now, after the inept confessions about Chile and the CIA, could American moral indignation again surge forth at the dabbling of the Soviet Union in other peoples' affairs, or even at a new Czechoslovakian débâcle? The guardian of the ideals of the free world has become like the rest of us – sinful, corrupt, and all naked to the view.

Curiously enough this is not all loss – far from it. The unconscious assumption of many Americans *vis-à-vis* the rest of the world, and particularly Europe, has grated on the nerves and susceptibilities of many Englishmen, Frenchmen, Germans, Italians, as well as Japanese and Indians. Many Americans acquired the national arrogance with which the British were afflicted in the nineteenth century and for which they were so heartily detested. There was an arrogance that expressed itself in loud voices, loud clothes, that regarded foreign languages as unnecessary and the dollar all-persuasive. American food, American habits, the American way of life possessed an obvious *virtù* that only purblind chauvinists could fail to appreciate. But it is remarkable how, in the last few years, beginning before Watergate, possibly due to a sense of shame over Vietnam, this attitude has begun to fade, and Americans in Europe are being absorbed into the anonymous background.

Remarkably, their voices no longer boom in the Piazza San Marco or the courtyards of the Louvre. Indeed, in Paris recently, they had faded so completely into the landscape that they seemed far less numerous than Japanese, and totally outswamped by loud-voiced Germans as secure in their Deutschmarks and the economic miracle as Americans were in their dollars and victories in the 1950s. And when one does make a casual acquaintance with an American tourist, there is none of the old bluster. One meets the same courtesy, the same warm-eyed, slightly naïve curiosity and delight in the strangeness and antiquity of Europe, but it is now mixed with a note of apology, and redolent with a sense of regret for what America has done to itself, like children who know that they have lost their innocence. The seven-foot Texan, with his ten-gallon hat, fat cigar in the corner of his mouth, a photographer's shop across his chest, booming away at uncomprehending natives, has vanished, leaving behind a more complex and sensitive human being of far greater interest; if perhaps with too great a tendency to hang his head for the short-comings of his government and society. A new lack of confidence, a mild sense of failure, and a touch of guilt, one or the other or all, has been a marked and new characteristic of the hundreds of Americans whom I have met in Europe during the last twelve months. Such an attitude, if crystallised, would be a pity, valuable, as it may be, in the convalescence that follows trauma. Americans and America should again take stock of those achievements, of which perceptive and friendly Euro-peans are well aware. America, for us, is still a very great country – not only economically and militarily, but also for its contributions to all that is valuable in human living.

Clumsy and inept almost to the point of incredibility the Watergate saga may have been, but there was always much in it to admire – the adamantine sense of law and justice that sustained Judge Sirica and which will bring him, rightly, a measure of immortality. The rectitude of Eliot Richardson and William Ruckenhaus; above all the capacity of the Supreme Court to act promptly, with complete impartiality and absolute justice – indeed the Supreme Court is the one vital part of the Constitution whose stature has been enhanced, not derogated, by Watergate. All Americans can be proud of the American press and the American courts of law; it is more than doubtful if either press or justice in any European country would have performed so admirably or with such awareness of the moral imperatives that faced them. As against the prevarications of the politicians or the dishonourable lack of candour in the White House, this was enormously impressive and won the unstinting admiration of all who have America's welfare at heart. Unfortunately the law, the press, the Supreme Court, are not the whole of the story. Certainly they have sustained America's image, but much else has weak-ened it. But perhaps worse dangers lie in the straws which many Amer-icans clutched at to sustain their spirits.

One hoped to see evolving out of the horrors of Vietnam and Cambodia and the frightful mess of Watergate a wise, more mature, more sophisticated America, less likely to be deceived by clap-traps about freedom and justice and liberty; more wary, more cynical of its own institutions as well as others', a revulsion from hyperbole and an acceptance of very limited expectations. But still this is not so – there is still far too strong a tendency to exaggerate America's world position and the achievements of Dr Kissinger. No one has greater admiration for his dedication, his patience, his diplomacy, his unceasingly physical effort, or his skill than I have, but the ends achieved are too often judged by the labour involved. Like his hero, Metternich's, his arrangements are made of gossamer, not steel; they will hold in light breezes, in the lull that follows tempests, but could vanish in a trice as soon as the winds of conflict begin to mount again. During the Watergate débâcle, Kissinger preserved America's *amour propre*, hence the inflation of his success. These successes were real, but modest, and have all the appearance, as Metternich's always had, of impermanence and fragility. More important, and potentially more sinister and dangerous to America watchers in Europe than Dr Kissinger's Middle Eastern diplomacy, is the momentous and growing investment by Arab States in American industry and commerce, whose consequences are little understood and rarely studied. And will those Arab States, so full of money, with growing interests to protect in America as well as in the Middle East, take a stouter weapon from Dr Kissinger's armoury and see that opposition favourable to their interests in America are not short of dollars? Chile may yet be a boomerang – *Realpolitik*, as Dr Kissinger should know, can be a deadly poison and viciously corrupting.

There is, therefore, a dangerous tendency to clutch at and to inflate the successes in foreign policy as a sweet consolation of the horrors of the domestic scene. If only America could quickly adjust itself to the facts of political life, that corruption of power has happened, and will happen, in all societies, great and small, that checks have constantly to be increased and then carefully watched; that Watergate is neither better nor worse, say, than the great Dreyfus scandal that wracked France. And that its greatest dangers do not lie in itself. It has been exposed, the guilty expelled, and, one hopes, soon to be punished. What is needed, and what all lovers of America passionately hope for now, is attention to the consequences. The most dangerous result of Watergate is the revulsion that sensitive men and women are increasingly feeling for politics and politicians. There was a tremendous surge of hope when President Ford expressed his intention to act with total candour and to use his power only after the most widespread consultation, tedious and laborious though that might be. And for a few brief days it looked as if the battered corpse of politics might be given a new life, renewed honour and respect. That was so necessary because America is about to be caught up in the rapids of inflation; and inflation corrodes social and political institutions with terrifying rapidity; far more rapidly, indeed, than Watergate. This we see happening in Italy and in Britain, and it will need all of Giscard d'Estaing's high intelligence and steely courage to guide France through the swirling waters of mounting inflation, yet he and his political system hold the high regard of most Frenchmen and women. Inflation is a world-wide phenomenon, uncontrollable by any one country, and so politicians, even Presidents as powerful as Gerald Ford, can only make a marginal difference, and then only if they can win the support of the major sectors of society as well as a consensus among politicians. To ride inflation, high intelligence and great political authority is required. Great political authority, powerfully based on the hopes and wishes of the American people, was within President Ford's grasp, but it was shattered by the pardon – not necessarily by the pardon itself, but by the manner of its doing – impulsively, secretively, with authority unshared. And so, sadly, the old doubts about politicians, about secret fixing – whether just or unjust – have flared up again. And so the hope of those who watch America with love and sympathy is again undermined and replaced with a mounting sense of despair. America stumbling like a wounded and bleeding giant is not what the free world wishes to see. Morally, if not commercially and financially, the leadership of the free world is not vacant. Will Europe take America's place? Inconceivable, not entirely – for Kissinger apart, the intellectual quality of Europe's politicians can hardly be matched in America, and morally, too – Dutch, French, Germans possess great moral integrity, and what perhaps is of even greater importance, they possess a vision attainable, if not yet attained, of a politically integrated Europe. What vision does America now possess for itself, let alone the world? And which political leader can clothe American ideals in a rhetoric that will touch the hearts and hopes of all men who pray for a wiser and saner world. By the sardonic irony of history, '76 is once again going to be a critical year for the destiny of America. 1776 filled the men of vision in Europe, as well as America, with hope and strengthened their sense of endeavour. We shall all be watching, in 1976, with anxiety. Hopefully the nightmare of Watergate will be past, the fever of inflation contained, and Dr Kissinger's gossamer threads strengthened into tenacious tendrils.

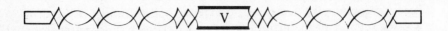

Salute to America: The Dark and the Light

I had first met Benjamin Sonnenberg at the Harvard Club at a charity dinner for the University's archaeological school in Greece. I sat by him; he asked me to ride in his limousine when we left for the exhibition of the school's work at the Museum of Modern Art. Later he insisted on taking me back to the Knickerbocker Club where I was staying. He made me promise to lunch or dine with him when I was next in New York. I thought nothing of it as I only had the vaguest idea of who he was and what he did. James Parton had introduced him to me and it was through James that he learned of my next visit and I was taken to luncheon at 19 Gramercy Park – a house of elegance and admirable taste – fine drawings, pictures, furniture and silver. The luncheon was for fourteen and fascinating – Alistair Cooke, Brendan Gill, Geoffrey Hellman, Bill Moyers and other journalists and broadcasters whose names I knew but whom I had never met. All of them seem to have been provided not only with a copy of *The Death of the Past* but also reviews of it, including the one in *Encounter* of which Ben himself insisted on reading the more laudatory parts at the luncheon. Then American custom took over – Brendan proposed my health in light verse and I replied in flat prose, but at least I was able to express my gratitude not only to Ben but to New York and America.

Ben pressed me to stay with him the next time I came to New York and I realised that he genuinely wished me to stay, so I did and I stayed with him every time I visited New York until he died. 19 Gramercy Park became a home. Also Ben opened up for me a whole new world. Indeed he launched me in New York museum society: and he advised me. He was one of the wisest men I have ever known: tough (he could be bleak), doubtless he had need to be ruthless to create the splendour in which he lived: millions are not easily made, even in New York. His house had become the theatre in which he played out his days. He had made a great fortune in being one of the first and finest practitioners of the art of public relations. He was short and round – not a heavy drinker but a heavy smoker, he became fat through hatred of exercise which he thought was a total waste of time better spent reading, talking or scheming. One of his favourite authors was Samuel Johnson, and like Johnson he believed in keeping friendship in constant repair and one of his ways was to flip through innumerable magazines (and magazines form a singularly large part of the literate New Yorkers' lives) and mark what might interest; so whenever I was in Texas, in Cambridge, in France, clippings would follow usually with a terse, sly or witty comment in Ben's immaculate hand. And if one was in a remote part of America, there was always someone he knew, like Stanley Marcus in Dallas, who could be relied upon to succour Ben's protégés.

Ben's house was run on a majestic scale – the only house in New York, I believe, to have a resident laundress; footmen, maids, cooks abounded: of course a secretary and a book-keeper and I expect others that I never heard of, all superbly orchestrated by his steward of the household, an admirable Englishman, called Horne. Ben's wife, Hilda, was never much in evidence – she spent months in Florida or on the Cape; at home she frequently kept to her own rooms and was not often seen. Ben was devoted to her and had great respect for her judgement on the purchase of works of art and their placement. However, Ben deserves a memoir to himself. His importance here, is that he promoted me and made me widely known in Washington as well as New York: in consequence it became very easy for me to get work, indeed by 1972 I was far better known in America, more admired too, than I was in Britain.

From 1970 to 1978 I worked harder than ever before in my life. I reviewed extensively; for four years I played a full part in running the history faculty at Cambridge, as well as taking on more and more work with American Heritage in an attempt to keep *Horizon* profitable and viable; undertook with Jules Prown the opening exhibition of Paul Mellon's great gift to New Haven – the Mellon Center for British Art: accepted the invitation of Little, Brown to edit the Library of World Biography; lectured constantly throughout America for these too were the years of the Bicentenary; reviewed constantly: produced at least three important scholarly articles. On the top of this I undertook to write nine scripts of *Royal Heritage* and produce a volume to go with the television series: this I partly succeeded in writing while I was running a seminar at the Graduate Center of the City University of New York and lecturing to undergraduates at Hunter College. There were weekends when I left on the night flight for London on Thursday, coped with affairs in Cambridge on Friday, started at the BBC about 10 am on Saturday and worked right through until Monday, with breaks for sleep and meals, until I caught the 11 am flight back to New York in time to prepare my classes and seminar for Tuesday. At times, it made the war years seem like child's play. And Ben was always there, encouraging me. Indeed Ben was one of the very few people I have met who gave me confidence about myself. Ben was himself so insecure that he quickly sensed it in others. I was surprised by his joy when Brooke Astor accepted an invitation to come to lunch to celebrate my book *In the Light of History*. Of course he knew Mrs Astor but she had never been to 19 Gramercy Park before.

Auspicious for Ben, far more auspicious for me. I was totally captivated by Brooke and still am – her vivacity, her intelligence, her warmth and the depth of her feelings about people and the world made her one of the most outstanding personalities I had ever met. And add to this her elegance and beauty – real beauty that age can never kill – and you have no difficulty in understanding why she is so deeply loved in New York. I got to know her quickly and well. For me Ben and Brooke were the centres of my New York life, year after year they opened new vistas – people, events, too numerous to recall. And one of my happiest moments was a dinner I gave for them both at the Knickerbocker, but I must write more largely about both before very long.

It was 'A Walk in Detroit' that sealed Brooke's friendship: it touched all of her social concerns. Other essays that follow owe much to Ben and Brooke and the circle of friends which they created for me. They have enriched these last decades of my life.

(i) Brooklyn Through English Eyes

In 1959 Daniel P. Moynihan gave me dinner at Gage and Tollner on shad roe and bacon (it became an addiction; every year since I've returned in March to eat shad roe) and then walked me around Brooklyn Heights and guided me across the Bridge. I was staggered. Again and again I was hit by the sheer beauty of New York as I had been in the winter of 1945 when I first saw Manhattan from the deck of the Queen Mary. True, the downtown skyline was more beautiful then, the skyscrapers were more elegant, less crowded, but even now who would ever tire of walking as I do, day after day, along the Esplanade and staring and staring across the river. Sharply one realises how water-borne New York is, a Venice of the Atlantic, no more American than Venice is Italian: cosmopolitan, money-haunted, the weirdest city in the world, the only one that looks truly of the twentieth century.

By now, I must have walked across the Brooklyn Bridge more than any other Englishman – I've never missed a chance for fourteen years, and so teaching for a year at both the Graduate Center of the City University at 42nd Street and Brooklyn College, there was obviously no other place for me to live than Brooklyn Heights. As my Manhattan friends, aghast and bewildered by my choice, pointed out, there is all the world of difference living in a place day after day and making a quick visit.

And certainly there are sharp disadvantages – it is shocking that an affluent community such as the Heights has such few good restaurants. One cannot eat at Gage and Tollner every night and, apart from one excellent but modest Mexican restaurant, there is little else. (The meat and spinach pies of the Near Eastern Bakery excepted.) And if one compares the Heights with Chelsea in London, as one should, for the income brackets are about the same and the inhabitants show the same strong mixture of the literary, the bohemian, the liberal and the rich, then the shops are dim indeed: no antique shops of merit, one good bookshop, the clothing shops and supermarkets tedious, ugly and boring.

Indeed, living for week after week quickly brings out the blemishes and makes one curiously aware of the vast indiscipline of American life. At 3 o'clock every afternoon, mothers collect their children from their nearby schools and the noise of their car horns is so insistent and so hideous that I became almost hysterical during the first two weeks. Getting a subway token is a free fight, and thanking the seller a waste of breath; indeed, thanking anyone – girls serving in supermarkets, taxi-drivers, bus-drivers – is like thanking the dead: no response. There is a movement in the Heights for almost every social problem, run by charming, leisured, concerned and elegant wives; could they start just one more – a Society for the Improvement of Public Courtesy? And also, please do something about their children: if they would read a little history, they would know that the human psyche is infinitely robust and certainly cannot be damaged beyond repair by restraint and discipline.

On my first day in the Heights I saw two small children trying to destroy a trash-can with their tricycles while their mother watched. When she was bored with waiting, she called them away while the battered can rolled along spilling its fetid guts onto the sidewalk. And is there any reason why eleven year olds and less should bellow four-letter words at the top of their voices? Within the home, often the children are charming and courteous, but in the street anonymity presumably descends and they can revert to the jungle. But of course, social discipline is not the Heights' strong point. Every street has one side marked 'No Parking at Any Time' and every street is full of automobiles: those from out of town get an occasional ticket.

The cost of living in the Heights is for an Englishman prodigious; the salaries unbelievable – garbage men under their new contract get as much as the highest paid professors in Oxford and Cambridge, firemen will get more; a maid costs far more than a fully trained, experienced secretary in Cambridge. And the food consumed – during my first month here I spent longer than I should in the A. & P. supermarket just watching what people took away – carloads of food, enough it seemed for an English village and probably an Indian city: no wonder so many boys look like baby brontosaurs.

I suspect that there may be more self-pollution through eating than social pollution through industry. When I get back I shall hold the English in thrall with tales of the prodigality of the Heights' dwellers' food habits, dragging home their hundredweights of food on special wheels, buying turkey legs by the score and steaks by the square yard. Irritating at times, worrying at times, but what a wonderland of variety – from the man across the block who always works between midnight and 5 am, to the boy who sits quietly on the Esplanade doing his embroidery, to the pseudo-cowboys of Montague Street and the weird Irish drunk of Court Street who still begs for, of all things, a nickel. And at nights, the Heights are beautiful; as in Amsterdam, the undrawn curtains and the half-open louvres give glimpses of mysterious, elegant interiors, glittering with chandeliers, adorned with books and pictures that bespeak sophistication and urbanity. The dappled light of the side-walk that moves with the wind is quite haunting. One is enfolded in a sense of privacy, of intimate living as one might be in an oasis. I feel at times, that alone and forever I could walk these streets day and night.

One learns to admire the natives of the Heights – these people are tough, they have courage; the old ladies moving with determination down Court Street on a dark night to the subway not knowing what may come with each step; the old gentlemen resolutely walking the Esplanade amid the hustlers whose belts and boots intimidate and threaten; and they bear with broken-down subways, buses like prison vans; their nights rent by the howl of sirens; and everywhere the taunting virility of gun-happy cops who seem to entice violence. A tough city, indeed, that is met with sharp wisecracks or worried understanding. No society is so self-critical, so preoccupied or so haunted by social problems.

Even though the jungle lurks in the Heights; and deeply foreign, even alien as the life here is for an Englishman (as my research assistant said: 'One would realise just how very foreign they are if they spoke a different language') yet I shall leave it with regret – a prey to nostalgia for these houses with their strong deep washes of grey and red, for the wrought iron, for the stoops and the lights in the streets and above all for the vista of downtown Manhattan and the Bridge; so huge, so incredibly, unbelievably huge and one hopes indomitable.

Of one thing one can be certain. If people can live in New York, they'll be in the Heights. I expect they'll be there even if Manhattan becomes the first Nineveh of modern times. And I hope that I shall still be staring at it from the Esplanade.

(ii) New York Vindicated

Last week a lodger in a small terraced house in Worcester, England, was charged with impaling two baby girls and one baby boy on the spikes of iron railings. A sixteen-year-old boy was sentenced for stripping, raping and kicking to death an eighty-year-old woman whilst robbing her of seven pence. An old-age pensioner in a middle-class London suburb was savagely mauled and battered to death by two adolescents, infuriated because he would not part with the few shillings that he possessed. Half a million pounds of platinum and diamonds was coolly stolen from Heathrow Airport at the point of a gun – fortunately unused. There was the usual weekly crop of wage-snatches and bank robberies. How easy it would be to devote an issue of this magazine to the muggings, beatings, rapes and slayings that are now a weekly feature of life in BOAC England, with its leafy lanes, thatched cottages, turreted spires, and of that cosy, idyllic London that a few restless expatriate Americans have recently fled to, like a clutch of chattering magpies, soon doubtless to take off again. They have found in London the same barred windows, double locks and burglar alarms that they required back home. Nor is Piccadilly much safer than Times Square. The map registering thefts at Scotland Yard, London's Police Headquarters, is so crowded with flags at Piccadilly (each one for a theft), that there is no room for more. And the pornography in Soho is just as bad as the pornography in 42nd Street, the hustlers equally obvious. Indeed, the dilly-boys at Piccadilly (teenage male prostitutes) are more flagrant than anything in New York. And as for drug addicts, they can be photographed any hour of the day or night in Jermyn Street, just a stone's throw from Piccadilly where, in the summer, European teenagers (15–18) collect in droves like mating terns, caught between drugs to the south and rampant pornography to the north, and almost certain to be fleeced if they hang about the Circus for long.

With judicious titbits from the *News of the World* and the *Sunday Mirror*, the two sensational London Sunday papers, add a few interviews with those who have been mugged or raped, illustrate with a clutch of photographs of the rampant strip-girls and dilly-boys, and what a picture the *New York Times* might give of London – every fact true, yet the picture totally false.

And this was what aroused the indignation of so many of my friends as well as myself when the *Sunday Times* of London devoted most of its magazine to depicting the horrors of New York, culled, picture-wise, mainly from the *Daily News* and based on two weeks' work by a reporter on the spot. The indignation was great, and anyone who cares to read the entire *Sunday Times* of London (and few do) may have noticed a slight attempt to back-pedal. In a recent travel section, there was a light and cheery piece by a girl journalist who admitted that in spite of friends' warnings she had enjoyed New York, actually walked in it after dark, and had not been mugged or molested. And she did mention that it was rather a remarkable and impressive city. This may ease editorial guilt, but it will convince no one. The picture of Jo Gallo's blood-spattered body carried more conviction. That is the true New York, the one that we hear about so endlessly in this country.

English journalists, English intellectuals, English academics, indeed English politicians, alight on the problems and evils of New York like blue-bottle flies settling on carrion – buzzing with delight. No doubt one element which none of them would like to recognise, is a ghoulish joy, a macabre revenge. For most of their youth America loomed over the world – magnificent, powerful, the paradise of plenty in a world of dearth. And so, like ugly women seeing an arrogant beauty suddenly corrupted with age, they cackle with glee. And, of course, what they have to say is saleable, profitable, viewable. The world is addicted to violence, to crime, to garish sexual titillation (imagine raping an old woman of eighty!). And here, of course, the American newspapers, television, magazines, publicists are as much to blame as anyone else. So a vicious picture of violence, crime and corruption satisfies the envious, and fills the pocket. And, of course, every fact is true. And so, when I tell my friends that I have just spent the happiest year of my life in New York, they think that I am mad: or worse, corrupted by dollars.

Not that I had a particularly lucky year, sheltered by chance from New York's crime and violence. Indeed, I experienced quite enough for one year. Within a month of taking a house in Brooklyn Heights, I was rung up by the police because my telephone number had been given by a suspect. I was baffled; they were baffled; but in the end they said the crime was so serious that they would like me to speak to the suspect on the telephone just in case anything emerged. And then came the most bloodcurdling yells down the telephone, a desperate black adolescent screaming 'Help me! For Christ's sake, help me. Help me!' Whatever question I asked, he just screamed for help. After a couple of minutes of this I heard a tired voice call out, 'That's enough, book him for first degree murder.' He had killed a cop. And for many, many days that voice rang through my drawing-room, and I can still hear it. A month later a store-keeper in the next street was shot dead at 10.30 am, as he went to open his store. Although it took place in the heart of Brooklyn, of course there were no witnesses. And then later, the whole area became a little uneasy as Jo Gallo lay in state at the funeral parlour in Clinton Street, And finally, in mid-afternoon, on Brooklyn Bridge, I had a bayonet put to my throat and I was relieved of $50 by an elegant young black wearing a hat like a cardinal's biretta. And so, if I had wished, I could have added my little autobiographical piece of New York's horrors to the dark and brutal picture of New York that now dominates the English, and, I expect, the European imagination – a concrete jungle where black jaguars prowl and rob and kill. But it still remains the happiest year of my life. And returning again to New York, one still feels the same lifting of the heart, the same sense of life being enhanced.

Firstly, what I can never forget any day that I am there (and what I suspect no committed New Yorker can ever forget either) is that New York is the most remarkable city built by man, and as day turns to night one of the most beautiful cities in the world. At twilight, brave the dangers, take with you one, better still, two stout companions, and walk across Brooklyn Bridge: the dark water, the busy ferries, the huge backcloth of glittering buildings should generate a sense of man's power and of his achievement. Or drive down Park Avenue or up Sixth, or through the Park. Or be a tourist and go and take a drink in the Rainbow Room at the top of the Rockefeller Center. And deny New York's beauty if you can. Beauty combined with power, both locked in achievement. And these buildings, and all they represent, shackle, I suspect, many New Yorkers to their city. There are cosier cities, more elegant cities, more historic cities, cities that are total works of art, but no other city, save Venice, is so uniquely itself as New York. And it is this visual experience of which New Yorkers should be inordinately proud. But the people of New York are finer, even, that its buildings.

No one loves more than a New Yorker to dwell on the horrors and problems of his city – the crime, the garbage, the violence, the racial tension, the corruption, the abuse of welfare, the horror of the schools, and the total failure of its government and its mayor. They forget, or wilfully ignore, the daring of the city, its bold experimentation, and its inexhaustible capacity for self-criticism. And even more consistently ignored is New York's benevolence. It is not a cruel city, on the contrary it might be argued that it is too benevolent. Where else are there nearly half a million illegal immigrants, earning, by their own standards, very high wages, paying no taxes, no social security, and after twelve or eighteen months allowed to leave with several thousand dollars, only to return a little later for more? In London, even a Ugandan Asian with a British passport finds it difficult to worm his way through the immigration authorities. Anyone landing illegally in England is hunted down, usually caught, and immediately deported. And, although the conditions in which these black poor live in New York are overcrowded, even shameful, they are princely by the standards of Bidonville in Paris, where hovels made of petrol tins are home.

And again, whatever the rights and wrongs of bussing, whatever its educational or social values, all arguable surely, none the less New York with the optimism and daring that has so often marked its administrative history, has experimented on a most extraordinary scale – indeed, on a scale which would make the hyper-cautious city councillors of London reel with fear. There the attempt to free children from the ghetto schools is timorous indeed.

And Forest Hills – controversial, bitterly fought, perhaps a Pyrrhic victory – but can you imagine public housing for Algerians in Neuilly or for West Indians in Wimbledon?

And the same is true of the policy of 'open admission' to the city colleges. Controversial again, certainly, and certainly it has created problems, many of them due not so much to its introduction as the faculty's obstinacy in accepting it. But to any Englishman, open admission to London University would be an inconceivable experiment, and require a revolution to bring it about. And what other city has responded so quickly to the employment of blacks and women, still dilatory by ideal standards maybe, but if compared with London, Paris, Brussels, Zurich, Bonn, or the like, extremely advanced. And surely no city government in the world would listen – officially – to the protest of the Gay Liberation Front about unemployment in the police force and fire brigade.

Many New Yorkers, I think, hate this experimentation, feel that it is responsible for the worsening of the city's ills and complicates rather than solves problems. Maybe, but bold social experimentation must lead to difficulties on the road to solutions, and it ought to be a source of pride to New Yorkers, for they are grappling more boldly than any city with the problems of multiracial society and of urban life.

An incomparable beauty, a benevolence towards the poor blacks pouring in from the Caribbean and South America, a bold, almost insanely bold, social experimentation – surely this is enough to weigh down the scale loaded with crime and violence, but there is far more to admire both physically and intellectually, great and small, in New York than this. The *Sunday Times* of London might take a look at Robert Moses; visit and photograph Jones Beach and Fire Island, and then try to find any public facilities of a comparable nature within fifty miles of London. Indeed, what metropolis is so well served with such magnificent parks, and carefully preserved wild country as New York? Is there a motorway within the vicinity of ten million people that can compare with the Palisades? And as for the parks, compare again the imagination of Olmsted's Central Park with the banality of Hyde Park. And dare we speak of museums – has any *Sunday Times* reporter visited both the natural history museums of London and New York? What in London compares with the Morgan or the Frick? Would anyone exchange Brooklyn Museum for Bethnal Green's?

And if we move from great art to the more ephemeral aspects of intellectual life, the balance between London and New York tilts overwhelmingly in New York's favour. If I wish to know in some depth what is happening in Chile, in Costa Rica, in Portugal or Greece, in Bangkok or Jerusalem, it is no use any longer looking to the *Times* of London, which has become increasingly a magazine of trendy triviality, but I have to consult either the *New York Times* or *Le Monde*. Apart from one splendid piece of journalistic enterprise about the thalidomide children, London journalism cannot compare with the boldness of America's – the *Washington Post*, the *Los Angeles Times* and, of course, the *New York Times* itself. In London now, there is no political comment of any distinction either in the dailies or weeklies, neither to the left or right. And surely in any metropolis one expects, one should have a right to, sophisticated comment on politics and power?

As with political journalism, so with literary journalism, or even the journalism of information. Londoners have to buy either *Time* or *Newsweek*. *The New York Review of Books* is sought in England more eagerly than the *Times Literary Supplement*; the literary pages of the Sunday papers have shrunk almost to nothing, and what there is is more often than not the tired reflections of ageing belletrists on their more esoteric interests – the lives of nineteenth-century bishops or the peculiar mating habits of the praying mantis. Only a fat book on the Tractarian Movement or fleas is certain of a review. The literary appetites of New Yorkers, always wolfish, are amply served, the Londoners' starved. And remember that London has nothing comparable to the *New Yorker*, or the *New York Magazine*. It lacks a magazine of comparable beauty to *Horizon*. All that literary journalism has spawned in London of recent years is *Private Eye*, a modest little contribution to satire. And the situation is deteriorating: both the *New Statesman* and the *Spectator* are in difficulties about circulation; only the *Economist* and the *Listener* thrive, although the *Listener* is under attack for being, it is felt, unfairly subsidised by the BBC: very cheap, very well edited, its circulation soars, whereas its rivals, becoming more expensive every year, sink. But the journalism of London, whether political or literary, is not to be compared with New York's. Nor, one might add, do Londoners buy so many books.

In the theatre, and in music, the two capitals are more evenly matched, but New Yorkers are too ready with their praise of the London stage, and often, in their perverse way, too deprecating of their own. Much of the freedom now enjoyed by the English theatre was pioneered in New York.

At first sight, I must admit, New Yorkers seem an unprepossessing lot. The crowds in the streets, unlike Rome, Paris, Stockholm, or indeed London, are rarely exciting to look at. Public courtesy would not seem to come naturally to anyone using the subways, buses, taxis, streets, restaurants or shops. I have waited so long in an empty shop for assistants too busy with their own affairs to cope with a customer that I have walked out, been so harassed by an aggressive salesman in another that I would never use it again, and amazed by the time-using complexities of purchase in others that would have seemed elaborate even to a French provincial department store. No, emphatically, New Yorkers do not set out with cunning charm and ready desire to please, to tickle dollars from the pockets of tourists. There would almost seem to be a conspiracy amongst New Yorkers to parade their vices, and to hide their virtues.

For in private, New Yorkers are immensely hospitable, generous, courteous and, above all, free, by English standards, totally free from any kind of social snobbery. Of course, it would be stupid to think there is none, and far more stupid still not to recognise a certain snobbery of wealth. Even so, accent, social origins, family background, the nature of one's education are of little significance to New Yorkers: one's abilities, one's wit, one's capacity for success, above all, one's professionalism (whether it be in repartee, tasting wines, writing books, or selling stocks) are the principal objects of their interest. And, I think, no New Yorker can appreciate how deeply refreshing and invigorating this attitude is to those who have suffered the crimps and cramps of English snobbery: its petty insults; its instinctive amateurism. Indeed, snobbery hangs like a cloud of smog over London.

And that is why so many Englishmen of talent feel a lifting of the heart as they drive from Kennedy across the wastes of Queen's towards the mid-town skyline. Here they know that if their talent is as good as they think it is, they will find a responsive audience, and an appreciation as life-enhancing as it is genuine.

This is a part of New York's intense humanity – that responds so simply and so directly to life. Few cities give off such a sense of man's energy and vitality, or indeed of his capacity to endure. There is no more moving scene than to see an old and not very prosperous New Yorker, black or white, making his way alone in the evening. They know the dangers, many have suffered violence, but they will not be denied either their city or their freedom.

And finally what other city has New York's infinite variety? The villages within villages, the towns within towns, scattered up and down the island: many so strange, so alien to America, yet utterly at home in New York. Walk in Williamsburg, saunter amongst the Syrian shops of Atlantic Avenue, hunt out the tiny Armenian community on Second Avenue. And New York can be more eccentric than any other city in the world. Where else can you buy second-hand food, or consult a cat psychiatrist, or buy false eye-lashes for your dog? Where else can you get specially printed prayers for truck drivers, go to an Arabic and Chinese movie on the same day, buy sea-horses dead or alive, rent a snore controller for your husband, give your family the surprise of its life with a dish of poi, pinnestek or sisi?

Violent, criminal, teetering on bankruptcy, and impossible to govern New York may be, yet it is a tonic city – life-giving, life-enhancing: a city to love and a city of which to be proud. More deeply than any city that I know, New York is suffering from a crisis of self-confidence. It is high time New Yorkers recovered from the searing shocks of the last ten years of politics and social revolution, rejected their masochistic delight in wallowing in criticism, and set about enjoying themselves and their incomparable city.

(iii) A Walk in Detroit

Late in the fall the sun still blessed Detroit, the blue sky was high, wide and handsome, too inviting to evade in a cab, too warm to be missed by one about to be plunged back into the mists and fogs of London. About 11 am on a Saturday morning I set out from my motel and walked down Woodward Avenue. After five minutes I began to feel uneasy, unsure as to whether I was awake or dreaming. Maybe I had strayed into a film set by Fellini. No human being was to be seen. Cars sped by, buses hummed and coughed, the sun blazed down, but as far as the eye could see the sidewalks were empty. After twenty minutes' walk I saw two white boys, carrying roller skates, waiting for a bus: ten minutes later two black youths slid round a corner and stared at a Cadillac through the windows of a showroom. And I saw no one else, no other living being, not even a cat or a dog, until I reached the art gallery, a walk of some two miles. And what a walk. Cracked and broken sidewalks, with grass and weeds growing through them; desolate parking lots, shabby automobile showrooms; and quite often nothing – just lots. Everywhere dirt, bits of paper, cigarette and chocolate cartons – the excrement of a consumer society thrown out of passing automobiles.

The art gallery, of course, was stupendous: wonderful pictures, splendidly displayed; room after room proclaimed the generosity of Detroit's leading citizens. But the walk from the art gallery to downtown Detroit, another mile maybe, was more searing, if less nightmarish. Broken-down snack bars, stinking of cheap food; grimy shops selling magazines and books; side-streets full of ageing houses, the street corners occupied by a few derelict Negroes. Here and there one or two young black people bustled about, but even they in their pink trousers and lime green jackets could not stifle the air of decay, of dirt, of hopelessness: a concrete city with a concrete heart that belied the generous warmth of the sun and that pellucid blue of the sky that drew my thoughts to fifteenth-century Florence.

What a contrast! There was a city as vast for its age as Detroit for its; there, too, had been families of fabulous wealth drawn from international trade. These families, the Medici chief amongst them, had set about their city. The *piazza* had been cleared and beautified with staggering works of art that have continued to give joy for hundreds of years and will do so for hundreds more. Church after church, square after square, bridge after bridge, street after street create a world of brick and mortar and stone that delights the eye and lifts the spirit – a city in which anyone, rich or poor, native or foreign, can dwell with pride. Nor is Florence unique; the more anonymous aristocracy of Venice deliberately created the beauty which we see. By deliberate act they cleared and paved the *piazza* and *piazzetta*, built the splendid façades and made the beauty that draws the world to it.

Cities do not grow beautiful by chance. None has: a fact forcibly brought home in *Paris in the Age of Absolutism*, a brilliant book by a young historian, Orest Ranum. Here we see how Paris grew, not only in people, in commerce, in riches, but also how it became a symbol, an expression of the aspiration of Louis XIV and his minister, Colbert, who wished to emulate Augustan Rome. The beauty of the Louvre, of the Palais Royal, of the surrounding bridges and *hôtels*, springs from their intention of making Paris a city of grandeur as well as of beauty. And what Louis XIV started, Napoleon I and III completed; the splendour of Paris is due to them and their architects. At the same time Paris never lost its human scale. For centuries, and still today, it is a city to be lived in, possessing all the contrasts that are needed – quietude and privacy in the midst of the multitude, sudden vistas, parks, gardens, fountains, places to wander in, places to sit in; above all, places to talk in.

Somehow the great European cities have preserved the quality which created the adjective 'urbane'. True, London is under strain, as streets of Victorian and Georgian houses are ripped out for Manhattan-style office blocks. Although the majority of English towns can still be lived in, patches of Detroit blight are visible in most – the waste areas between the suburbs and the commercial centre, which in American industrial cities has become a chronic disease, an inhuman nightmare land of loneliness and violence. The automobile, the basis of Detroit's fabulous prosperity, started the long death agony of the American city by opening up vast suburbs that gave space, a sense of country, and abolished from sight the poor and the black. The only American metropolises, apart from San Francisco and New York, which still possess something approaching the grace and amenities of European cities all pre-date industry – New Orleans, Savannah, Charleston, Boston and a few other New England towns.

This tragedy goes far deeper than mere physical appearance. Cities, purposely created, are life-enchancing. If you do not believe me, then study the life of Dr Samuel Johnson or, better still, read Dorothy Marshall's *Dr Johnson's London*. Turn to the other volumes in Norman Cantor's excellent series *Historical Cities* of which these are a part. Then look at a kindred series put out by the University of Oklahoma Press, *The Centers of Civilisation*. And having read, think hard and long about Detroit, Chicago, Pittsburgh, Baltimore and the rest – above all Detroit.

In Dr Johnson's day London, with its beautiful squares and parks, its amusement gardens and theatres, its taverns, concert halls and academies, produced a brilliant civilisation that was thoroughly and totally urban. When tired of London the rich and fashionable went sometimes to the countryside but just as frequently to the beautiful spa cities – Bath, Tunbridge Wells, Brighton, Harrogate and the like – so that they could still enjoy the civilities of urban life. Returning to London, they experienced an invigoration of the spirit, a sharpening of the intellect. As Dr Johnson said, 'Whoever is tired of London is tired of life.'

Of course, it was not all Georgian elegance and refinement. There were slums and there were poor: the sick, the starving, the illiterate and the violent. There were mobs and ghettos, but it was a community, the living centre of culture, the seedbed of genius, complex and human – never a desert of concrete lots and growing weeds.

As I said earlier, many of the most beautiful of European cities were the creations of a man, a family or a small class of men. Even the staggeringly beautiful city of Bath was due almost entirely to one man – Ralph Allen. Yet scarcely one large American city has captured the imagination, the energy and the dedication of those who have derived their wealth and power from them. Outside Detroit lies one of the greatest industrial complexes the world has ever known. The stupendous generosity of the Fords to the world through their Foundation has been commensurate with their mountainous riches. Nor have they entirely forgotten their native city: benefactions to universities, and the art gallery's world-renowned pictures bear witness to their private benefactions. These, however, are but diamonds embedded in cinders scattered across a desert of broken and dirty concrete. If one thinks of what the Medicis and the great Florentine families did for Florence, the plight of Detroit sears one's soul. Surely these great empty wastes could have been planned and modelled to create a city to live in. Yamasaki has shown what could be done with his elegant and entirely human-sized buildings at Wayne State University. If only that university and the art gallery had been surrounded by squares enfolding gardens and fountains as a setting for crescents and terraces of housing to suit the whole range of Detroit's needs! If only the Fords had built a palace in the heart of Detroit and lived in it – if only they would! Then there might be a Florence in Michigan. After all, Florence was and is a great industrial city. The idea is not outrageous.

To cure the ills of American cities, the rich, the middle-class and the professional families must live in them again, and attempt to recreate the civilities and urbanities that rightly belong to great towns. American architects (such geniuses with an office block or public building) must design homes within the city landscape. Perhaps it is too late, the disease too far gone. Perhaps one should destroy these decaying corpses and plan a world that consists of suburbs and centres – industrial, commercial, cultural. Perhaps the city is rapidly becoming merely historic and so has no future: or a future only for the poor. If so, humanity will be the loser, for city life at its best has been one of mankind's greatest achievements.

(iv) Secular Heretics

In late February 1967 a stark naked man stood near the sanctuary of the Glide Memorial Church in San Francisco; about him men and women, waving incense, chanted to the throb of the Congo drums; topless belly dancers wove in and out; psychedelic colours flashed across the church; and time and time again the sad, humanity-haunted face of Christ was projected above the crowd. Adolescents caressed and loved by the altar or withdrew to another room provided with a plastic bed. And so it went on until the early hours of the morning when the church elders 'lost their cool' and called it a day.

In Cologne about 1325 the Brethren of the Free Spirit met in their luxurious secret chapel: there a live Christ celebrated mass, a naked preacher exhorted the Brethren to return to primeval innocence, to strip, to love: for those who had become one with God there could be no sin, no church, no property. Love and the ecstatic experience was all. The church of the pope and the kingdoms of princes were evil. Take from them all that was needed, cheat them, lie to them, for innocence and love were beyond crime as well as beyond sin. The celebrants responded to the preacher and loved hard, there and then. What better place than a church for copulation that was beyond sin?

In Hampshire in 1649 William Franklin and his soul-mate and bed-companion Mary Gadbury found God within themselves, gave up work, lived in voluntary poverty, rejected sin and encouraged their little flock of Ranters to revel in obscenity, promiscuity and drink. They were not alone, little bands of these religious hippies buzzed like wasps' nests throughout Cromwell's England. They were stifled, not by the savage laws of the Commonwealth, but by their first cousins, the Quakers, whose early philosophy was hip with a difference. The first Quakers, sometimes walked naked through the villages of Leicestershire: both to show disapproval of the accepted world of materialism and darkness and to proclaim their salvation and their purity as Children of Light. They too rejected the religious establishment as well as the differences of social status; wearing their hats in church to demonstrate one and calling all men 'thou' to prove the other. And they would not pay tithes. They went to gaol. Nor would they take oaths, or fight, so off to gaol they went again. And although they eschewed physical love outside marriage, the love of all men and women, whatever suffering it might bring, lay at the heart of their creed.

Much of the content of hippie philosophy has a long history in such religious heresies: even to drugs, for Ranters and Free Brethren and Spiritual Libertines used alcohol in excess to provide ecstasy: and as for promiscuity clothed in an aura of religiosity, this almost stretches back to Adam himself. The hippies, ignorant of history, are but a part of a chain stretching back into the Middle Ages and beyond. Why do these philosophies, heresies, call them what you will, recur so frequently in Western society? And is the present-day hippie world illumined by the light of the past?

The hippies are secular heretics, for they reject the moral principles of society, claiming to return to a purer, less hypocritical morality. What is common to this new secular heresy and religious heresies of the past, to which it possesses so many resemblances, is that it has occurred in a very affluent society. The Brethren of the Free Spirit, who were so similar to the hippies, flourished in the prosperous towns of Flanders and the Rhine where society and the Church had grown materialistic, given to wanton luxury and guilt-free extravagance. Also, as now, it was a time of war and of social dislocation. And the same conditions prevailed in England in the days of the Ranters and early Quakers. The philosophy of the marketplace had spread like bindweed over ancient morality and stifled it: political and social anarchy, with turbulence and riot, combined with seemingly meaningless civil war, gave a loathsome luminosity to the material world in the eyes of the Ranters and Quakers. Better get right out of it, and dwell with Brethren, led by the inner light.

Such antipathy to the material world and to the world of government, order, discipline and force goes, however, deeper than heresy. It is a constant theme in most religions except the Chinese. Sometimes the Church has contained it and been revivified by it. Think of St Francis, the son of a prosperous merchant, who divested himself of all material things and treated all that lived – birds and beasts and insects – as aspects of God. He pursued poverty like a lover and preferred the broken, the tormented, the simple and the foolish. A hippie-saint if ever there was one. He and his brethren battened on the conscience of the material world that they despised – taking the food, the alms, the shelter as the hippies did in Haight-Ashbury. Indeed some founders of religion seem uncomfortably close to the hippies. Beyond St Francis looms a larger, more formidable figure, who amidst the vast riches and stupendous power of the Roman Empire had no use for it, nor for riches, nor for strife, nor for hypocrisy, who preferred a prostitute to a prude. In the West, religion that is intense, personal and deeply felt has always been at odds with the world it has to live with.

Yet no matter how closely one presses the resemblance of this new secular heresy, with its total rejection of the principles and morality of the middle-class establishment, to the religious heresies and movements of the past, or indeed sees it as a part of the cycle of rejection of materialism which has been a constant factor in Western life and thought, there remain very important differences. The hippie world is compounded not only of social heresy but of acid. Here surely is the break with the past.

Drugs date back, at least, to the neolithic revolution, when men first discovered wine and beer: both were given sacred and ritualistic functions, which they have maintained. This is true of all communities, primitive and advanced, communist and capitalist. Almost the whole of humanity has been sodden, at some time or another, with alcohol. And its use is deeply embedded in social rituals. Billions of gallons of wine, spirits and beer are needed to sustain the social conventions of group activity. Minor drugs and narcotics, after much initial opposition, also secured social acceptance, and became a part of the social ritual. After all, James I of England hated tobacco as much as Harry Anslinger hates hemp, and coffee houses were thought by Charles II to be dens of decadence and political treachery; but the public craving would not be denied.

Artists, particularly from the nineteenth century onwards, sought powerful hallucinations through drugs. Opium, laudanum, ether and hashish were plentiful in bohemian and artistic circles in nineteenth-century Europe, a process which reached its zenith in Rimbaud, who deliberately attempted a '*dérèglement de tous les sens*' and wrote psychedelically of the colour of vowels. But this experimentation was a means to art, an attempt to heighten consciousness for art's sake – not a way of life.

In the hippies, therefore, two historical strands have intertwined in an odd way – social heresy and the artist's quest for heightened perception through drugs. The need for the latter is, of course, due to the absence of God. Ecstasy and elation could be achieved by the mystical heretic through ritual, fasting, contemplation or flagellation, so long as they were intensified by a sense of God within and without. For the hippie, God is scarcely existent, replaced by a vague sense of the oneness of humanity which is quite insufficient to create the heightened consciousness needed for hallucinations or ecstatic experience.

The hippies' ancestry, however, is European rather than American, which, perhaps, is one of the reasons why their impact has been so shocking. During the nineteenth century the American artist occasionally toyed with decadence or drugs but, like Poe, he was an oddity. There were no Coleridges, no Baudelaires, no Rimbauds, no Verlaines, no Wildes, not even a Byron or a Shelley. The American bohemians were a tiny sect and their free-love utopias were small, isolated and without dramatic social impact. In America the need to fly from materialism, from the grossness of a conscious world, was assuaged by the West, either actively or imaginatively. Nature, wild and untamed, was there in abundance to soothe a Thoreau or to ease a Parkman. Nothing was easier in nineteenth-century America than to contract out of urban, commercial civilisation. Now it is impossible, as it has been in Europe for many centuries. Not because there are not enough ponds for putative Thoreaus, or Oregon trails for embryonic Parkmans, but because the myth has grown feebler: myths can only be sustained and given meaning by the needs of society. This aspect of American life – half-dream, half-reality – has lost its social dynamic. Pioneer America is meaningless, not only to hippies, but to the nation at large. It has been commercialised to package tours down the Grand Canyon or up the Santa Fé trail. Escape is easier within oneself. Indeed, there is nowhere else to go.

Furthermore, America is beginning to be afflicted with those ills which beset Italian and Flemish towns of the late Middle Ages – a contraction of opportunity for their middle class or their artisan young. Medieval heretics were often drawn, as were the earlier Quakers, from the class of skilled artisans in times of depression and economic contraction, or in periods of rapid social and technological change which proved inimical to their crafts. The hippies are largely the waste-products of extensive university education systems; the drop-outs who are creatively or intellectually unsuited to the intense competitive system of Horatio Alger America. The acceptance of failure and withdrawal from society are deeply satisfying solutions to stress, anxiety and strain – especially if there is the ultimate safety net of middle-class parents. Religious heresy was rare amongst the abject poor. They preferred saints and miracles, and hippies are not common in the black ghettos of America.

And therein lies a danger, for although individuals and groups can opt out of the political and moral structures of society, the majority of the nation cannot. And opting out changes nothing but the individual. No religious heresy of total or partial withdrawal from society has changed a nation for better or worse. Advancement in social and political justice can only come through political action, revolution or civil war, as indeed the history of America demonstrates. If the hippies develop a philosophy of active civil disobedience the picture may change. If they do not there will be enormous *political* danger in the growth of hippiedom. The aesthetes and decadents, as well as many sensitive liberals, withdrew likewise from active policies in Germany in the 1920s and 1930s. Politics for them were corrupt, violent and dishonest, and withdrawal seemed to possess a higher morality, to be a more sensitive reaction. A withdrawal of a large segment of the younger generation of the middle class from participation in politics may easily lead, as it did in Germany, to a situation ripe for totalitarian politics. One of the most disquieting aspects of the hippie world is the cultivation of the Indian and the withdrawal from the Negro and his problems which create the central crisis of American politics. Lucy may be in the Sky with Diamonds but it is the Negro in the ghetto who matters.

But will this secular heresy grow? After all, medieval heresies rarely lasted. They were quickly destroyed if not obliterated. They were sporadic fires which only ravaged briefly the healthy body of the Church. And even the Ranters were quietly absorbed by the Quakers who disciplined themselves to live alongside if not within the society they despised. (Will this happen with the hippie rural communities which are growing such splendid vegetables?) Other less ecstatic and more socially-oriented heresies such as occurred at the Reformation, however, established themselves successfully. Printing in the fifteenth century broke down the localisation of medieval heresy: social dislocation and economic change in the sixteenth century gave new heresies opportunities for growth and victory denied to heresy in the Middle Ages.

Indeed, the potential for the growth of heresy is in direct proportion to the means of communication that are available. At the present time secular heresy has an even greater communications system at its command than that exploited by every means of modern communication

– press, radio, television and film. Hence their message and their way of life spreads like a virus, leaping from state to state, from country to country, from continent to continent in the briefest possible time. And they provide by their dress, their buttons, their posters, paint and pot quick bucks for the commercially adroit. The consumer society they hate manures and fertilises their growth. And like the great religious heresies of the Reformation which succeeded in establishing themselves as ortho-doxies, this new secular heresy has begun to spread internationally in a way the beats never did: nor for that matter the London teddy-boys or the mods and rockers. Groups of hippies have emerged in London, in Cambridge, in Oxford, even in the provincial towns of England. Leicester has its flower people and its park has witnessed its first love-in. The Provos in Holland will soon be riding their white bicycles with tulips in their hair and bells on their handlebars. Already there are feeble attempts, and they will grow stronger, to give these seemingly spontaneous growths international organisation and common propaganda.

For any religious or secular heresy to succeed requires a social context that will nurture and strengthen it. In return it must meet the aspirations and create the opportunities not merely for a handful of folk but for considerable and diverse sections of a community. This was true for Christianity, for Lutheranism, for Calvinism, for the Quakers, Unitar-ians, Mormons, Methodists and the rest, all of which began as heresies. It is as true of intellectual heresy as of religious. Is there a resonance between the hippies and new situations in our society which may echo louder and more clearly in the near future? Maybe. Youth has achieved a freedom and an affluence that in previous societies was limited to the aristocracy and to very small sections of the rich middle class. What was once the privilege of a narrow segment of society has acquired a mass basis. Throughout history youth, especially its élite in intelligence and creativity, has rarely been drawn to the adult world, but it was forced to accept it and to obey it. The weight of society was too great, the structure of family life too firm, the acceptance of the Christian morality of the Churches too widespread for more than rebellion and rejection on the part of gifted individuals clustered in small groups. Most children and adolescents accepted, worked, obeyed and joined the adults. Those days may be over.

The opportunity for youth to rebel successfully is made easier because society itself is no longer sure either of its institutions or its morality. After all both were derived from a basically agrarian and craft-based society. The unitary family proved a remarkably viable basic unit in pre-industrial society and so did the extended family in the Orient. In the early stages of industrialisation the family proved adequate though far weaker; but it may be doubted if it will survive into a world moulded by technology and science. Certainly its sanctions are crumbling at every level. Few fathers today possess a tenth of the authority of their grandfathers, either over workers or children, and the father is the core of the family as we know it. One has only to contrast Jewish and Negro family life to see the truth of this statement. To the sensitive young the social structure of the adult world must seem hypocritical and luminous with decay, as ripe for revolution as the Tsardom of Nicholas II. And I suspect that attitude is acquiring the force of truth in Moscow as well as New York. Because social institutions have lasted ten thousand years, it does not mean that they are eternal: ten thousand years is a very brief span in the history of mankind.

The family, as an institution, may have reached a danger point; just as the aristocracy did in 1789 or the Roman Catholic Church at the time of the Reformation. The situation, oddly enough, is not dissimilar. · Institutions that are unsure of themselves, given to practices that are at odds with their avowed ideals, often crumble before a sharp radical attack, so long as this has a wide base, and this is the current situation between youth and its social targets in the adult world – marriage, monogamy, family life. It may not be too far-fetched to conceive of the Western world being caught up in a new type of social upheaval: a social revolutionary young attacking the institutions not of political life but of adult living. Possible, but, I think, unlikely. For the hippies do not possess the most important weapon in all revolutionary movements – a coherent ideology that interlocks belief and actions, that combines philosophy with the strategy and tactics of action. If one looks back at the successful historical movements or the triumphing political and social revolutions of the past, they have always possessed, as well as deep emotional drives, a strong intellectual content. An active ideology – coherent, rational within its own principles – marks Calvinism as well as Communism, the Quakers as well as the Jacobins. But the hippie world is a flight from the intellect and all that the intellect implies. It does not wish to dominate reality but to flee from it: to mock the adult world, not capture and change it. It possesses attitudes but not an ideology.

The hippie movement remains adolescent – confused, emotional, idealistic, protest rather than propaganda, an experience but not an ideology. And its social criticism remains merely a personal expression, not a dynamic of political action. In this it relates most closely to those estatic heresies of the Middle Ages that were also savagely anti-clerical, that dwelt with bitterness on the riches, the greed, the corruption of the clergy, and the simplicity and poverty of Christ: the contrast between the ideal and the reality. In this, the hippies' criticism, by implication and by action, of the straight world – its self-indulgence, its hypocrisy, its materialism – may lie their greatest contribution to society. The alarming gulf between avowed intention and action, as in Vietnam, is leading to moral bankruptcy. The American Dream, like America's Manifest Destiny, is dissolving, giving way to a future not of hope but of nightmare.

If the hippies force us to look at ourselves morally and spiritually naked, then well and good – but they may provoke a blinder and less sensitive reaction. They are playing as dangerously with social passions as any heretic played with religious passions in the Middle Ages. And remember how society turned on *them*, how its inquisitors tortured them, burnt them, extirpated their women and children, rooted them out, purged society of its danger. America, faced by insoluble problems, made frantic by riot and by the prospect of moral defeat, may vent its spleen and crush all liberal attitudes, using as one of its excuses the social nonconformity of the hippies. Heresies without ideology or the discipline necessary for political action have usually ended in disaster.

The hippies are a part of a social and historical process, and many strands are united in their beliefs and actions; but so far in man's long history no movement that has ignored power has ever succeeded, and all groups who have made a cult of social anarchy have either been defeated or destroyed. In the absence of a political creed and of a programme the hippies must be regarded as a symptom, not a social force – they are a living phantom bred by the decadent hypocrisy of so much of America's social and political morality.

(v) Middle-Class Bombs

A middle-class girl blows her parents' house sky-high in the middle of Manhattan. Other young people from respectable and affluent family backgrounds are caught planting bombs.

The spectrum of violence ranges from these extravagant extremes to brutality of language and gesture. But to violence of some kind tens of thousands of middle-class American boys and girls are committed. It bodes unthinkable future disasters. Will Americans have to learn to live with campus riots, burning of public buildings, and obscenity used as a social and political weapon? If so, why? Would it not be better to reduce the number of students at some universities, close others, and get back to instruction – back indeed to the good old days of the 1950s, when students in crewcuts conformed, never questioned their professors, and cheerfully joined the corporations?

To most middle-aged Americans the student revolt is as startling, as unlooked-for as an outbreak of yellow fever. Yet, oddly enough, it is the result of a condition with deep historical roots, going back some 400 years or more in Europe, and a number of generations in America – a fact of which the students themselves, amongst myriad others, are unaware. None of the authors involved in the protest movement whom I have been reading recently seems to be conscious of history, or indeed of any need to look at the past in order to discover the source of their problems.

But, first of all, one more general observation. It seems to me, an Englishman, that America has become too hysterical about protest, too hysterical even about riots and the occasional bomb. Although the country is, by European standards, extremely tolerant of personal violence, including murder, it has experienced little organised violence employed for ideological ends. There was, of course, a little in the struggle for trade union recognition, and I am aware of both the Revolution and the Civil War. But Europe has lived with bomb-throwers, arsonists, and rioters for decades. It has grown used to the ugly extremes of rabid nationalism and class tension. And it is hard for Americans to grasp that they too have a class war as well as racial tension on their hands. Indeed America, with nowhere to expand, heavily urbanised and racially divided, is rapidly acquiring a European type of society, and with it similar problems.

There is, however, a vital difference. The image, the dream, that America manufactured for itself – of an open, expanding, liberal society, full of opportunity, where the good life was easier to find than anywhere else, where individuality was prized more than anywhere else – no longer matches the facts. The contrast between dream and reality, seen with clarity by the young, is intensely depressing, for the reality is a diminishing of opportunity, a contraction of idealism, a visible network of corruption, oppression, and greed. Of course, mixed with the evil is much good. much idealism, much aspiration, but the uncritical acceptance of old-fashioned American social values is well-nigh an impossibility now for any intelligent and sensitive man or woman under twenty-five.

If one is still puzzled, just buy these books that I have been reading. They are typical enough of the growing volume of protest literature. Michael Myerson's *These Are the Good Old Days: Coming of Age as a Radical in America's Late, Late Years* is the most disturbing, the best written, and the most committed. Myerson possesses the toughness, rigidity and political acumen of the true revolutionary intellectual – a common enough phenomenon in Paris or Milan, or even London, but comparatively rare in an American city until these last few years. Like many other revolutionaries, however, Myerson has a marvellous way with facts. He accuses the free world of wholesale destruction of human life, but never mentions Stalin's liquidation of the Russian peasantry.

His rhetoric is convincing until one steps aside and looks at it critically. He is a type that will become increasingly common in the United States.

More sympathetic but duller is Paul Cowan's *The Making of an Un-American*, a rather naïve and narcissistic account of the author's experiences in the Peace Corps and his gradual realisation of the nature of American imperialism – its fear of social revolution in Latin America, its paranoia and its greed – and of the hypocrisy of the American ideals which he grew up to believe. Indeed, Cowan represents yet another strand of America's radical youth: the sensitive, self-involved, highly articulate, but politically ingenuous intellectual. It is hard to conceive that a European youth could have been so politically unsophisticated as Cowan was after so prolonged an education.

More provocative, and closer to the campus, is the young Englishman Richard Zorza's *The Right to Say 'We'*, a highly emotional, hectically written book about the Harvard riots of 1969. Again there is a sense of naïveté, of touching adolescent yearning, and, interestingly enough, of the value of direct political experience in developing maturity.

Except for Myerson, who is at least aware of the 1930s, there is in all these authors a dangerous dislocation from the past, and thus no attempt to analyse a situation, only to blame it. History, I fear, is irrelevant to the young. They do not know that they are the heirs of a long tradition of student revolt evident in Latin America and Europe for two or three generations. Even more, they consider as unique situations and experiences that have been common to youth throughout history. They never realise that they, as well as their elders, are manacled by time.

The student crisis is the culmination of two factors: for several centuries the young have been excluded from the adult world, including its amusements. (In the sixteenth and seventeenth centuries children partook of every aspect of adult life, its bawdiness as well as its solemnities.) The second factor is the result of the growing complexity of society, which places ever greater demands on education, requiring it to produce not only knowledge of crafts but also conventional patterns of personality. For generation after generation a type of Christian gentleman was trained to occupy places of authority. True, a few rejected the mould for which they were destined. But for most, education and social behaviour based on capitalist and patriarchal society were inseparably linked. This was achieved by segregating the young and regulating their lives to an incredible extent. Such training was, of course, largely confined to the affluent middle class, the owners of society.

The growth of science and technology, the collapse of empires, the filling-up and urbanisation of America, and two devastating mass wars have broken the old patterns, while leaving children and adolescents subject to the old disciplines. But authority has been undermined; long-accepted social roles have lost their universality of appeal. Once they were gone, the sacrifices demanded of children and youths appeared ever more meaningless. Why should they go without sex, without the excitement of drugs or alcohol? Why, above all, should they accept a career, that offered little joy for the sake of a dubious future?

For a century and a half students have been exploited in the interests of the adult world from which they were excluded. Massed together as never before, drawn increasingly from social groups who never expected to enjoy authority or power, is it surprising that they should rebel? The old world of childhood and youth that served our ancestors so well, yet at so great an emotional cost, is crumbling, and it cannot be saved. The tirades of Agnew will be as useless as the imprecations of Canute. Tides cannot be stopped – diverted, channelled, maybe, but not stopped. Youth is surging back into the adult world, and they have every right to say 'we'. Student protest is the foam on a tidal wave that will swamp and change society.

(vi) Crime Against the Person

For years I have been an addict of Brooklyn Bridge which from the catwalk recalls, with its gothic arches and flying cables, the nave of a splendid mediaeval cathedral. After a nostalgic luncheon with Alfred Kazin, standing by the spot where Walt Whitman printed the *Leaves of Grass* and looking into the Pilgrims Church, where Charles Dickens preached in Brooklyn Heights, it seemed natural enough to walk across it once more. Broad daylight, middle of the afternoon, there seemed no danger in that. And yet, leaving Alfred in the middle of the bridge and looking back towards Brooklyn, I knew it was going to happen. and yet stupidly I returned. I had seen him lounging by the pillars, a young elegant black in a curious Cardinal's biretta. As soon as I drew near, he approached and asked for a quarter. Putting on my best English accent, I told him I did not understand. Drawing a short bayonet from his coat and pointing it at my jugular, he said 'You understand this?' and demanded all of my money. Fortunately it was divided, a half on each side of my wallet, so I gave him half, which he took and fled. I had noticed twenty or thirty yards away a bicyclist dismount and sit on the broadwalk. After the black had run off he cycled by and naturally refused to give chase. Indeed, to make certain that he was not involved, he dismounted and sat down again – glum and silent. The emergency telephone was naturally out of order, the police station nearby had been closed. The police once found were courteous and mildly interested. I waded through a huge rogues' gallery of photographs, but to no avail. Yet the experience haunted me for days, like an automobile accident for which one was not responsible. One thought of all the actions one might have taken and did not. But worse was a sense of anxiety and hostility that I felt, combined with apprehension, every time I saw a young black at a lonely street corner or empty sidewalk or subway passage: feelings I had never experienced before. Hostility, fear, hate: are these the emotions with which, as mugging spreads, our society has to live?

Month in month out the figures mount as personal violence spreads not only to the suburbs but to countries and cities like France and London which have been comparatively free. The statistics pile up, computerised, analysed, and become the base for the pontifications of psychologists, sociologists, criminologists and moralists of every kind. It is poverty; it is large families; it is the absence of a powerful father; the presence of too savage a father; the breakdown of family life; bad housing; bad schooling; social deprivation of blacks; decay of morality; the spread of radicalism with its hatred of private property. And, of course, drugs. All muggers, it would seem, are desperate for a fix. And not to be beaten in the rush for headlines, the medicals have muscled in too. Violence is often genetic, an extra male chromosome sends you murderous and berserk. The TV panels give us selected brews of these experts who wrestle portentously with statistics with a glum pessimism; their cures as widely divergent as their diagnosis – severe sentences; milder sentences; medical treatment; rehabilitation through love; street vigilantes; increased boys' clubs for adventure activities; more jobs; better housing; better street lighting; more police on the streets; and so on and so on. However, there is one professional whose views are never asked on these panels – namely the historian. Crime on the streets is rarely considered in the perspective of time. If it were, there would be less blather about the decadence of our time, or indeeed its public violence. By comparison with times past, it is only moderately violent and moderately criminal. Also, for reasons that are historically credible, it may be likely that crimes of violence, particularly assaults on the person will, towards the end of the present decade, begin to decline – and whatever fashionable nostrum there is then in vogue will be hailed as the curative process. This is not to deny that roots of crime push deep into the structure of society, drawing sustenance from its fissures and strains and deep pools of misery, or that social control is without effect. But there are other seismic movements at work.

What historical evidence we have about mugging on a large scale derives largely from Europe.

And crime in Western Europe was intense, widespread and rapidly growing from the sixteenth century until the middle decades of the nineteenth century when there was some easement which lasted until the end of World War II when growth again became very rapid. In 1890 or 1930, strolling about the West End of London or the main Boulevards of Paris, you were unlikely to be mugged: riding the countryside on a bicycle or walking it on foot you were just as unlikely to be robbed. Little girls and boys had an excellent chance not to be raped. A vast change from the previous century. By the standards of England or France of the eighteenth century even modern New York is relatively crime-free. Highwaymen festooned London, robbing coaches in Hyde Park in broad daylight with impunity; travellers making the journey to Yorkshire without being robbed blessed their luck, Rape, often of the very young, was depressingly commonplace. House-breaking ran neck and neck with mugging in prevalence and audacity; late in the century even Buckingham Palace was broken into and robbed. Gang violence and mob violence were endemic. Compared with the Gordon Riots in London in 1780, the ghetto riots in America of the late 1960s appear like a holiday fiesta of unruly children. In four days of riot 300 people were killed, $50,000,000 of damage resulted from 36 separate fires. All prisons were broken open, then put to the torch. In more peaceful days any bourgeois who angered the mob was likely to have his house pulled down about his ears. Petty thieving knew no bounds. Nor was the countryside much more peaceful: gangs of professional robbers terrorized France in the late eighteenth century, often murdering for sheer pleasure – raping, beating to death, cutting throats and often stripping and coupling the cadavers: sometimes they would feast, drink and dance around the corpses. As for child criminals, boys and girls, London and Paris were full of them: they increased in Paris during the revolutionary period and lived in droves in early nineteenth-century London. The shutters of French houses and great formidable doors bespeak a bourgeoisie rightly terrified of violence and theft. England was little better.

And let it be stressed, we know of only a fraction of the crime committed: most then as now, went unrecorded and unpunished, perhaps 90 per cent. The severity of punishment, then as now, was no deterrent. Men were quartered, broken on the wheel: children branded, at times burnt alive: it only made juries reluctant to condemn. A great deal of this crime, then as now, can be laid at the door of poverty, so long as it is realised that it was provoked by the presence of affluence. All-embracing grinding poverty does not, as the villages of India demonstrate, provoke widespread violent personal crime. What eighteenth-century London and Paris provided was the sight of obvious and increasing affluence, dangled before the eyes of desperate men and women. There was more to steal. Almost any prosperous bourgeois in eighteenth-century England had a gold watch, gold trinkets, golden guineas in his pocket and expensive clothes in his trunk. He was a plumper target than his grandfather and great-grandfather had been. But poverty combined with opportunity to steal was only one thread in a complex social situation.

More important, perhaps, than opportunity, was the age of the criminals. As the average life was about thirty, these were youthful societies. Even so, in the late eighteenth century and early nineteenth a larger proportion of the population were children and adolescents. Then, as now, a great proportion of violent crime was committed by young men between fifteen and twenty-five, and it is not surprising that as the growth of violent crime levelled off towards the end of the nineteenth century, for this too is the time when the proportion of the young men under twenty-five diminished. Of course, contemporaries pointed to a more effective police force, to the deterrent nature of prison sentences and to the closer correlation between criminal and punishment, for no longer were children hanged for theft, or servant girls burnt alive for attempting to poison their mistresses. All of these things may or may not have had their effects. It is, however, doubtful: most crime goes unreported and undetected and certainly unpunished, so that deeper social factors must have been at work. Violent crime has always been a young man's game (true, many continue in their thirties and forties, but the commitment to crime usually happens in adolescence). Perhaps what industrial society has failed to do this last three hundred years is to provide adequate activities for the aggression of adolescents, particularly those – mainly the poor – whose social lives provide none for them either in commerce or in the professions. Since the sixteenth century, affluence dangled before the poor and deprived has excited both cupidity and hate; the growth of great urban centres has created opportunity for anonymous violence; so crime has been endemic, becoming epidemic as the adolescent population has grown or fallen.

Soon the proportion of our own adolescent age groups that have swollen so greatly since World War II will begin to fall. And with that, doubtless, will fall the mugging and raping. At least for those who are violently robbed there is one mild consolation, it was worse in earlier times. This is not the first age in which the young poor have taken their personal revenge on the elderly rich.

(vii) A Drug is a Drink is a Smoke

New York, vital, beautiful, opulent, is smeared with slime – poverty, decadence, decay and drugs. Amidst the power and glittering riches there are pools of human debris, lives broken by abundance as well as poverty.

Who can ever forget the haunting story of young Friede, crawling the gutters of the Lower East Side in a hired car with his girl dead in its trunk, wandering aimlessly like some mindless, battered insect, stopping and starting, remembering and forgetting, caring and not caring? Wealthy, well-educated, replete with advantages that would have seemed paradisiacal to the hungry and ambitious adolescents of Latin America or Africa, he and his girl frittered their lives away with dope. Dick Schaap in the piece of effective reportage, *Turned On*, brings back the sad, grey story, nauseating in its futility and witlessness. At the thought of such young wasted lives the bile rises: surely the Narcotics Bureau should be strengthened; surely the penalties imposed on pushers and traders should become really punitive.

The Friede case was but one sensational event in what is rapidly becoming a flowing tide that will engulf more and more of the younger generation in drugs. Universities are particularly prone: Oxford and Cambridge, Harvard, Yale, and Berkeley acquire increasing numbers of addicts, as well as experimenters playing, it is true, mainly with hemp and LSD rather than with heroin. What the youth of America and England do today, the youth of Europe, East and West, will do tomorrow or the day after. There will be other sensations, other Friede cases, perhaps even more terrible and more haunting: personal tragedy will sear homes from which want, disease and cruelty have been banished. Why can this be?

The spread of drugs gives the castigators of our civilisation a wonderful time. They trot out all the old clichés about youth's loss of Christian morality, about the breakdown of the family and marriage, the artificiality of modern life with its emotional emptiness and boredom in an age of machines, the lack of those deep satisfactions felt by the peasant and craftsman, hungry and downtrodden though they were. Is the very affluence that gives youth much leisure but too little work, much security but too little direction the key to its wantonness? If the bread line were just around the corner would the desire for dope vanish? After all, the youth of Athens and Cairo are not riding high on LSD, amphetamines, heroin, and the like. Few Jeremiahs have had it so good as those who prophesy the doom, and revel at the decadence, of today's Western youth. And too many, far too many, ordinary decent liberals go along with them, at least half the way. Where drugs are concerned, much of the adult population suffers a semantic blockage and, as ever, they rarely think historically. It is hard to get drugs into perspective.

What society in recorded history, save perhaps a few of the most aboriginal, has not tolerated, indeed sometimes, welcomed, the use of stimulants or drugs? None that I know. Once invented – maybe very, very early in the Neolithic revolution – the use of alcohol by kings, priests and people spread like a bush fire. The earliest farmers in England were buried with their beer beakers, presumably to enable them to wassail through eternity. And peasant societies do not just take alcohol; they get drunk. Look at Brueghel's pictures, or at films of festivals in Nepal or the Andes, or wherever primitive agrarian production is the dominant way of life. In industrial society, of course, millions of men and women get high on alcohol week in and week out. The mutilated and lifeless bodies that result from automobile accidents by drivers overdrugged with alcohol are the price society seems willing to pay for its addiction to drink. Add to the wrecked cars the broken homes of alcoholics, their self-destruction, the huge waste of social capital invested in human lives that drink brings about year after year.

Yet temperance is akin to crankiness. Without alcohol, magazines as well as men would wilt. I am addicted enough to loathe the prospect of a world without wine. We accept alcohol, we have socialised it, and we have shut our eyes to the immense damage that total addiction causes because we handle our own addiction competently, well within the tolerance that our temperaments and physiques permit. But let us be honest: we need a chorus of Gertrude Steins chiming in our ears, 'A drink is a drug is a drug is a drink is a drug'.

'What about Islam?' one may inquire. 'There, surely, is freedom from alcohol.' Yes, but not from hashish, which is as common in Islam as drink in the West. In most Oriental and Near Eastern societies as well as in Mexico, the Caribbean and Central America, marihuana has been socialised as alcohol has been by us, although almost certainly at a lower cost in human wastage. Addiction is less, the results physically not so destructive. That is why *The Marihuana Papers*, edited by David Solomon, should be carefully studied by anyone concerned over the growing spread of reefer smoking in North America and Europe. What is regarded as perfectly normal and respectable in Karachi, Cairo or Algiers, is anti-social and illegal in San Francisco, Boston and New York.

The outlawing of marihuana makes odd reading. Way back in the 1930s Fiorello La Guardia set up a high-powered commission of doctors, biologists, educators and sociologists. They found that marihuana was not being peddled in high schools, that it was not breaking up families, plunging adolescents into degradation, or inflicting physical or mental breakdown on its users. Indeed, on the face of this evidence, reefers would seem to be far less harmful than not only alcohol but also tobacco – another killing drug that we permit, knowing its evil, long-term effects on the human body. But as yet no government in the world, whether bright red or deep blue, whether dictatorial or democratic, has made anything but token gestures to reduce or suppress tobacco addiction.

Once more let us have a chant by Gertrude Stein chorus, 'A drug is a drink is a smoke is a drug is a drink'.

James I hated tobacco – a beastly, filthy habit that he naturally associated with subversives as well as decadents. New drugs to those who do not use them always seem the peculiar prerogative of subversives. When James I's grandson, Charles II, came to the English throne, he grew very apprehensive about the spread of coffee-drinking and particularly coffee-houses, where he felt opponents of his régime came together not only to indulge in the brew, but to breed sedition. He subjected them to rigorous control, even thoughts of suppressing cafés altogether, but again the drug won. As did tea. Tea was initially regarded as such an effeminate drink that the heavy manual worker sneeringly stuck to his early morning beer; however, once his prejudices were overcome, he found a deep reddish brown brew of Indian tea to be a more effective stimulant. In fact, energised by tea, he was a better worker. But still a drugged one – as are the caffeine addicts of America or Europe.

Drugs everywhere abound. And when anything abounds there is investment, private and public. Vast fortunes can be, indeed are being, made from alcohol and nicotine, caffeine, and the host of minor drugs and sedatives and stimulants that we all use. Because of these strongly vested interests there is always resistance to anything that will cut sharply into profits. Thus, whatever their drain on human life, nicotine and alcohol are not going to be added to the Narcotics Bureau's list. Moreover, human beings are odd, curiously persistent, and often very lawless where legal restriction cuts across their needs: if the industrial West wants to adopt marihuana, or anything else for that matter, punitive actions will be as useless as Prohibition was in the 1920s.

It should be realised that drugs become less harmful when socialised: if alcohol could be purchased only in the company of alcoholics it would be infinitely more dangerous. With technological advance more drugs will become easily available; like most human addictions, they need long, dispassionate and scientific appraisal. Perhaps sensible permission is indicated rather than punitive prohibition. For a society that bans marihuana and permits alcohol is ripe for the satire of a Swift. However, we are not alone in our folly; after all, Islam permits marihuana and bans alcohol. Will man ever be truly conscious of its absurdities? To that question the historical perspective gives a gloomy answer.

(viii) The Death of the Outback

I have just come across one of the most moving books that I have ever encountered. Normally one re-reads books; this one is to be looked at time and time again, looked at and thought about, looked at and brooded on, especially by those who reside in, or whose roots go back to, remote places. The subject, I am sure, will not seem promising. It is Newfoundland or, rather, that part of it which so many of us, looking down from a plane, see as a wilderness of ice and rock and forest, rarely giving a thought for those who dwell there. Farley Mowat and John de Visser went and lived amongst the outporters, the fishermen and their families who inhabit the rugged, gale-scarred coast lands, far from St Johns, let alone the mainland of the United States or Canada. These simple people, descendants frequently of Portuguese, Basque and Breton fishermen, who may have begun to roost on Newfoundland's rocks a century before Columbus sailed, live lives of great simplicity and constant struggle against climate and crueller sea. Seals and whales and fish sustain their modest existence, which is depicted by John de Visser in some of the most poignant and dramatic pictures I have ever seen. Almost as vividly Farley Mowat describes these Newfoundlanders. By reaching back into their past and indicating their bleak future he gives depth to our understanding of them. *This Rock Within the Sea: A Heritage Lost* may look like a coffee-table book; it is in fact a requiem not only for a part of Newfoundland, but for a way of life.

When man lived by hunting, space was essential to him, and he steadily penetrated the most inhospitable terrain; neither the tundra nor the tropical forest nor the scorching desert nor the wild coasts of Tierra del Fuego daunted him. His exceptional intelligence and retentive memory; his capacity to name and distinguish the tiniest details of his environment; above all, the cunning of his hands that fashioned tools from rock and bone and wood made it possible for him to master those forbidding lands, to breed generations of his kind century after century, millennium, after millennium. In the remoter areas – the Arctic islands, the Australian desert, the Amazonian jungle, and far distant Patagonia – once the environment had been sufficiently dominated to maintain a steady subsistence, there was little change; it was in these places that the European discovered some of the most primitive tribes of mankind: primitive, yet with miraculously developed skills that enabled them to survive. And this was true even of the Onas of Tierra del Fuego, who were almost as civilised as the aboriginal Tasmanians, whom the English hunted to death in the nineteenth century.

Indeed, reading and looking at *This Rock Within the Sea* led me to reread E. Lucas Bridges' *The Uttermost Part of the Earth*, a brilliant book and a masterpiece of its kind. Published in 1948, it tells of the Onas, who lived in the gale-blown islands, straits and fiords of southern Tierra del Fuego that reach out to Cape Horn – almost certainly the wildest country in the world and the loneliest. The Onas did not even know how to make fire; except for a cloak of fur, they went naked (sensible since their dugouts often capsized in those turbulent waters, and they swam like fish). Although they had no idea of God or gods, their social lives were complex, threaded with ritual and highly communal. The Onas coped with their hostile environment, and their population, which neither grew nor diminished, stayed in balance.

Then the white men arrived, bringing sheep, for which they needed labourers. Thus the Onas were clothed and reduced to daily toil. The white men also brought measles and so killed off the Onas almost completely. A story of simple tragedy that could be told of most of the earth's remote places. But to this old tale *The Rock Within the Sea* adds a new ironic twist. For it would seem that time is taking its revenge on those who with their superior technology pushed out the primitive peoples. They are now following them into limbo.

The modern world has little use for the marginal lands and the people who struggle to live off them. Factory ships and modern trawlers decimate small fishing communities as easily as herring – as easily as the amenities of modern civilisation shrivel faraway isolated towns and villages. Farley Mowat and John de Visser bitterly blame the government of Newfoundland for the steady depopulation of its outports and for the dreadful sense of loss that these simple fishermen and their wives feel when they have to abandon their homes. Certainly not much wisdom or compassion has been shown. Optimistic growth centres that have been created have rapidly turned into dying communities of the unemployed. Uprooted and lost, the middle-aged and the old wait stoically for the end of their time; the young bolt to Canada, to Quebec and Montreal, to a new life of neon lights, pop groups and opportunity.

But government policy or no government policy, this would have happened. The world is contracting, not expanding. So in the Newfoundland outports the people are leaving, as they are leaving the Faroes, the Hebrides, the northern isles of Norway; even localities nearer the great cities – the Auvergne in France, the Appenines of Italy's deep south, the Pennine Chain in England are emptying too. Nor is America immune – the drift from Vermont, from Maine, has long been pronounced. Modern life no longer requires the marginal lands on which our grandfathers waged so stern, so bitter a fight with nature.

To realise just how bitter and stern the fight can be, turn to John de Visser's magnificent photographs, particularly those that illustrate the chapters called 'Bastions of Courage' and 'It Won't Be Very Long'; linger over the last haunting picture of this group. These human beings clung like limpets to their barren rocks. They had no flowers, no trees, hardly any soil; potato patches had to be made by hand; only the sea yielded a harvest and the bleak mountains an occasional windfall. The sense of aloneness, particularly in sickness and in death, must have been profound – and the sea, of course, constantly sucked in its victims.

Lives lived so starkly, so remotely, so intimately with nature at its harshest bred trust, compassion, neighbourliness, resourcefulness – qualities that contrast strongly with the delinquency and violence of our towns. Onas did not lynch each other; the outporters never locked their doors. Such communities did, of course, have their vicious sides, their ignorance and superstition. As with most isolated groups, the Newfoundlanders could get prodigiously drunk. And doubtless bitter feuds were handed down from father to son. Pity should be reserved for those who have been caught in the inexorable extinction of their ways of life and not for the ways themselves.

Nothing can stop this withdrawal from places either hostile or remote. It will go on and on until they are empty, save for an occasional temporary community of technicians – radio specialists in Thule, uranium miners in the Yukon, or here and there, where the climate is good, a tourist resort – Hiltons on the Caymans or the Cocos. But the great expansion of men and women into every corner of the earth in order to live there generation after generation is over. The great contraction has begun; the great conglomerates, the great antheaps will replace them. One can only hope that out of the upheaval which they generate will come a balance as delicate, as supremely viable as that which the Onas created for themselves in Tierra del Fuego or the outporters of Newfoundland.

(ix) The Beauty of America

The beauty of America never ceases to amaze me. In my own country, upstate New York would be regarded with reverential awe, and much of New England considered one of the most glorious of heritages. Yet how insignificant even they become when placed alongside the staggering beauties of the West. There is scarcely an inch of Great Britain, save for the seashore, that is not man-made. Fortunately, tens of thousands of square miles of America have not yet been scarred by humanity. This, however, may not be for long, unless we become more aware, both in England and in America, of man's relationship with his environment. Certainly many Englishmen and even more Americans are troubled.

Other Western countries – except perhaps for the Netherlands, perched on that great sewer of Europe, the Rhine – are less worried, while Africa, India, the Far East, and Central and South America seem blandly indifferent. Of course, even in those latter regions there are devoted men and women with their own particular concerns about wildlife or ancient monuments. Here and there, as in Kenya, governments have been forced to protect their vanishing game, though maybe as much for the sake of tourist traffic as for the safety of the animals. But only in America and Britain has conservation become a vital political issue. Some Western European nations are now following in their wake, and the fascinating aspect of this change is that the most highly urbanised countries are the most preoccupied with their rural surroundings. Perhaps only industrial societies can afford the luxury – and the cost – of proper environmental care.

Long, long ago, 10,000 years or so, when men were relatively few, there was no problem. Moreover, just as the Australian aborigines of today exploit their environment with great care, it is likely that prehistoric man exercised caution in his hunting – sparing the pregnant female animals, taking the young only occasionally. But the neolithic revolution, which led to agriculture and the domestication of animals, altered all that. Sheep-breeding ruined the ecology of central Spain. The primitive farmers of Britain stripped the north and west of its woodlands. The Mediterranean coast of Africa and its hinterland are other man-made disasters produced by careless farming. Many will remember how close Oklahoma came to turning itself into another vast desert – again through wanton, thoughtless exploitation.

Peasants do not care. For them, with rare exceptions, the country is hostile and has little aesthetic appeal. No English farm labourer bothers about the tin shacks, pylons or junk heaps that disfigure the land. Our concern with our environment is relatively recent, less perhaps than one hundred years old, and for most of that time it has been a minority movement, an obsession of antiquaries, animal lovers, vegetarians and do-gooders. There was nothing in it for the politicians.

The changing attitudes to nature, to the wild environments and man's spoliation of them, began with Romanticism, arising in the most urbanised parts of Western Europe, and were almost entirely confined to the sensitive members of the middle class. Only towards the end of the nineteenth century, with the popularity of the bicycle and the growth of hiking clubs, did the artisan and the working man get his opportunity to appreciate the splendours of nature, and its capacity to refresh with space, solitude and the hypnotic sense of timelessness. And so were bred those small societies for the preservation of antiquities and the protection of wildlife. Yet the men and women who gave their energies to save our heritage were mostly conceived of as obstinate cranks, thwarters of progress, lunatic opponents of profit, and therefore probably cryptocommunists or pinkos. Although they had their victories, great and small, winning a national park in the Rockies, saving a terrace of houses in Savannah, their sense of urgency affected only a few politicians. Only if connected with tourism did it acquire real bite; then the politicians' voice would bellow forth to save the bison or the redwoods.

Now suddenly, there is a new awareness, a horrified realisation that man may destroy himself more efficiently by ruining his environment than by manufacturing nuclear weapons. Agrarian society was destructive; industrial society is a billion times more so.

The real danger, however, is industry plus reproduction. And here let me recommend to you a disturbing yet penetrating article by Charlton Ogburn, Jr, 'Catastrophe by Numbers', in the December 1969 issue of *American Heritage*. Ogburn's statistics are appalling. It is not food that is the problem – science may easily take care of that – but resources, space, and the rate at which we destroy and pollute our environment without any thought of future generations. DDT works, so use it and damn the consequences. It's the same with oil and gasoline. And, above all, it's the same with children. We want them, we will have them. Conservation is not just preserving this piece of the Rockies or that old street of brownstones. It has become a massive problem of social education and social engineering, in which law and coercion will have to be used.

This brilliant article of Ogburn's should be in every school, in every home. Man's greed, his blind satisfaction of his own appetites must be checked; and there are signs that, at last, governments are putting the needs of the people before immediate profits.

If anyone doubts the value of such social discipline, such concern with the welfare of the majority of men and women and their environment, let him buy *The American West*, by Ann and Myron Sutton. In it the beauties of the West, not only its mountains, canyons and deserts but also its animals, birds and insects are displayed in the most magnificent photographs I have ever seen. Here is a heritage of incomparable splendour, stretching from the arctic wastes of Alaska to the tropical waters of Baja California. Enjoy the photography, then read the text, and you will understand in what jeopardy this great treasure stands, how it already has been violated and corroded, and that only through the relentless and dedicated fight of committed men and women, occasionally backed by state or federal aid, has so much been preserved.

But time is short. Within thirty years another 100 million Americans will be eating up the space and the solitude, clamouring for the oil and the minerals, spewing out their consumer waste. Indeed, as Charlton

Ogburn stresses, the key to conservation is the control of reproduction: without that, defeat is certain, for we should remember that man is nature's most formidable parasite. Quaint though it may seem to us now, our tax systems may have to go sharply into reverse – bonuses for bachelors, high taxes on large families. That could happen within a decade, and even then it may be too late.

(x) The Future Without the Past

The next fifty years – exciting, terrifying, or just plain unbearable? The future used to be a matter for the imaginative novelist, for a Jules Verne or an H. G. Wells, and as far as technological development was concerned the latter was quite brilliant in his forecast. But those days are over. The computer is more precise than the imagination, and although it cannot devise an invention, it can be terrifyingly exact about development. The number of people who, barring global accidents, will be alive in 2017 is easily assessed, and so is where most of them will be living – in America, it seems, in three to five megalopolises. The racial structures of these great cities can be forecast but not, of course, their race relations. Nevertheless the information available is huge, and information can be used. The American Institute of Planners, to celebrate its fiftieth anniversary, called a conference of exceptional importance to discuss the future of man's environment: to ponder on the problems the computers tell us will be ours. Its first series of papers has now been published – *Environment for Man: The Next Fifty Years*, edited by William R. Ewald, Jr. The result is a stirring, stimulating, baffling book, in which brilliance of analysis is to be found side by side with impenetrable opacity of thought. Yet it is a volume that everyone who is concerned with the quality of life should read.

Universities in the United States have devoted considerable facilities in men, money and space to urban research, the pathological aspects of city life – suicide, alcoholism, drug-addiction and delinquency. Biologists, too, have now entered this arena, formerly reserved for sociologists and psychologists; overcrowded rats stop reproducing, they find, and some birds become maniacally aggressive if their territories are invaded. *Ergo* human beings. . . . But, as John W. Dyckman says in his essay 'City Planning and the Treasury of Science' (by far the wisest of these papers): 'It is virtually impossible to assign meaning to these findings. Urbanisation is a process which stands for a whole cluster of other processes, and for scores of social and economic variables'.

And men are neither rodents nor birds. Hong Kong, the densest of human colonies, breeds furiously, and mankind clusters like gannets without going mad with rage. The effect of urban environment on people is exceptionally complex; the danger lies in concentrating on mechanical shortcomings, congestion, pollution, noise, substandard architecture. Easy to measure and turn into socio-political debate, they have been the happy hunting grounds for planners. From these preoccupations developed a derogation of city life, a stress on its unnaturalness for man, a growing mythology that is preoccupied with a city's anonymity, the loneliness of its crowd, its destruction of family life, and its rootlessness. The city, in fact, of Satan. And to highlight its evil, an even sillier mythology has grown up about the satisfactions of small rural communities, the contact with nature, the face-to-face living, the naturalness of craft; we are told that making things by hand gratifies man in a way that constructing objects by machine never can. Beyond the city is a golden world of environmental harmony, which the city will continue to destroy until totally replanned.

This nonsense, which reaches back to Thoreau, is particularly prevalent in Christopher Alexander's contribution. It is totally unhistorical. Anyone who has worked in the annals of peasant culture or studied the records of small towns knows that these communities are as riven with jealousy, envy and hate, as capable of cold indifference, of neglect, of alienation as any group of city or suburban dwellers. And nothing is more absurd than some qualities that are now attributed to families. One such non-historically based concept is that the modern city has taken education out of the family circle and so lowered the prestige of the father. Outside simple agrarian and peasant societies, education in the family has been the habit only among the unskilled. The apprentice system and the education of the rich well away from home have been constant factors in Western civilisation. Even amongst the poor, domestic service in other families provided what education they received.

One is appalled by the lack of historical dimension in so much modern sociology as well as urban studies. This is particularly true of the American Institute of Planners' conference. Often they express themselves with warm-hearted rhetoric. They know slums and ghettos exist and that they should not. They realise the social tensions of cities, the hatred and fear between the rich and the poor; the splendour of the former's environment, the ugliness of the latter's. At no place, however, does the conference discuss the nature of political action required to effect change. In many ways these planners are like generals deep in the tactics and strategy of war without an army to fight it. Social progress and the improvement of cities have been due to two fundamental processes: one, technological advance, which could be quickly exploited for private profit; the other, radical political protest.

Stanley J. Hallett and Calvin S. Hamilton, who come near to a discussion of the need for action, are aware that politics and planning are intertwined, but the solutions they offer are social, not political. They are great believers in 'cross-fertilisation', in the foundation of mixed groups to participate in planning activity, in democratic decisions at the small-group level. This is splendid until one is brought up sharply by this naïve admittance: 'The most difficult task is to get cross-fertilisation between neighbourhood groups such as the Negro ghetto and the white affluent middle-class neighbourhood groups.'

This is, of course, the core of the matter. How can planning work in a society that has sharp social divisions due to disparity in wealth as well as difference in colour? How can planning work if profit, personal or corporate, must be a more urgent motive than control and conservation? So long as society is structured as it is, there will be slums; the looming towers on the fringe of Harlem are more hygienic at the moment than the old slums; they have more amenities – light, air and no rats – but they are not the environment of the future. By 2025 they will be decrepit, sordid slums. Without political action, no amount of thinking about environment, no amount of planning the optimum space and minimal communal facilities can be effective, except for those who possess the advantages already. And that means political action of a radical nature. The history of the last hundred years shouts this fact aloud. Human beings are like carrion crows, not Christians. They will not give up what they have to the poor; they have to be scared before they will disgorge.

Environmental problems get too easily abstracted from social problems – and the latter from their historical roots. These planners tend to define all problems in terms of architecture, communications, sociology and psychology, and to leave class structure and politics alone.

Curiously, they neglect the enticements and attractions of urban life. The city, after all, has for centuries been a magnet for human beings, who have flocked into them whatever the conditions. Urban slums have always been more desirable to men than rural poverty and subjection. The greater social freedom of cities, the greater diversity that they offer to the eye as well as the mind, the heart as well as the head, have, for the majority of men, always outweighed the disadvantages of over-crowding, noise, disease and even, in the earlier periods, the higher chance of death. But planners are more concerned with health than joy. Again, the root cause is a lack of both historical sense and knowledge.

What one misses so far in this conference is the dimension of time, any analysis of how men have secured control of environment, or in fact what has caused them not only to achieve it where they did, but also what has attracted men to and held them in vast incoherent industrial or environmental congeries. Indeed, though unfailingly stimulating and at times brilliant, this book views the future without the past – a sad comment on the declining social authority of historians.

Appendix I:
Date and Place of Publication

Part I

1 Balls of Cotton and Parrot's Feathers. Review of Cecil Jane and R. A. Skelton, *The Journal of Christopher Columbus* in *The Spectator* (June 1969).
2 The European Vision of America. *American Heritage* (August 1976).
3 The World Beyond America at the Time of the Revolution. In J. H. Plumb, *Men and Places* (Cresset Press, 1963).
4 *New Light on the Tyrant George III.* George Rogers Clark Lecture. The Society of Cincinnati (Washington DC, 1978).
5 British Attitudes to the American Revolution. In J. H. Plumb, *In the Light of History* (Penguin, 1978).
6 America and England, 1720–1820. The Fusion of Culture. Harvard Art Gallery Exhibition Catalogue (April 1975).
7 The French Connection, 1776–1782. *American Heritage* (December 1974).
8 The Peacemakers. Review of Richard B. Morris, *The Peacemakers* in *New York Review of Books* (March 1966).
9 In Search of Benjamin Franklin in *New York Review of Books* (January 1972).
10 Franklin Unbuttoned. Review of Claude-Anne Lopez, *Mon Cher Papa, Franklin and the Ladies of Paris* in *New York Times Review of Books* (December 1966).
11 A Little Revenge. Review of Willard S. Randall, *A Little Revenge: Benjamin Franklin and His Son* in *New York Review of Books* (May 1985).
12 Inventing America. Review of Garry Wills, *Inventing America: Jefferson's Declaration of Independence* in *Bookworld* (July 1978).
13 *Man and Monument.* Review of Marcus Cunliffe, *George Washington, Man and Monument* in *Sunday Times* (January 1959).
14 George Washington's Chinaware. Review of Susan Grey Deitweiler, *George Washington's China* in *House and Garden* (May 1983).
15 The Ordeal of Thomas Hutchinson. Review of Bernard Bailyn, *The Ordeal of Thomas Hutchinson* in *The Times Literary Supplement* (June 1975).

Part II

1 Slavery, Race and the Poor. In J. H. Plumb, *In the Light of History* (Penguin, 1972).
2 Plantation Power. In J. H. Plumb, *In the Light of History* (Penguin, 1972).
3 The Problem of Slavery in the Age of Revolution. Review of David Brion Davis, *The Problem of Slavery in the Age of Revolution* in *The New York Times Book Review* (February 1975).
4 Slavery and Human Progress. Review of David Brion Davis, *Slavery and Human Progress* in *The New York Review of Books* (October 1984).
5 American Slavery, American Freedom. Review of Edmund S. Morgan *American Slavery, American Freedom* in *The New York Review of Books* (June 1975).
6 A Nightmare World of Fantasy and Murder. Review of V. S. Naipaul, *The Loss of El Dorado* in *Bookworld* (April 1970).
7 The Royal Navy and the Slave Trade. Review of W. E. F. Ward, *The Royal Navy and the Slavers* in *Bookworld* (June 1969).

Part III

1 History and President Kennedy. Unpublished.
2 The Private Grief of Public Figures. *Saturday Review* (January 1967).
3 Where Do We Go From Vietnam? Review of Philip L. Gegelin, *Lyndon B. Johnson and the World* in *Saturday Review* (June 1966).
4 Another Year of Defeat. *Saturday Review* (October 1968).
5 Nixon as Disraeli? *The New York Times Magazine* (February 1973).
6 Inflation, Frustration and Tea. *The New York Times Magazine* (June 1973).
7 The Fatal Flaw. Not previously printed. Written 1976.
8 Brooklyn Through English Eyes. *The New York Times* (June 1972).
9 New York Vindicated. *The New York Times* (July 1973).
10 A Walk in Detroit. J. H. Plumb, *In the Light of History* (Penguin, 1972).
11 Secular Heretics. J. H. Plumb, *In the Light of History* (Penguin, 1972).
12 Middle-Class Bombs. *Saturday Review* (August, 1970).
13 Crime Against the Person. *Horizon* (1973).
14 A Drug is a Drink is a Smoke. *Saturday Review* (May 1967).
15 The Death of the Outback. *Saturday Review* (April 1969).
16 The Beauty of America. *Saturday Review* (March 1970).
17 The Future Without the Past. *Saturday Review* (July 1967).

Appendix II: Notes

New Light on the Tyrant George III

1 Bernard Bailyn, *The Ideological Origins of the American Revolution* (Cambridge, Mass., 1967), 144–59; J. H. Plumb, 'British Attitudes to the American Revolution', in *In the Light of History* (1972), 70–87; Sir Herbert Butterfield, *George III and the Historians* (1957); John Brewer, *Party Ideology and Popular Politics at the Accession of George III* (1976).

2 'Chatham', in Thomas, Lord Macaulay, *Historical Essays*; George Otto Trevelyan, *The American Revolution* (1899), 6 vols.

3 Sir Lewis Namier, *The Structure of Politics at the Accession of George III* (2nd edn 1961); *England in the Age of the American Revolution* (1930); Sir Herbert Butterfield, *George III, Lord North and the People 1779–1780* (1949); Ian Christie, *Myth and Reality in Late Eighteenth Century British Politics* (1970).

4 John Brooke, *King George III* (1972). This is by far the best biography of George III, although the interpretation of the many political crises of his reign leaves much to be desired. Nevertheless Brooke's character of George III is close to the truth; it is based on a wealth of material derived from the Royal Archives and he has put every eighteenth-century historian, including myself, very much in his debt.

5 Sir Lewis Namier, 'King George III: A Study of Personality' in *Personalities and Politics* (1955), 39–58; J. H. Plumb, *The First Four Georges* (1956).

6 Ida Macalpine and Richard Hunter, *George III and the Mad Business* (1969); but see the review of this book in *The Times Literary Supplement* of 8 January 1970 and correspondence in subsequent issues, particularly that of 12 February 1970.

7 John Brewer, op. cit.

8 Sir Lewis Namier and John Brooke, *The House of Commons 1754–1790* (1964), Introduction.

9 Brooke, *George III* 56–8.

10 J. H. Plumb, *Royal Heritage* (1977), 161–2.

11 See Bailyn, op. cit. 35–40; also Bernard Bailyn, *The Origins of American Politics* (New York 1968).

12 Plumb, *Royal Heritage*, 182–3; John Charlton, *Kew Gardens*.

13 Romney Sedgwick, *Letters from George III to Lord Bute*, (1939), lv, lviii–ix.

14 J. H. Plumb, *The First Four Georges* (revised edn 1975), 151.
15 Brooke, op. cit., 304–6; Plumb, *Royal Heritage*, 169–70.
16 Ibid., 168.
17 Ibid., 179.
18 Sir Oliver Millar, *The Later Georgian Pictures in the Collection of Her Majesty the Queen* (1964); also *George III, Collector and Patron* (Catalogue of the Queen's Gallery exhibition, 1974), 18–20.
19 Brooke, op. cit., 301–2.
20 *George III, Collector and Patron*, 9–10.
21 V. K. Chew, *Physics for Princes* (HMSO, 1968), Introduction.
22 *George III, Collector and Patron*, 25–6.
23 Ibid., 61.
24 Ibid., 6–7; Brooke, op. cit., 302–4.
25 W. J. Bean, *The Royal Botanical Gardens* (1908).
26 Brooke, op. cit., 291–2.
27 Sir Herbert Butterfield, *George III, Lord North and the People*.
28 Romney Sedgwick, op. cit.
29 John Adams, *Collected Works* (Boston 1851–6), viii, 255–9.
30 Brooke, op. cit., 310–14.

British Attitudes to the American Revolution

1 For a discussion of the influence of these dissenting radicals, see Caroline Robbins, *The Eighteenth-Century Commonwealth Man* (Harvard, 1959), 320–77, an invaluable book on an obscure and difficult subject that still needs further detailed study.
2 J. C. Miller, *Origins of the American Revolution* (London, 1945), 145. 'Although it must be recognised at the outset that some factions of the Whigs such as John Wilkes, John Horne Tooke, Joseph Priestley, Richard Price and Catherine Macaulay, adopted a liberal, conciliatory position in the dispute between Great Britain and the colonies, it cannot be claimed – as has so often been done – that they represented English public opinion.' Also Eric Robson, *The American Revolution in its Political and Military Aspects, 1763–83* (London, 1955), 38, 80.
3 Groups which, I might add in passing, are badly in need of more detailed research, and one can only wish that many European cities had received the same scholarly attention that Carl and Jessica Bridenbaugh have given to Philadelphia.
4 See N. McKendrick, *Transactions of the Royal Historical Society*, 5th series, vol. 14 (1964), 1–33. I am deeply indebted to Mr McKendrick for the transcripts of the Wedgwood MSS here quoted.
5 *Barlaston MSS*, J. W. to B., 24 February 1776.
6 Ibid., 22 December 1777.
7 R. J. Fitton and A. P. Wadsworth, *The Strutts and the Arkwrights, 1758–80* (Manchester, 1958), 159.
8 *Barlaston MSS*, J. W. to R. W. Mr Holland of Bolton, Lancs. [n.d], *c.* November 1776.
9 G. H. Guttridge (ed.), *The American Correspondence of a Bristol Merchant, 1766–76* (Berkeley, California, 1934), 2.

10 Philip Davidson, *Propaganda and the American Revolution, 1763–1783* (Chapel Hill, North Carolina, 1941), 43–4.
11 Ibid., 139–52.
12 *Barlaston MSS*, J. W. to B., 7 August 1779.
13 Ibid.
14 Lord Brougham, *Historical Sketches of Statesmen who Flourished in the Time of George III* (London, 1839), I, 303–4.
15 G. H. Guttridge, *English Whiggism and the American Revolution* (Berkeley, California, 1942), 76–7.

Index